QUANTUM
THEOLOGY

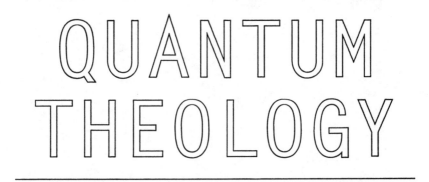

QUANTUM THEOLOGY

DIARMUID O'MURCHU, M.S.C.

A Crossroad Book
The Crossroad Publishing Company
New York

1997

The Crossroad Publishing Company
370 Lexington Avenue, New York, NY 10017

Copyright © 1997 by Diarmuid O'Murchu, M.S.C.

Printed in the United States of America

Library of Congress Cataloging-in-Publication Data

O'Murchu, Diarmuid.
    Quantum theology / Diarmuid O'Murchu.
        p. cm.
    Includes bibliographical references and index.
    ISBN 0-8245-1630-3 (pbk.)
    1. Quantum theory. 2. Physics – Religious aspects – Christianity.
3. Theology. I. Title.
BL265.P4048 1997
231.7–dc21   96-49656
                                              CIP

Contents

Acknowledgments

This book feels more like a *process* than a *product*. It draws together the ideas and dreams of many people. In recording my gratitude, I do not differentiate between the living and the dead, because in a quantum world, these are merely two dimensions of the one-life experience.

Theologically, I belong to the Catholic tradition, often perceived to be restrictive and legalistic. For me, it has been a fermenting ground of many questions and few answers, abetted by inspiring people to whom I owe so much. Chief among these are Pierre Teilhard de Chardin, Ladislaus Boros, John Macquarrie, Karl Rahner, Mary Daly, Ursula King, Sallie McFague, Gustavo Gutiérrez, Leonardo Boff, Mary Grey, Katherine Zappone, and Thomas Berry.

Scientifically, I am very much a late developer, and I cherish deeply those colleagues and friends whose patience and tact opened up for me the wonders of science, reassuring me, time and again, that what I was talking (writing) about made a great deal of sense (and, occasionally, a good deal of nonsense!); in this context, Paul MacAlevey and Chris Elliot merit special mention. I have engaged with scientific exploration as much through books as through people; from a quantum perspective, ideas are rich in potential whatever their source. Whether through personal or written contact (sometimes, both), I wish to record my indebtedness to David Bohm, Stephen Hawking, Ilya Prigogine, Paul Davies, Danah Zohar, Kitty Ferguson, Peter Russell, James Lovelock, and Rupert Sheldrake.

Dialogue is an invaluable resource to clarify ideas and unearth their deeper meanings. My special thanks to those who have befriended and encouraged me in my quantum explorations, particularly Frances O'Kelly, Elizabeth Smyth, Kathleen Lyons, Sion Cowell, John Woodcock, Maura Corbett, John Doyle, David Smith, and the provincial of my religious order, Ciaran MacCarthaigh, for his continuous support.

In preparing this manuscript for publication John Eagleson was meticulous with detail and gracious with advice. I very much appreciate his painstaking effort and his personal interest in this work.

Debbie Thorpe of Godsfield Press was always gracious and generous in offering advice and information. It is through her consistent support that this book is seeing the light of day. To Debbie and to Mike Leach of Crossroad, I record my deep gratitude for taking the creative risk of publishing this work. I hope the outcome will give you good reason to take such risks again.

Part One

The Invitation

The picture of reality coming to us from contemporary science is so attractive to theology that we would be fools not to use it....

— SALLIE McFAGUE

Chapter 1

You Are Invited...

New evolutions as profound as those of Einstein and Heisenberg are waiting for a new generation of more daring and integrated thinkers.
— DAVID FINKELSTEIN

The vital act is the act of participation. "Participator" is the incontrovertible new concept given by quantum mechanics. It strikes down the term "observer" of classical theory, the one who stands safely behind the thick glass wall and watches what goes on without taking part. It can't be done, quantum mechanics says.
— JOHN WHEELER

We are entering a new age. The European civilization which we have known for the past two thousand years is giving way to a global civilization....As we enter this new civilization, the meeting place of East and West, and the nations of the world, will be science.
— BEDE GRIFFITHS

Can you remember the last time you received an invitation? It may have been to a party, a family function, a game of golf, or a cup of coffee with the neighbor next door. What did it feel like to be invited? Pleased, delighted, excited, apprehensive!

Invitations are very much part of our culture, and perhaps for that reason we take them somewhat for granted. Nonetheless, we rarely turn down invitations, and when we do, we feel we have to offer a reason of substance.

Invitations tend to excite us. We look forward and anticipate. Often we dress up for the occasion. We hope to meet new friends or renew old acquaintances. We feel good that we have been included, and often we record our appreciation by gift or donation.

Most of our invitations relate to predictable experiences. If I am invited to a wedding, I have a good idea what will happen on the

3

occasion; there are bits I look forward to and parts I may seek to avoid. If, on the other hand, I am invited to an event that is likely to be quite unusual and unpredictable, I may well hesitate and offer a plausible excuse for staying away.

I open this book with an invitation:

> *Come with me on a journey of exploration; let's link arms in a trajectory whose direction and destiny we'll discover as we go along. Enter into the experience of searching, seeking, exploring, and, I hope, discovering. Participate in the task rather than remain a mere observer.*

You are invited to a strange, weird, and paradoxical experience. We'll roam down alleys and byways we have rarely been before. We'll encounter strange, intriguing figures, puzzling over incomprehensible quagmires. We'll connect, interlink, and form networks around unusual and even contradictory experiences. And somewhere on our journey (perhaps many times), we'll come to the edge of an abyss beyond which there exists — we know not what, but somehow it will seem appropriate to have got this far.

If, at this stage, you are feeling confused and ambivalent, that's fine. Just stay in touch with those feelings; they'll be useful to you later. You'll be expected to use your head (brain), but far more importantly, your heart. It's not what you can grasp intellectually that will be crucial, but what you can dream in your imagination, sense with your intuition, and feel with your heart. The journey is all about an *experience:* of a world awakening to its own inner meaning and mystery, a world we can no longer comprehend purely in scientific terms nor in exclusively religious dogmas, but in the emerging dialogue that enables both fields of learning to meet and interact in a new way, which I have chosen to call "quantum theology."

Is this another book about science and religion? Not really. We're operating out of a different paradigm, one in which we wish to discard the simplistic dividing lines of old dualisms. We live in a unified world; it's the connections rather than the divisions that engage our wisdom and imagination. And we celebrate the great paradigmatic shift, whereby *cosmology,* rather than *theology,* is now emerging as the queen of the sciences. We believe that creation itself is fundamentally sacred, the touchstone from which emanates the eternal yearnings behind theological dogma and scientific certitude. I acknowledge that these sentiments may be disturbing, even repugnant, to scientists and theologians alike; it is not my intention to offend, but as a seeker for truth on the edge of the new millennium, it is my

duty to engage with those strange insights which arise in the personal
and collective unconscious of our time.

Before you accept the invitation, carefully consider what you'll
need to bring with you, and what you'll need to leave behind. We'll
need to travel light because the landscape is vast and the heat will be
intense at times. It's your inner resources and not your external baggage that will be important to us. Bring all the reserves you can of
imagination, intuition, creativity, and your capacity to marvel. And
please bring along your wild (wo)man, your deep feminine part, your
hurt child, your wounded parent, and, above all, your flamboyant
artist.

You are unlikely to need your passport — because we consider the
whole planet to be home; your fixed religion — the landscape we'll
encounter cannot be contained in any one, or even in all, the major religious systems; your official academic qualification — in our
wholistic pursuit, this is likely to be an obstacle rather than an as-
set. And please leave at home your religious and scientific ideologies
along with the dualisms you have inherited, which you tend to use to
divide life into right and wrong, earth and heaven, God and humankind. Our expedition is about discovering the connections which
help to forge unity and not the differences that fragment and divide.

It all sounds very utopian! But what's wrong with utopia? Why
resort all the time to reductionism and rational logic, playing around
with inert facts and figures, striving to control and manipulate planetary* life? We have been playing that game for a long time, and it's
not getting us very far. Perhaps our human and planetary destiny is
more in the pursuit of utopia than in the creation of a mechanized
universe! At least, let's be open to entertaining the idea!

The invitation is about participation, not mere observation. We
are not journeying *in* the universe but *with* the universe. We are not
concerned about living in an evolving world but co-evolving with
our world. We are parts of a whole, much greater than the sum of its
parts, and yet within each part we are interconnected with the whole.

You may draw hope from the fact that this journey has been tra-
versed before. Mystics, artists, poets, and prophets have been along
this highway. Even a few scientists and theologians ventured out; indications are that they didn't get very far, probably because of excess
baggage. The mystics seem to have been the most successful, the ones

---

*Throughout the text, I use the word "planetary" with either specific reference to Planet
Earth itself, or to planetary life in general. The context will disclose which usage is
intended.

that realized that their pilgrimage was not to a holy shrine without, but to a sacred place within. And that interior search is personal, interpersonal, planetary, and cosmic all at once. Mystics are quite adept at discerning the underlying unity that maintains and nurtures the tremendous diversity we experience in everyday life.

Consequently, it's a journey with a purpose, but not necessarily with a destiny. There may be no end — and possibly no beginning. To many people that feels very scary. But in a universe where all is one, where "beginning" and "end" are constructs of the human mind (and not necessarily helpful any more), then the possibility — and the invitation — to embark on the journey is open to everybody.

So what's the purpose? To understand the nature of *light*. This is what all the great religions have been about. Scientific pursuit, from our prehistoric ancestors to the architects of modern technology, has been preoccupied with light. And all pilgrims, whether to Mecca, Jerusalem, Allahabad, Amristar, CERN, or Fermilab are in search of light. In all our hearts — even at the heart of the universe itself — we detect a divine echo which, in verbal form, might well coincide with Einstein's statement: "For the rest of my life, I'll be trying to understand the meaning of light."

Once upon a time, three wise beings followed a star that led them to what they considered to be the Light of light. In the complex world of today, we follow not one, but many stars, and in our quantum world, discovery may not be at the *end,* but *within* the journey itself. It is for this reason that you need to come equipped with a heart capable of understanding rather than a brain capable of comprehending.

So the invitation is to search for the light. And the enlightenment we seek may be in the exploration rather than in the discovery. Consequently, we are invited to travel light, so that, hopefully, we are unencumbered and more favorably disposed to receive. If we can risk all, and trust the process, then the chances are we'll arrive at truth, because the mystery we move within is fundamentally benign and benevolent.

Are you prepared to take the risk...? R.S.V.P. while the daylight lasts!

What Do We Mean by Theology?

A paradigm shift in theology must include this very important claim — that there is a new way of reflection, a new procedure of interpretation, a new orientation of knowledge.... Theology interprets, interrupts and transforms.

—REBECCA S. CHOPP

Theology is ruptured as the poor speak of God, and through this process of rupture, theology is converted into a critical theory of human freedom.

—GUSTAVO GUTIÉRREZ

Theological reflections about the Goddess are described as thealogy which is seen as fundamentally different from traditional male-oriented and male-dominated theology. Thealogy gives primacy to symbols rather than to rational explanations, which are so prevalent in theological thought.

—URSULA KING

Theology is essentially a Christian concept, derived from the Greek combination of *theos,* meaning God, and *logos,* meaning word. In the Christian context it is closely related to the notion of *revelation,* the belief that there has been a divine disclosure (of who and what God is), outlined in sacred writings which Christians call the Scriptures.

All the great religions have a sacred book (or books) which is considered to be a deposit of divine truth: the Bible for Christians, the Koran for Muslims, the Guru Granth Sahib for Sikhs, the Vedas, Upanishads, or Epics for Hindus. Some (e.g., Muslims and Orthodox Jews) consider these sacred texts to be God's own words, which should never be tampered with, modified, or changed; in other words, they should be accepted at their face value and literal meaning. In this case, there is no need for a formal religious interpretation,

7

nor for that quality of reflection which Christians associate with theology.

Other religions, such as Christianity and Hinduism, consider the sacred texts to be divinely inspired, but not to be taken literally. They acknowledge that the texts were originally compiled in the language and thought forms of a particular time and place and, consequently, the message underpinning the text needs ongoing re-interpretation and fresh application to changing cultural conditions. And for Christians, this is primarily the task of theology.

Of course, it's not quite as simple as that. Over the centuries, Christians have had different understandings of theology. Up until about 1000 C.E., theologians focused mainly on spelling out the deeper meaning and practical implications of the Christian Gospels, especially the meaning and significance of Jesus himself. Around the twelfth century, a new theological impetus emerged, largely pioneered by St. Thomas Aquinas, who considered theology's task to be that of "faith seeking understanding." The theological horizon was expanding, and a creative undercurrent began to unfold.

Unfortunately, the Reformation in the sixteenth century, and the reactions to it from Catholics and Protestants alike, greatly jeopardized the enlightened vision of the high Middle Ages. Fear and suspicion drove both sides into theological enclaves. Protestants pursued an exclusive allegiance to the Word of God, paving the way for a rather cerebral, intellectualized, dehumanized quality of religion, while Catholics developed a strong sacramental and canonical (legal) approach, which became a measuring stick for who was, and who was not, deemed to be *in* or *out* of the Catholic Church. Within these restrictive and artificial confines, theology became an ideological criterion for allegiance to one or other camp. It was only a matter of time until theology assumed an idolatrous significance: "Our God, and not yours, is the real one," adding sectarian bite to the slogan of early Christendom which claimed: "Outside the church there is no salvation."

Perhaps the greatest tragedy of the theological developments in the post-Reformation era is that the spiritual insights of other religions — and the spiritual unfolding taking place outside formal religious contexts — was totally ignored. Worse still, it was condemned as being pagan and ungodly.

The year 1960 marks a new theological threshold for our time. Something fresh and vital in the collective consciousness of our planet and its peoples burst forth. In the North, we risked being playful and flamboyant once more as Jesus freaks and flower people paraded our streets and university campuses. In the South, the colonial oppression of centuries began to crumble; in 1960 alone, *seventeen* African nations achieved their independence. Theology began to reclaim its central commitment to the new world order envisaged by Jesus in the proclamation of the New Reign of God (the Kingdom). Henceforth the theological horizon would continue to expand. The nature and meaning of that expansion is central to the considerations of the present work.

Theology and Religion

This rather patchy historical backdrop is necessary to understand many of the dichotomies we take for granted today, especially the rigid and staid distinctions between sacred and secular, earth and heaven, God and humankind, church and state, religion and science. But it is even more significant if we are to appreciate the volatile, confused, and creative nature of modern theology, grappling with the paradigm shift of contemporary evolution (see Küng and Tracy, 1989).

I have already hinted at a distinction between religion and theology. As indicated above, theology as a science takes its subject matter from formal religion (from sacred texts). This would seem to suggest that theology and religion are inescapably intertwined. One of the great merits of Protestant theology throughout the nineteenth and twentieth centuries was its development of the notion that the task of theology was to purify religion of its ideological and idolatrous trappings. When religion tended to opt for one or other specific understanding of God, life, church, sacrament, etc., seeking to make that understanding normative and obligatory for all time, theology posed fresh and challenging questions, highlighting the need to be less dogmatic and more open and adaptable to change.

This notion that theology serves as a corrective to narrowly defined concepts, ideas, and practices is not unique to the nineteenth and twentieth centuries. Biblical scholars of the Christian tradition argue that this is very much the mind and attitude of Jesus in the Gospel narratives. It obviously resonates with the notion of "faith seeking understanding" (adopted both by Anselm and Aquinas) and underpins much of the theological reflection and research taking place in our world today.

The etymology of the word "theology" (*theos-logos*) also suggests the need for an open and creative horizon of exploration. *Logos* can be understood in the narrow linguistic sense of a special set of words which state what reality is, or determine what it should become. This literary understanding and application of concepts is very much the subject of modern linguistic analysis, highlighting the relative nature, on the one hand, and the symbolic significance, on the other, of all spoken language and written text (see Alston, 1989, and the valuable feminist critique in Nye, 1990).

From within the Christian tradition itself is a rich, inclusive, global sense of *logos,* which dominates the opening verses of John's Gospel, and is specifically outlined in the Hebrew Scriptures, where *logos* is translated as *dabhar,* meaning wisdom as a creative, divine energy. The task of theology, therefore, could be understood as an exploration of that wisdom which awakens and sustains the creative impulse of life. Central to this inquiry is the ability to *listen,* to be open and receptive to the life-giving energy of the divine *logos.* According to Collins (1995, 226), "It is increasingly in the cathedral of the environment that our contemporaries are rediscovering a way into the realm of the transcendent; they are discovering the sacred presence that stands behind the natural world."

It may sound sophisticated and grandiose, but in fact humans have been exploring spiritual meaning from time immemorial. When we examine primitive (so-called) and prehistoric religious behavior, we find a wealth of custom, ritual, and ceremony, not bestowed by a formal religion, but invented by the human imagination as a means to discern, accommodate, and internalize the primitive fascination with mystery.

Long before we humans ever invented the formal study of theology, people *did* theology. They grappled intuitively and ritually, sometimes in awe, sometimes in fear, with the encircling mystery of life. Long before they thought of God as a divine being, they felt and celebrated a sacred presence which evoked in them feelings of amazement and trepidation, respect and intrigue, but above all a reassurance that, despite everything, the ultimate mystery of life is benign and benevolent.

Over the millennia — some seventy thousand years — we humans lived in a spiritual ambience.[1] We sought and discovered meaning in the events and experiences of daily life. We sensed the frightening, yet benevolent, power of the divine in the rhythms of nature, in the changing seasons, in the warmth of sunshine, the light of the moon, the destruction of storm and thunder. The entire universe was alive with potential meaning, perceived for over thirty thousand years as a Divine Mother of prodigious fertility and nurturance; fortunately there were no theologians around to accuse us of pantheism.

Then came the Agricultural Revolution (around 8000 B.C.E.) and with it the insatiable desire to control the precarious elements of life, including the religious ones. We began to take over the planet and claim it as our own, dividing it into segments, later known as continents and nations. We began to master and control the environment, and we didn't know when or where to stop. We even invented warfare so that we could conquer and control every alien force.[2]

Prior to this time, quite a different worldview prevailed. Despite occasional tendencies toward cannibalism and other macabre practices, Planet Earth was revered as the Great Mother Goddess, birthing forth a prolific variety of life, the sacredness of which dominated all other concerns. Prehistoric cosmology sometimes engenders a sense of fear and trepidation, as people confront the vast unknown, but far more prevalent is the feeling of being at home in Planet Earth, nurtured and sustained by its egalitarian and prodigious creativity. Consequently, rivalries between nations, races, and religions were largely unknown and warfare, as a dominant mode of declaring superiority, is very much an invention of the postagricultural era.

The craving to dominate took on diabolical proportions. Tribal and ethnic groups vied for ultimate supremacy, as Planet Earth was carved into sections and nations. Finally, we humans tried to conquer and control the Godhead itself, that divine, mysterious force, that fascinates, puzzles, and frightens us. And how did we decide to do it? *By inventing religion!*

Religion is one of the great anomalies of our evolution as a human species. It is the instrument with which we tried to gain supremacy over the Godhead itself, by anthropocentrizing the divine power and molding it into a system of duties and expectations of *our* making. In the name of religion we have invented a litany of gods, many made in our own image and likeness, and not a few serving as projections of our own distorted will-to-power. Religion is the greatest idolatry of all time, and in many ways, the most dangerous also.

The major religions known to us today came into being in a time span of about forty-five hundred years (3000 B.C.E.–1500 C.E.). Formal religion is a very recent visitor to Planet Earth. It has been around for about 5 percent of humanity's spiritual journey, which began to unfold about seventy thousand years ago.

That religion should have arisen as part of the ethos of the Agricultural Revolution is understandable. One could even argue that it was appropriate and necessary for that phase of our evolution as a human species. What we cannot escape is that we as a species have outlived that phase of our evolutionary development and so, quite appropriately (it seems to me), thousands of people are leaving religion aside, no longer feeling the need for it. One of the most precarious dilemmas of our time, however, is the vacuum created by the demise of formal religion.

Theology and Spirituality

Most of us have grown up with a religious legacy. Even those who have never partaken of a formal practice of their faith carry within them cultural norms and expectations. Our surrounding culture is heavily tinged with religious symbol, feeling, and expectation. I don't wish to deny that religion has brought benefits to our lives and to our planet. My concern is that it is, and for some centuries has been, overshadowing a more fundamental human aspiration, namely, *spirituality.*

The word "spirituality" has several meanings. I use it with a very basic connotation: *the human search for meaning.*[3] All of us, all of the time, operate out of a sense of being connected to an inner core of meaning. Thompson (1990, 196) even suggests that the autonomic nervous system communicates and transmits information in order to enhance meaning. A DNA helix can validly be spoken of as carrying meaning because it bears information which is transmitted, received, and interpreted in terms of protein structures used to build the body and enhance the quality of life.

Throughout life, we humans are exploring meaning, searching for it, and imposing it where we feel it doesn't exist. We cannot do otherwise; it's our very essence as human beings. We're creatures of meaning and the drive toward meaning comes from deep within — not just within ourselves, but also, I dare to suggest, from deep within creation itself. In this context, therefore, spirituality is *planetary* (and cosmic) as well as *personal* — which may be another rendition of the feminist claim that the personal is political.

From the beginning of our evolution as a species, we have been exploring and expressing our spirituality — with both its light and shadow. Not everything in our spiritual unfolding is necessarily good — but *always* activated for a perceived good. The spiritual search, the pursuit of meaning, has several mediations and expressions. We worship several gods, many of which are false, including some of the most cherished in our formal religions.

Our spiritual identity is inescapable; without it we simply wouldn't exist. How we enculturate and express it is a separate question, which I have explored in another book (O'Murchu, 1986). Religion is one aspect of our spiritual unfolding, but only one. Our spiritual evolution as a species took place for an estimated seventy thousand years without formal religion, and there are many indications that we are, once more, evolving spiritually into a nonreligious ambience. As a human species we are outgrowing our need for formal religion.

It seems important that we differentiate between *spirituality* and *religion*. Spirituality is inherent to the human condition — also to planetary and cosmic growth; in my estimation, religion is not. Spirituality has an enduring quality, coterminous with human evolution; religion serves a transitory and temporary purpose.

Theology, therefore, has a great deal more in common with spirituality than with religion. Theology belongs to the primal and primordial aspirations that underpin the search for meaning, predating religion by thousands of years. When our ancient ancestors grappled with the mystery of life, even at the "primitive" stage of prearticulate speech, they were already doing theology. They were connecting with the divine energy; they were opening their hearts and minds to divine wisdom.

By adopting theology as a religious phenomenon, and using it — as happened for much of the Christian era — as a tool to suppress and oppress others (pagans, infidels, heretics, among a range of other *labels*), we humans were debasing one of the oldest and most sacred of the sciences. Since it is also one of the most creative and subversive fields of exploration, it is understandable, if regrettable, that we sought to curtail its influence.

Contemporary Theology

Formally, theology still belongs to official religion, and in its general usage it is almost exclusively a Christian concept. Informally and unofficially, it is a powerful ferment for thought, reflection, dialogue, and provocation. It is emerging as one of the most multidisciplinary of all the sciences and in recent years has assumed new political, global, and cultural significance (see Lash, 1986; Hopper, 1987; Liechty, 1990; Krieger, 1991). The new theological agenda is multifaceted, as can be gleaned from four recent developments which I outline briefly.

Liberation Theology

Liberation theology is probably the single greatest development in contemporary theology. Born out of the experience of oppression and exploitation in South and Central America, it sets out to establish that Christian theology is primarily about liberation in this world rather than salvation in a life to come. Freedom from all forms of oppression, from all that undermines personal and planetary well-being, is considered to be a central goal of the New Reign of God (the Kingdom) that Jesus proclaimed.

Liberation theology is very pragmatic in its orientation. It considers systemic or structural oppression (rather then individual sin) to be the underlying cause of injustice and exploitation. Consequently, it seeks political strategies that help to bring about necessary change; it rejects capitalism, which it considers to be synonymous with the colonial oppression of the West, and often opts for a socialist alternative as the best approximation of the liberation it seeks to achieve.

In its Latin American context, this is largely a Catholic development and is accepted, only with great caution, by the guardians of Catholic orthodoxy. Contrary to public opinion, Rome's apprehension about liberation theology is not so much about its political undercurrent as its hermeneutical strategy.

Traditionally, the starting point for Catholic theology was the revealed Word of God in the Scriptures and in tradition as expounded by Catholic teaching. The theological task was essentially reflective, unearthing the deeper meaning of immutable truths and outlining their application to daily life through a series of guidelines and laws. In this approach, theology began with the mystery of God and ended with the human condition. It was a linear, deductive, top-down approach. Historically such theology blossomed in all Christian circles, particularly since the Reformation of the sixteenth century.

Liberation theology adopts a whole new method. It begins with human beings in their struggle for liberation. It names that struggle for what it is in both its personal and political dimensions. It reflects on that struggle in the light of history and in the light of revealed truth; from these inspired sources it conjures ways of action to initiate and implement the liberation God intends for all people. In the light of that *reflection* and *action* (praxis), it formulates its theodicy: the God the people come to know, the God they encounter, in the struggle for liberation.

Liberation theologians are committed to *doing* theology, not just preaching, teaching, or writing about it. The base communities have emerged as a new way of being church, an ecclesial implementation of the praxis of liberation. In this new context, the theory and practice interact in novel ways as the theologian and the "ordinary" people enter into the same struggle and explore strategies for the human and earthly realization of God's new promise: "that they may have life and have it to the full" (John 10:10).

As a new paradigm, therefore, liberation theology marks the dethronement of academic, cerebral theology which, in many cases, had become an intellectual preoccupation for theologians and an oppressive ideology of the churches. It creates a fresh theological approach by beginning, not with divine revelation (as traditionally understood), but with the God who discloses meaning and purpose in the daily struggle for human and earthly liberation. It is this fresh starting point, and the novel context it demands for its articulation and implementation, that makes liberation theology essentially *new* (for a more detailed survey, see Ferm, 1986; for a critical analysis, see McGovern, 1989; for the ecological implications, see Boff, 1995).

Feminist Theology

Feminist theology was very much a trend of the 1980s. It is not just about women's ordination, inclusive language, or women's rights within the churches, although it includes all these. It also espouses quite stringent efforts to give women a greater voice and more shared responsibility in church life, particularly at the levels of ministry and decision-making.

The kernel of feminist theology is much deeper, namely, the rediscovery of the *feminine* in men and women alike (also in the culture generally). Initially, this demands a critical reassessment of what feminist theologians consider to be three oppressive values underpinning our current way of interpreting reality. Feminist voices express concern and protest about many specific issues, but fundamentally all criticism and campaigns are rooted in an outright challenge to *patriarchy, androcentrism,* and *sexism.* These are three different but interrelated aspects of the patriarchal will-to-power which — according to the feminist critique — has outlived its usefulness and no longer serves the best interests of people or the cosmos (see King, 1989, 20ff.).

Patriarchy refers to those masculine orientations of possession and control, setting the authoritarian male over against everything else in life (nature included), which is understood to be there for the conquering.

Androcentrism is a one-sided approach to all relationships — whether human or earthly — whereby the male is projected as the stronger, the better, the holier, the more authentic.

Sexism has been defined as an exclusive ordering of life by way of gender. While biological sex is given, gender is socially and culturally constructed and must be learned.

Feminist theology adopts two dominant orientations. It seeks to respect and cherish *experience,* particularly women's unique capacity to trust their feelings and emotions and perceive reality in the totality of its emergent unfolding. It seeks to overcome the traditional dualism of emotion and intellect, of the rational and the irrational, the heart and the head. Consequently, feminist theology tends to have a strong *wholistic* sense. Everything in life is assumed to function as an organic whole, often distorted by the masculine compulsiveness to fragment and differentiate. To rediscover this underlying unity and inherent harmony is one of the primary goals of feminist theology (see the comprehensive overview in Ross and Hilkert, 1995).

As a new paradigm, feminist theology endorses the methodology of liberation theology, namely, that we do theology on the foundation stones of our experience. But it sharpens this orientation by its quite deliberate choice to forego all *dualisms.*[4] Even the polarization of good and evil is rejected, because, it is claimed, it allows us to disown the shadow without examining its causes. We do not transform the darkness by dismissing or trying to overcome it, but by engaging with it in all its complexity.

Life does not consist of opposites, most of which are *man*-made constructs which empower the masculine consciousness to conquer and subdue. Life is essentially one, where opposites are better understood as complementary values. This outlook has profound ramifications not merely for theology, but for all branches of contemporary wisdom and learning.

As a new theological paradigm, feminism forges deep links with long-lost sacred traditions. Foremost among these is the rehabilitation of the notion of the *goddess,* the female personification of divinity that preceded patriarchal religions by at least thirty thousand years and exemplified a breadth and depth of spiritual versatility unknown in the largely cerebral theology of more recent millennia. Those striving to rehabilitate the goddess (e.g., well-known names such as Rosemary Radford Ruether, Carol Christ, Charlene Spretnak, Merlin Stone, Miriam Simos, otherwise known as

Starhawk, and others cited in Orenstein, 1990) invoke a new form of theological discourse known as "thealogy."

Creation Theology

Creation theology follows closely on the heels of feminist theology. Like feminist theology, it advocates a profound respect for the earth and for the created order, which it perceives as unequivocally the work and wonder of God, despite its pain, suffering, and incongruities.

The major shift of emphasis here is on the notion of the "world." Traditionally, Christian theology considers the world to be transitory and not worthy of deep trust and love. In fact, a great deal of Christian apologetic, right from the time of Christ, is about the "end of the world," an expression of a deep human dissatisfaction with the created order and a desire to "escape" to the realm of true life and lasting happiness. In the latter half of the twentieth century, our attitude to the world (and especially to the earth) has changed quite dramatically. For a start, we no longer identify the *earth* with the *world*, as we did for much of the Christian era. We are now more disposed to wonder and marvel at the complex grandeur of our universe and the intriguing life potential of Planet Earth itself.

We are also a great deal more clear-sighted and informed about the "end of the world." We know our world has existed for at least fifteen billion years and will continue to evolve over millions of years into the open-ended future, unless jeopardized by human interference. Our evolutionary story[5] also informs us that life on Planet Earth evolved without any assistance from humankind for 95 percent of its evolutionary time scale, and that awareness profoundly alters our attitude to creation and to our participation in its growth and evolution.

Not only have we a new sense of our world, how mysterious and sacred it is, but we humans are invited to confront the anthropocentrism whereby we set ourselves up as the masters of creation and set in motion a dangerously idolatrous task of ridding the world of all *we* consider to be evil; ironically, we have potentiated the power of evil almost to the point of a total global catastrophe.

Creation theology invites a fresh reformulation of some central tenets of the Christian faith (as outlined by scholars such as Fox, 1984; McDonagh, 1986; and by feminist writers such as Halkes, 1991, and Ruether, 1992):

a. To examine critically our world-denouncing spirituality.

b. To reexamine our notion of original sin, which tends to convey a sense of the world being essentially prone to sin and evil when, in fact, it is primarily the fruit of an original blessing, benign and life-giving in its fundamental orientation.

c. To reverse our masculine tendency to dominate, manipulate, and exploit creation for human benefit. No longer do we understand the earth to exist primarily for the benefit of us humans. The earth exists to manifest the beauty and grandeur of the creator; it is an "alive" planet with a capacity to grow and survive, endowed with a resilience that we humans cannot match (a topic we explore in subsequent chapters).

d. To rediscover our role as co-creators with God, participants in the transformation of the world into the "new heaven and the new earth," a notion captivated by Leonardo Boff in the statement: "The world is the arena for the historical realization of the Kingdom of God."

e. To appropriate the interdependence and interconnectedness of all life forms. We humans find our true identity by collaborating interdependently with all other forms, not by "lording it over them" and assuming that all others exist for our benefit.

f. To befriend the pain and darkness of our world in a spirit of justice and peace. In seeking to overcome pain and disease, we humans have accentuated rather than reduced the suffering of the world. Most meaningless suffering is, directly or indirectly, the byproduct of human greed and interference, and not the fault of alien, cosmic forces.

As a new paradigm, the main contribution of creation theology is the attempt to reclaim the world as the arena where God works out the drama of revelation and salvation. Since all the great religions assume that our world must not be taken seriously — because it is only a temporary abode as we move to the real life in the world hereafter — the new creation theology provides a creatively subversive challenge. For Christianity, with its central God-figure becoming incarnate, as a full human being in a full earthly sense, the implications for christology and ecclesiology are substantial and will be reviewed in subsequent chapters.

For many disillusioned Christians, creation theology, with its accompanying ground-based spirituality and ecological ambience, has rewakened hope and meaning. It has provided a new context for re-creating the church at the heart of the world, a church where people find and experience real communion as they commune more deeply with the God who enlivens all that exists.

Theology of Multifaith Dialogue

In the 1960s the Reformation rift between Catholics and Protestants began to heal, after some four hundred years of coldness and in-difference. Ecumenism became a leading theological challenge for Christians of all shades of opinion. Unfortunately, it has become an intellectual preoccupation for scholars and specialists and has largely lost the rank and file of Christian society.

Meanwhile, a new ecumenicity is beginning to emerge. This time, representatives of the major world religions — Christianity, Judaism, Hinduism, Buddhism, Islam — are exploring common ground. This is not likely to lead to a new world religion, but to a deeper appreciation of the common elements shared by all the religions.

This development is almost exclusively a Christian one (see Hick and Knitter, 1988; Tracy, 1990). The great Eastern religions are wary of it, while Muslims — considering their own religion to be the only true one — participate in a very limited way.

Theologians of multifaith dialogue tend to adopt one of three positions:

a. *Exclusive:* Because Christianity is understood to have the ful-ness of truth, then it must be granted a status higher than any or all the other major religions. In its most extreme form, this conviction led to the formulation: "Outside the church there is no salvation." Only evangelical theologians, of whom George Lindbeck is one of the more enlightened contemporary figures, tend to hold this position today.

b. *Inclusive:* Christianity still has priority, but its sense of revela-tion and salvation are so global that it can be understood to include all the aspirations and possibilities of the other ma-jor faiths. Christ is considered to be the normative revelation of God, but salvation is possible through religions other than Christianity. Most Christian theologians today adopt one or other variant of this position.

c. *Pluralist:* All religions are equal and valid paths to the one di-vine reality. Each is right for its own cultural, communal, or personal context. Each religion is understood to be a cultural, historical attempt at contextualizing the one divine plan of revelation and salvation. This is not to say that all religions are equal, or that one religion is as good as another. Rather, it declares that each religion is right for its time, that each offers a partial and limited view of reality, yet each can genuinely lead us to God and communicate God's design for ourselves and for the world.

As a new theological paradigm, the multifaith dialogue is only beginning to create an impact, and it seems that it will be quite some time before the religions will feel free and safe to participate as equal partners in the dialogue. Meanwhile, the dialogue raises even more acute concerns beyond the formal agenda of multifaith research:

a. The perception that all religions, even the so-called revealed ones (Christianity, Judaism, and Islam), are human attempts to construe and contextualize God's revelation to humanity.

b. The fact that each religion — and religion in general — perpetuates forms of idolatry which have caused, and continue to cause, immense pain and suffering in our world.

c. The possibility that the religions, understood in evolutionary terms, properly belong to the Age of Patriarchy (c. 8000 B.C.E.– 2000 C.E.), and may have diminished importance for humanity as we move into a new evolutionary epoch.

d. The fact that although in the past religion was the chief means through which people explored and articulated their spiritual desires and their search for meaning in life, today increasing numbers of people are discovering their spiritual identity in contexts other than those of formal churches or religions.

As a new paradigm the theology of interreligious dialogue relativizes the very foundations that theology has always taken for granted, namely, religion and religious belief. As that basis is progressively eroded — which does not necessarily mean a world engulfed in atheism and agnosticism — theology will begin to outgrow its narrow religious niche in preference for the open arena of the world. Some people would consider this to be the end of theology, and, indeed, multifaith dialogue is only one of a number of recent developments that pushes theological exploration toward renewed and enlarged horizons.

Conclusion

These theological trends, and a host of others that could be named,[6] invite us to engage in a new theological discourse. The *spiritual landscape,* rather than the *religious tradition,* has become the arena for theological exploration. And the theological excursion may no longer begin with God and work downward; rather, it will originate in the human experience of searching and seeking and move outward to embrace ever wider horizons of life and reality. Like the universe itself, our theological parameters are expanding, not contracting. The *context* in which we do theology is becoming as important as the science of theology itself (see Bevans, 1992).

To this day the Christian church claims a monopoly over theological discourse and conscientiously believes that it has a duty to safeguard the purity and integrity of doctrine. Meanwhile, theological exploration — by which I understand the human attempt to grapple with divine-human co-creativity in the world — is outstripping not merely its ecclesiastical context, but even its religious one. The emerging theological agenda is based on questions from the *world* to the *world;* the earthly and cosmic dimensions can no longer be ignored or relegated to a secondary role. If the churches and religions wish to be involved they seem to have little choice other than dialogue with the world of our time.

Instead of feeling threatened and responding in a negative and defensive fashion, surely the churches and the religions can find here a moment of liberating grace to allow and enable the world to take future responsibility for that treasure which the churches and the religions have reserved to themselves for so long. Are our churches and religious institutions broad-minded and big-hearted enough to cut the proverbial apron-strings and entrust the theological heritage to a new parent or, perhaps more appropriately, to its own emerging maturity?

This book sets out to explore another theological horizon: the mystery and meaning inherent in the quantum theory. This is not an attempt to make science sacred, godly, or holy; rather, it is an exploration of the divine co-creativity emanating from one of the most ingenious scientific discoveries of the twentieth century. Nor is it a new way of exploring the dialogue between science and religion (outlined in comprehensive review by Rolston, 1987, and Barbour, 1990). No, it is a great deal more, embarking upon a creative threshold that will push both the scientific imagination and the religious fascination to new frontiers unknown to previous generations.

Quantum theory in its strictly scientific sense studies the nature of reality at the microscopic level, beyond the perceptions and comprehensions of our daily observations. But even the early proponents of the theory could not lay aside their intuitive hunches that this theory points to something much larger and more engaging, with far-reaching implications not merely for the scientific pursuit itself, but for our comprehension and understanding of life at every level of existence. Alongside the strictly scientific understanding, creative thinkers of our time are unearthing philosophical, metaphorical, and mystical ramifications to the quantum vision; it is these latter dimensions that will concern us primarily in the present work. First, however, let's review some of the central notions of the theory itself.

Chapter 3

What Is the Quantum All About?

Anyone who is not shocked by Quantum Theory has not understood it.

—NEILS BOHR

It is more important to have beauty in one's equations than to have them fit experiment.

—PAUL DIRAC

I want to support the view that the foundation of reality itself is a unified, indeterminate maze of possibilities.

—DANAH ZOHAR

Science is a strange and fascinating world. It has echoes of discovering hidden secrets and conquering alien forces. It sets about unraveling mysteries of the universe, but also mysteries of our own bodies, such as the make-up of DNA. On the other hand, science provides the knowledge and skill to build bombs and demolish natural habitats, in the name of "progress." For some, it is the ultimate wisdom that will enable us to get rid of the God of superstition; for others, it is the ultimate atheism underpinning humankind's irrational craving to be totally in charge of the universe.

Science is presumed to be the invention of the seventeenth century and more specifically of the technological revolution of the twentieth century. But from time immemorial, people have been asking scientific questions and experimenting with scientific solutions. Magic and witchcraft are prehistoric equivalents of contemporary science. The ancient Greeks speculated that the world consisted of air, water, earth, fire, and ether; they also laid the foundations for geometry, a form of mathematics still in use. For a great deal of our human history, science, religion, and philosophy were considered to be one, a wholistic perception whose inherent wisdom we seem to be rediscovering at the present time.

Our daily lives are immersed in the culture of science. Every time I switch on the television set, use a camera, take an aspirin, run a water tap, drive a car, or play a computer game, I am interacting with my world in accord with scientific wisdom and discovery. Science is what makes the world go round. All the technology we use — day in, day out — for a vast range of purposes, is the product of scientific discovery. At one level, there is nothing mysterious in it; at another level, it is mystery all over.

The Classical Model

That type of science with which we are quite familiar in daily life we call the classical model. It is characterized by:

a. *Cause and effect:* I push the switch and the television comes on. Everything happens as a result of something that causes it to happen.

b. *Determinism:* Retaining the example of the television, it is predictable that the set comes on when I push the switch — assuming, of course, that both switch and set are in working order. Everything in the universe is assumed to work in this predetermined, predictable fashion.

c. *Wholes comprising a certain number of parts:* The TV is a whole (machine) in its own right, consisting of a specific number of parts. If the set does not work, it has to be the result of faulty or damaged parts. Repair or replace the parts and all will be well. Everything in the universe works in similar fashion — or so we are often told!

The classical worldview was — and continues to be — neat, efficient, and so easy to comprehend. We knew where we stood with it — at least we thought we did until the nineteenth century, when it began to dawn on the scientific community that in trying to explain the world, we had, in fact, been explaining it away. Face-value impressions were considered to be objective and reliable; what the neutral observer detected and verified in experiment was considered to be reality as reality was.

Atoms, as the basic units comprising all life[7] in the universe, were first named by the Greek philosopher Anaxagoras (500–428 B.C.E.).

Atoms were considered to be indivisible and indestructible (hence the term "elementary particles"), a view that prevailed until the nineteenth century, when physicists such as John Dalton, J. J. Thompson, and Ernest Rutherford began to analyze the composition and nature of the atom. This led, at the beginning of the present century, to the splitting of the atom and the identification of a proliferation of subatomic particles, now numbering over one hundred.

The exploration and discovery of subatomic particles still goes on. The approach is very simple and seems to make sense: continue to break things down into smaller and tinier pieces and eventually you reach the original bit (or bits) out of which all others emerged. Once we have discovered the original bit(s), then, we assume, we will know how the universe began, how it is intended to work, how various forces within it can be conquered and controlled, and how it will eventually end. We will have a complete understanding of life as we know it, and, more importantly, we humans will be totally in control. The oft-cited quote from the French mathematician Pierre Laplace (1749–1827) is quite unambiguous:

> An intelligence knowing at any given instant of time, all forces acting in nature, as well as the momentary positions of all things of which the universe consists, would be able to comprehend the motions of the largest bodies of the world and those of the smallest atoms in one single formula, provided it were sufficiently powerful to subject all data to analysis; to it nothing would be uncertain, both future and past would be present before its eyes. (Quoted in Davies, 1984, 38)

This oft-quoted passage highlights the subconscious (and frequently conscious) drive that underpinned and motivated a great deal of scientific research throughout the classical era. It has reaped many benefits for humankind and for our world; unfortunately it has also generated enormous human exploitation and no small share of ecological catastrophe.

According to the classical approach, all elements in the universe are stable, isolated, independent of each other, and operate as in a machine where each part functions in order to make the whole (machine) operate effectively. This model was virtually unassailable until Albert Einstein formulated his relativity theories in the early years of the present century. These were the first of several discoveries in the twentieth century which rocked the classical paradigm in vogue for the previous four hundred years.

Einstein's special theory of relativity claimed that time and space are not two separate entities, but that together they form a space-time continuum, and that energy and mass are, in fact, two aspects of the same phenomenon. Things can be understood only *relative* (i.e., in relation) to each other, not independent of, nor isolated from, each other, as absolute values.

In 1915, Einstein went on to outline his theory of general relativity, in which the framework of the special theory is extended to include gravity, i.e., the mutual attraction of all massive bodies. According to Einstein's theory, the force of gravity has the effect of curving space and time. This means that three-dimensional geometry, developed by Euclid and adopted by Newton, was no longer adequate to measure and describe space and time. Our world is not a flat plane, but a curved space and the degree of curvature depends on the mass of (the amount of stuff in) an object. And all objects move and interact relative (in relation) to the curved nature of the space-time continuum, a curvature which effectively holds everything in place and enables the universal life process to function as a great whole (see Swimme and Berry, 1992, 260).

Einstein's theory of relativity is an eminently rational theory, uniquely capable of predicting and measuring the motion of objects such as stars and planets. When we want to express the theory in ordinary language, however, we run into serious difficulties since our conventional notions of space and time cannot be extended to include the nature of reality postulated by Relativity theory. In other words, our common notions of reality are limited to our ordinary experience of the physical world and have to be abandoned whenever we extend this experience.

Philosophically and spiritually, however, relativity theory raises provocatively new questions, which theologians generally have not yet acknowledged or addressed. The theory evokes a novel sense of how we perceive and understand reality in terms of a four-dimensional space-time continuum. And Einstein's famous equation, $E=MC^2$ (C being the speed of light), alters the view that mass is a form of indestructible matter and instead becomes a form of energy, capable of being modified and transformed. Beyond its strictly scientific significance, relativity theory is a powerful metaphor inviting the human imagination to transcend the rational, calculable, sense-perception observations of our daily existence. Beyond the experience of life based on the immediacy of our senses is an alternative worldview opening up realms of mystery and fascination for the intuitive imagination, that sphere of human living so pauperized by the excessive rationalism of recent centuries.

The Quantum Theory

Equipped with this new sense of openness, excitement, and exploration, scientists in the 1920s really began to push the frontiers of the human imagination; even Einstein himself could not keep pace. The classical concept of a world of solid objects, governed by deterministic laws of nature, came under fresh scrutiny. There began to emerge a distinctive sense of an alive universe, and instead of being isolated, everything seemed to connect, interact, and interrelate. The time was ripe for a massive quantum leap![8]

Scientists have always been fascinated by light — its speed, its nature, its purpose. In classical science, light consists of a long series of particles, forming a string of energy which, on hitting its target, illuminates it. But in the 1920s, the German physicist Max Planck postulated that all radiation (whether light or heat) is not emitted continuously, but appears in the form of energy packets. Einstein called these energy packets "quanta" and recognized them as fundamental aspects of nature. The fascinating thing about these quanta is that one could never say for sure whether they were particles or waves of energy, whether they could be said to exist at definite times and places or whether they tended to exist as probability waves. Today they tend to be understood as nonlinear waves, known as solitons, whose very existence makes sense only in terms of the medium to which they belong, namely, the information-rich subquantum field, hence the definition offered by Laszlo (1993, 138): quanta are observable soliton-like flows within an otherwise unobservable subquantum medium.

Quantum theory offers a new way of analyzing heat energy and poses fresh questions regarding the nature of reality at the microscopic, subatomic level. Scientists continue to unravel the intricate implications and applications of this theory. Meanwhile, scholars of other disciplines detect far-reaching implications of the quantum theory for their respective fields of exploration (e.g., Chopra, Zohar, Wheatley), leading to radically new understandings of this theory, often baffling and bemusing to mainstream scientists. When viewed and explored within a multidisciplinary context, quantum theory assumes profoundly challenging implications for human and planetary life.

It is at a perceptual level that the theory evokes a new way of viewing and understanding our world. In essence, it states that everything we perceive and experience is a great deal more than the initial, external impression we may obtain, that we experience life, not in isolated segments, but in *wholes* (quanta), that these bundles of energy which impinge upon us are not inert, lifeless pieces of matter, but living energies; that our naming of the living reality we experience will at least be a probability-guess at what its real essence is (an essence best understood by interacting with it experientially rather than trying to conceptualize it at an "objective" distance).

A homely example of the quantum vision of reality is the wooden desk I use every day. Externally it seems to be a dead, inert material object, which I can dismantle into its constituent parts and destroy if I wish. But if I take any fragment of the desk and place it under a powerful microscope, I will notice that it is a sea-bed of minute, "moving" particles. In the quantum context, I am invited to view my desk as something that is *alive* (as described in endnote 7). The "life" is crystallized in the timber, tightly packed and condensed, but comprising the same particles that make up my body and everything else in the universe.

Truly, my desk may be described as a pulsating conundrum of crystallized energy. Even the sweat, toil, devotion, and creativity of those who made my desk belong to its essential nature and may be having a minute but nonetheless real effect on my feelings and thinking as I write these words. My desk is a constellation of living energy which, at very fine and sensitive levels, is affecting my psyche, just as I am affecting it.

In a similar vein, Ferguson (1994, 5) writes:

> My chair is a blur of uncertainty which I am allowed to think of as imaginably tiny particles whizzing around in a fuzzy manner. I know I mustn't think of those particles as "things" in exactly the sense I think of the chair as a "thing" — something that can be pinned down in the accurate way we expect to pin things down. I wonder whether a chair consisting of "non-things" can itself fairly be called a "thing," and why I see it as such.

The indeterminate, undefinable nature of the particle-wave duality is a central tenet of the quantum theory and of the extended application under review in this book. Not merely does it seek to outgrow the classical distinction between wave (momentum) and particle (position), but it postulates a new phenomenon, called the "wave packet," wherein the subatomic particles (e.g., electrons) are neither fully particles nor fully waves. While we can measure waves and particles on their own, the exact properties of the duality always defy precise and accurate measurement. Fuzziness, uncertainty, and probability are the crucial features of existence at this deeper, quantum level where, as Zukav (1979, 275) reminds us, we are dealing with a piece of action best described as a set of *relationships*. Our human desire for neatness, precision, and clarity seems to be a misleading delusion, an inherited "controlling" device of the patriarchal mindset, that seems to have outlived its usefulness.

For newcomers to quantum theory, one of the most difficult concepts to grasp is the collapse of the wave function that occurs just after an observation has been made. The wave function in effect represents what in quantum theory is called a "superposition of states," in other words, the simultaneous coexistence of several different possibilities, such that each possibility has its own specific probability of being observed. When the observation is made, only one of these possibilities materializes; the wave function has "collapsed" to the one possibility which has now ensued. In less simple situations, a few (rather than just one) possibilities may materialize. Again, there are far-reaching implications to this aspect of the central theory. For millennia — even in prehistoric times — humans experienced life as an overwhelming array of potential and possibility. Indeed, the patriarchal urge to dominate and control may be understood as an attempt to reduce the awesomeness of life to manageable proportions. Our problem now is that we consider the primary reality to be that which has ensued from our reductionistic exploits. And this is beginning to prove deeply dissatisfying to the human spirit. Intuitively we know there is so much more to understand and experience.

The collapse of the wave function is a timely reminder to us that we are enveloped by a universe of enormous diversity and vitality, all of which we cannot engage with simultaneously, without being overwhelmed and confused, but which we can assimilate in condensed or unique bundles, arising from our interaction with our world. The process that leads to the collapse of the whole into one or other outcome is another of the great quandaries of quantum theory: to what extent do our perceptions bring reality into being?

Do We Create Our Own Reality?

The impact of human observation on the world of particle physics remains largely unresolved. In classical Newtonian physics, the observer or experimenter was an external agent who was considered to be totally neutral and objective. Nowadays, we believe that the observer is always involved in the process of observing and, in spite of his or her best efforts to the contrary, will *always* influence the experiment and its eventual outcome. In a participatory universe, there is no such thing as a neutral observer.

According to quantum theory, not only is the observer involved, but the observer actually brings about what is being observed. What we observe in the world around us is what we choose to observe, and our very act of observing brings reality into being. Whether, therefore, the wave/particle is manifested as a wave or as a particle depends on which one the observer is seeking. This is known as the Copenhagen interpretation of which Neils Bohr and Werner Heisenberg were the most ardent advocates, and for which James A. Wheeler (and his notion of a participatory universe) is one of the most committed contemporary proponents.

This could be considered to be a narrow interpretation of the Copenhagen school. There is also the view which claims that the quantum world is *actual* — things really happen in it — but not *real,* in the sense of containing *res,* things, as we perceive and identify various aspects of reality. "According to the Copenhagen view," writes Thompson (1990, 99), "until the observation is made particles have ambiguous, 'ghostly' states and then the observation 'reduces' the particles to the determinate states we observe." This view seems to acknowledge an objective reality which we humans perceive and know only in a piecemeal and limited way.

Zohar (1993, 21ff.) adopts a similar view, considering reality as a vast sea of potential for which the scientist (and, indeed, each one of us) acts as a midwife — evoking, at any one time, one or more aspects of the vast underlying potential. She cites the example of language acquisition: all infants are born with the potential to learn any one or several of the world's existing languages (they can, and do, utter all of the eight hundred or so phonemes which make up these languages), but each will develop his or her linguistic abilities in accord with the linguistic repertoire of the surrounding culture. Potentially, the whole of our reality is always greater than that which we perceive or engage with in daily life. (On this and other aspects of the quantum theory, see Polkinghorne, 1984; Herbert, 1985; Russell, Murphy, and Isham, 1993; Zohar, 1990, 1993; and a valuable contemporary overview in Horgan, 1992).

One of the initial challenges to the Copenhagen view came from Einstein in his collaborative experiment with Boris Podolsky and

Nathan Rosen, the EPR experiment, which demonstrated that if a beam of light is put through a magnetic field (called a Stern-Gerlach device), the field splits the beam into two equal, smaller beams. If we modify the spin status of a particle in one beam, there is an instantaneous change in the other so that its spin is always equal and opposite that of its twin. The effects on the second particle take place without any direct human interference (observation). Alain Aspect's experiment of 1982 (described below on p. 57) provides a much more convincing confirmation of what the EPR experiment demonstrates.

The role of the experimenter strikes at the very heart of to-day's scientific ideology. There are some quite serious methodological questions here, some with enormous ethical import. Contemporary science works on the assumption that the human mode of perception, understanding, and comprehension — at this stage in the evolution of humankind — is the highest possible form of wisdom both now and for the foreseeable future. That the human (scientific) mind can be in error — which it often is — is something that the scientific community is notoriously reluctant to acknowledge. By and large, scientists dislike metaphysics, but they play an intriguing metaphysical game with its own language and concepts when they describe the scientific process of experiment-verification-proof, selectively forgetting that the whole scientific edifice has been constructed, influenced, and interpreted by fallible human beings. Even those ardently committed to the quantum vision are culpable of ignoring, or at least underestimating, the complex and limited nature of human understanding.

The debate on the role of the observer has been advanced in recent times. The insights of Gestalt psychology, which initially flourished in the 1920s (when the quantum theory was first conceived) pioneered by scholars such as M. Wertheimer, K. Koffka, and W. Kohler, regained prominence in the 1960s, making the bold claim that humans do not think or perceive in piecemeal fashion, but wholistically. For example, I look out my window at a nearby house. An image registers in my brain (what the scientist calls the collapse of the wave function). I can describe the image of that house, noting its various features. As far as I am concerned, I have mentally examined the house and ignored everything else in the surrounding environment.

According to Gestalt psychology, I have perceived a great deal more than the house. I also noted in my mind the total geographical/situational context, to such an extent that if that same house was situated elsewhere, my perception — in minute details — would be considerably different. In other words, *innately* I perceive in wholes, not in parts; my brain is tuned to perceive wholistically.

Wholistic Consciousness

The work of Karl Pribram (1971) in the 1960s and 1970s confirms these discoveries in his holographic model of the human brain. The brain, functioning as a hologram (described below on pp. 55–56), interprets bioelectric frequencies, not at individual centers, but throughout the brain. Information is not localized but spread throughout in wave-like, frequency patterns along a network of fine fibers on the nerve cells. Only such a model could interpret and understand our holographic, wholistic universe.

Danah Zohar (1990, 1993), acknowledging the holographic model of mind and consciousness, seeks to push the quantum vision even further. She proposes a quantum, mechanical model of consciousness to explain how the brain and its neurons can act in a coherent, unified way. The necessary physical mechanism, which functions at normal body temperature, seems to be similar to the "pumped system" of electrically charged molecules (dipoles) first described by Herbert Frohlich (1968). When energy is pumped into electrically charged molecules, a threshold of excitation is reached beyond which the molecules begin to vibrate in unison. They do so increasingly until they pull themselves into a highly ordered form known as a "Bose-Einstein condensate." When all membranes vibrate sufficiently to pull themselves into the most coherently possible form of order, we have a Bose-Einstein condensate, with the aid of which we can distinguish conscious from nonconscious systems: In Zohar's own words:

> Evidence for coherent states (Bose-Einstein condensates) in biological tissue is now abundant, and the interpretation of its meaning lies at the cutting edge of exciting breakthroughs in our understanding of what distinguishes life from non-life. *I think that the same Bose-Einstein condensate among neurone constituents is what distinguishes the conscious from the nonconscious. I think it is the physical basis of consciousness.* (Zohar, 1990, 67–68).

Zohar works on the assumption that consciousness is a property of all living systems and, in a quantum context, becomes the basis not merely for awareness, but more importantly for *relationships,* an innate potential for mutual cooperation between all beings and systems within the one quantum universe. In this model, the dualistic dichotomy between observer and that being observed itself breaks down; the collapse of the wave function leads only to reductionistic confusion. Instead, it is suggested that observation gives way to relationship, a complex mode of interacting, fluctuating between giving and receiving, until a sense of *resonance* (see Taylor, 1991; Metzner, 1987) emerges, whereby the individual parts (giver and receiver, observer and observed) lose their dualistic, independent identities, but rediscover a sense of the "quantum self" in the interdependent relationship of the new whole, which might be anything from the marriage of two people to a newly felt bond with the universe itself.

Living systems are by their very nature neither subjects alone nor objects isolated, but both subjects and objects in a mutually communicating (and defining) universe of meaning. At a deep level, each living being is implicated in every other. Each suffering, each extinction, affects us and impoverishes us. Similarly, we partake of the joy and creativity of each individual organism. The capacity of organisms to evolve thus depends on their capacity for communication. This deeper truth has been ignored by neo-Darwinian theory, which sees evolution only in terms of competition of the fittest in the battle for survival. Ultimately, it is not the individual species which evolves as much as all living systems connected interdependently within a coherent whole.

Contemporary advocates of the quantum theory, while acknowledging the historical significance of the Copenhagen interpretation (which, among other things, claims that the observer influences — to the point of determining — the outcome of any experiment or observation), no longer adhere to its anthropomorphic impact. We humans do not and cannot determine the final outcome, except by a quality of interference and control that is often deleterious rather than beneficial to progress and growth.

We humans are not the masters of creation; we are participators in a co-creative process that is much greater than us and probably quite capable of getting along without us (as happened for almost fifteen billion years before our species evolved). If we are to influence global and planetary life, we'll do it in cooperative interaction rather than in competitive strife. Our interrelationship with life — at both the micro and macro levels — is a learning process of mutual interdependence, and not that of exploitation, combat, and warfare, a lethal process which is almost certain to destroy us in the end.

We can now return to some of the key concepts of the quantum theory and explore their meaning in the light of our new vision.

Cause and Effect

In a quantum universe, all life is understood to operate within the context of relational interaction. Everything is affected (rather than caused) by everything else. The poet Francis Thompson seems to have imbibed this view when he wrote: "Thou can'st not stir a flower without disturbing a star." At the observational level, my action of turning on the TV may be described as cause and effect. The quantum vision invites (and challenges) me to the realization that such an "effect" is only possible in an electromagnetic universe; my ability to move my hand in order to push the switch is also affected by the universal law of gravity. There is a great deal more to switching on the TV than mere cause and effect. In fact, cause and effect has to do with the "part" which can be fully understood only within the wider, global "whole."

Determinism

In a quantum universe, nothing is predictable, and the idea of life being in any way determined is abhorrent. Quantum theorists very much like the word "probability" (for which Heisenberg's uncertainty principle[9] is a basic tenet). Surprise, expectancy, wonder, creativity, beauty, and elegance are the kind of words that enable the quantum scientist to make sense of reality.

There is a shadow side to this description which goes something like this: if the universe is not determined by an external agent (e.g., God, as both Newton and Einstein believed), then we can begin determining and controlling it for our own self-aggrandizement. Let me emphasize: this is *not* quantum theory in its purity (if there is such a quality of theory); this is an aberration of what the original theorists conceived. Throughout the 1940s and 1950s it became the dominant orientation of the scientific and medical communities, and it still prevails, although its prevalence is beginning to wane in the face of recent scientific awareness and the challenge of a growing wholistic consciousness.

In abandoning determinism, the proponents of the quantum theory were, inadvertently, advocating a quality of mystical receptivity: be open to the unfolding (evolving) nature of life at all levels. Life is not determined by blind external forces; it is affected, for weal or for woe, by the quality of our respect for its inherent processes and our willingness to interact with (relate to) all life forms in a gentle, non-exploitive, cooperative manner. Modern ecology, with its acute sense of planetary homeostasis, is deeply in tune with the original dream of the quantum physicists.

The Whole Equals the Sum of the Parts

Although quantum theory is widely accepted in scientific circles, there are very few scientists who understand it fully or who claim to be able to explain it in a simple and succinct way. I would submit that quantum theory is complex, but not necessarily complicated. The human body — a prime example of quantum theory at work — is highly complex, yet exhibits an amazing sense of order, rhythm, and purpose.

What makes the human body special is the complex interaction of so many forces and energies that we do not (and cannot) observe in everyday life. There is no scientific, sociological, or psychological means of measuring the intimacy and exhilaration of courtship, the eroticism of sexual embrace, the ecstasy of contemplative prayer, the gripping excitement of sport or achievement, the placid serenity of a beautiful sunset, or, alternatively, the rending terror of pain and suffering or the mental and physical exhaustion of agony and torture. In all these situations, and in many others, what is happening in the *whole* person can be neither analyzed nor understood in terms of some or all the *parts* of the human personality.

For the quantum theorists, the fact that the whole is greater than the sum of the parts underpins all reality. For everything in life, there is more to it than meets the eye. The real essence, and the real meaning, is deep within, which in effect often means both inside and outside the object we are observing.

Like many discoveries in the early years of the twentieth century, it took some thirty to forty years before the new quantum awareness seeped through the sturdy barricades of rationalism and conservatism. Eventually the barricades began to crack and crumble. It all hit us in the 1960s as "bundles of energy" seemed to be cascading from all quarters. Among the leading discoveries was that of the quark assemblage, generating a precocious sense of excitement that the long-sought fundamental "building blocks" might at last be nailed. But nature was speaking a different language, and its quantum significance we'll review in a later chapter.

In modern physics, the image of the universe as a machine has been transcended by the alternative perception of an indivisible, dynamic whole whose parts are essentially interrelated and can be understood only as patterns of a cosmic process. At a subatomic level, the interrelations and interactions between the parts of the whole are more fundamental than the parts themselves. There is motion, but there are ultimately no moving objects; there is activity, but there are no actors. There are no dancers; there is only the dance itself! (See Capra, 1982, 83.)

To join in that dance, we need to shed a lot of fears and inhibitions — not a few of which are religious in nature. It is only by participating that we learn what the dance is all about. The day of the neutral observer is well nigh spent!

Part Two

The Dance

Yet that fierce memory of freedom's dance will yet prevail....

–Mary Grey

Chapter 4

Energy, Movement, and Rhythm

Subatomic particles do not just sit around being sub-atomic particles. They are beehives of activity.
— GARY ZUKAV

Modern physics pictures matter not at all as passive and inert, but as being in a continuous dancing and vibrating motion, whose rhythmic patterns are determined by the molecular, atomic and nuclear structures.
— FRITJOF CAPRA

If our senses were fine enough, we would perceive the slumbering cliff as a dancing chaos.
— FRIEDRICH NIETZSCHE

Energy is the substance of life, the unrelenting wellspring of pure possibility, escalating and undulating as in a great cosmic dance. Life throbs with energy and potential, the Chinese *ch'i*, the homeopaths' vital force, the Reichian "orgone energy." It unfolds amid movement, connection, and relationship, defying, from the scientific point of view, concrete description or definition, but evoking in the mystic primordial images of some great dancer dancing the world into being.

Dance is an elegant form of movement, characterized by great freedom and spontaneity. As we are moved along by the rhythm and tempo of the music, we experience a sense of being danced rather than we ourselves performing the dance. Yet, dance is a highly organized activity governed by set postures, specific movements, and standard combinations.

The structure is important to get the dance into its rhythm. Once the inner movement takes over, the external structure becomes less important. And often the "external" movements become natural and spontaneous. The inner and outer blend into one.

Dancing is one of the few experiences left to us that has not been mechanized. Indeed the rise of pop music and its accompanying subculture — with its tendency to be spontaneous in movement and rhythm — may well be a subconscious protest against our over-mechanized world. A modern disco is a powerful symbol of protest against mechanization: people dance and move to a whole range of beats and rhythms; participants act out a vast array of feelings and emotions. Some dance on their own, often lost in a fantasy world (it would seem); others dance within a range of different combinations. Frequently, the music is blaringly loud, aggressive and belligerent in tone and quality. To the outsider, it can easily convey the sense of being a great escape or a confusing chaotic melee, but for the dancer, it is an experience that often defies rational explanation.

The desire to dance is deeply ingrained in the human psyche. It is also woven into the tapestry of evolution itself and has become a powerful metaphor to understand and explain the nature of planetary and human life. As a cultural phenomenon, dance is one of the earliest modes of human communication. Campbell (1976, 282ff.) suggests a strong biological link with our animal ancestry. Just as animals dance to a range of ritualistic behaviors to express their creativity, so we humans, from a very early stage of our evolution, used this medium to express and explore significant life experiences.

Huizinga (1950) coined the term *Homo Ludens* to indicate the human need for jest and playfulness. But the very process of exploring and expressing this playfulness takes on planetary and cosmic dimensions. All play — and particularly dance — assumes a wider cultural significance. It is as if creation itself dances with the dancer.

Going right back into the twilight of our human story, at least to six hundred thousand years ago (when we think fire was first brought under human control), our human ancestors danced. Dance was one of their chief forms of communication — with each other, with nature, with the cosmos, and with the life force (God). Dance emerged as a primary medium to make sense and meaning out of life. Dance became the connecting link with the "ultimate source," the medium used to establish archetypal communication with the heart of reality. Dance is the first, most ancient, and most enduring form of *religion*.

Dancing to Our Sacredness

Today we use the notion of "sacred dance" to denote forms of circle or liturgical movement that awaken and convey religious sentiment. In anthropological and evolutionary terms, *all* dance is sacred. For thousands of years before the development of formal religion, we humans did not draw the currently dualistic distinction between the sacred and secular. In its origin and evolution, dance is fundamentally spiritual, and its primary innate function is to facilitate contact with the sacred and the divine.

Not only did our ancient ancestors dance to the sacred, a practice often dismissed by Christians as pagan worship; they also danced in order to articulate and celebrate what Wosien (1974, 110) calls the wonder of existence. External action and inner experience were given symbolic, ritual expression, activating a process of wholeness and integration. Dance became the primary medium to explore and articulate the human search for meaning.

Long before spoken language became a feature of life (probably about a hundred thousand years ago), a highly elaborate, symbolic form of communication existed among people. Long before religion was ever taught, preached, or codified in sacred texts, it was lived and celebrated in ritual play and dance.

Modern versions of sacred (circle) dance illustrate something of the effusive richness of these ancient forms, particularly the group dimension, the circular aspect, and the sense of interconnectedness. According to the ethnologist Joachim Wach (1958, 137), dance was a means of affirming the cohesion of the group in its communion with nature, with the ancestors, and with the source of life. Everything was experienced as a wholeness, not in rigidly, fixed form however, but as a conglomerate of movement and energy, often chaotic, but at a fundamental level, characterized by rhythm, pattern, and interconnectedness.

Thus, many of the great experiences of prehistoric dance were related to aspects of the hunt, the changing seasons, transitional moments in human life (e.g., birth, death, rites of passage), and the precarious events of nature (e.g., rainfall, storms, drought). The dance was a core experience of creative imagination, a moment of human/divine transformation, a space-time connection with the creative life force, which thousands of years later, formal religion named as "God."

Perhaps the greatest disservice that formal religion has rendered to our world is its tendency to disrupt the dance. It tried to project God out of creation into the "divine" realms of the church (on earth) and heaven (in the world beyond). It has led us into a speculative, cerebral mode (of thought and action), which ultimately was not about devotion and worship, but an insatiable desire to control the capricious power of the Deity. We tried to sever the divine connection with the heart and with the imagination and substituted the head and the soul in their place. Faithful to the spirit of the Agricultural Revolution, we fragmented the spiritual realm of human experience, just as we had begun to fragment the one planet into nations, races, and ethnic groups. Instead of the dance, we invented formal rituals which, in time, became structures without a spirit, insipid formalities devoid of feeling and imagination.

So that the reader can keep pace with the quantum leap that I am exploring, I make the following observations about formal religion, pointers that will recur several times throughout this book:

a. Formal religion is a very recent visitor to Planet Earth. It began to emerge — with Hinduism — about 3000 B.C.E. and could be said to have ceased with the rise of Sikhism in the seventeenth century.[10] In terms of human evolution, dating the emergence of Homo sapiens to about 100,000 B.C.E., formal religion has flourished for merely 5 percent of that time.

b. As indicated earlier, humans have grappled with religious issues — and the spiritual meaning of life — for thousands of years. Anthropological evidence for this exploration can be traced to about 70,000 B.C.E. (outlined in another work, O'Murchu, 1986), but further research is likely to date it even earlier than this. Consequently, humans were evolving and developing as *spiritual* creatures for thousands of years before adopting an identity of *religious* allegiance, through one or other formal religion.

c. In today's world, we often confuse *religion* and *spirituality,* giving the impression that one can be spiritual only by adopting and practicing a formal, official faith system. Around our world, however, are millions of people who do not belong to any specific church or religion, but still grapple with spiritual questions and strive to live out of a spiritual value system. This fact, combined with the diminishing influence and impact of formal religions — especially in the Western world — would seem to indicate that the religions are in decline, while the revitalization and rediscovery of spirituality engages the human heart and imagination in a range of new and exciting ways.

d. Although theology, in its formal sense, is about religion and its official teachings, there has been a notable (unconscious) shift on the part of theologians to include wider spiritual concerns in their reflections and writings, particularly among feminist theologians (e.g., King, 1989; Zappone, 1991; McFague, 1987, 1993; Grey, 1993). In the past twenty years, theology has moved significantly from being a highly academic science that began by postulating a higher being (God) and argued deductively toward the religious meaning of all reality. Most forms of modern theology (as outlined in chapter 2) tend to begin with people's experience. Through a process of reflection and dialogue centered on that experience, people begin to name their spiritual feelings and values and may (or may not) eventually contextualize this exploration in terms of one or other religious creed.

How we do theology is changing, rapidly and dramatically, and the subject being explored in this book, quantum theology, accelerates that change, even to a degree that could alter the whole landscape of theological discourse.

Dance of the Gods

Let's return to the dance — interrupted when religion came along! But that disruption serves to remind us that Hinduism, the oldest of the formal religions, retained strong elements of the dance. The three most worshiped divinities in India today are Shiva, Vishnu, and Shakti, the Great Mother. Shiva is one of the oldest Indian gods and is often portrayed as the king of dancers. According to Hindu belief, all life is part of a great rhythmic process of creation and destruction, of death and rebirth, and Shiva's dance symbolizes the eternal life-death rhythm which goes on eternally. Capra (1976) and Zukav (1979), in attempting to understand developments in modern physics, draw liberally on this ancient Indian wisdom, as does the theologian Moltmann (1985, 304–5) in outlining his ecological doctrine of creation.

The third great divinity, Shakti, also appears in Hindu tradition as Shiva's wife, and in many temple sculptures the two are shown in voluptuous, sensuous embrace. Hinduism, as distinct from Christianity, displays a magnificence and celebration around fertility and sexuality, and the human sexual encounter is understood to have global as well as personal significance. The procreative energy is a primary expression of the dance, which itself is inherently creative — for person and planet alike. The dance of Shiva symbolizes the dancing universe itself, expressed in the ceaseless flow of energy going through an infinite variety of patterns that melt into one another.

Most of the formal religions have retained some semblance of this rich inheritance. Examples that spring to mind include the swirling dances of the dervishes in Sufism (the mystical branch of Islam); the elaborate dance ritual of the lamas in Tibet; the fingernail dances that prevail in Thailand to this day; the Taoist Chiao festivals of China; the Zoroastrian dance at many popular shrines in Iran; the revival of sacred (liturgical) dance in contemporary forms of Christianity; and undoubtedly most impressive of all, the spontaneous and exuberant worship dances of native African and South American peoples. Hinduism, however, is unique in retaining a more explicit tradition, with many of the great epics, e.g., the *Ramayana,* "preached" in dance (the Ketjak dance of Bali) rather than in word; this is clearly linked to an older strand of immense spiritual and anthropological import.

Dance as a Scientific Metaphor

It is, perhaps, for this reason that a number of contemporary physicists (Capra, 1976; Zukav, 1979; Sahtouris, 1989; Swimme and Berry, 1992) draw strong links between modern developments in particle physics and the image of our world portrayed as a cosmic/sacred dance. An oft-cited example is the dance of Shiva, the Hindu God who symbolizes and integrates the apparently conflicting cycles of creation and destruction, birth and death.

Modern physics has shown that the rhythm of creation and destruction is not only manifest in the turn of the seasons and in the birth and death of all living creatures, but is also the very essence of inorganic matter. According to quantum theory, all interactions between the constituents of matter take place through the emission and absorption of virtual particles. More than that, the dance of creation and destruction is the basis of every existence of matter, since all material particles self-interact by emitting and reabsorbing virtual particles. According to modern physics, subatomic particles engage in an unceasing, pulsating process of creation and destruction. The subatomic world is one of rhythm, synchronized motion and continual change (see Ferguson, 1994, 60ff.).

To understand the dance, scientists rely heavily on mathematics as an interpretative tool. With the ascendency of the dance metaphor, the language of mathematics has correspondingly changed from dots, lines, and circles (what we call linear geometry) to sets, matrices, integrals, series, and probabilities. With the introduction of computers, numerical equations and geometric figures have given way to graphics and images of great elegance and beauty. Foremost among these is the Mandelbrot Set and the new progeny of mathematics known as *fractals* (see the illustration on the following page).

The current fascination with fractals owes its origin to the pioneering work of Benoit B. Mandelbrot (1977), of the IBM Thomas J. Watson Research Center in Yorktown Heights, New York. Mandelbrot coined the term "fractal" in 1975. (For a brief and valuable overview, see Jürgens et al., 1990.)

Fractals enable us to measure and describe "irregularities" in the world of our experience, e.g., weather patterns, cloud formation, jagged coastlines, the dripping of a water tap, the fibrillation of the human heart. Let us take as an example a piece of jagged coastline, which, on observation, seems to have a chaotic, irregular shape, devoid of any obvious design. Using modern computers, we can create a simulation of that piece of coastline. As we magnify the image on a computer, we note that specific sections are repetitions of the overall structure (like the repeating patterns of the dance). As we move into detailed analysis, we discover that each part is a replica of the whole. By obtaining an accurate measure of one small piece, we can deduce a measurement and calculation of the entire coastline.

In fractal geometry, the basic elements cannot be viewed directly, as in Euclidean geometry. Fractals are expressed, not in primary shapes (dots, lines, circles, etc.) but in algorithms, mathematical procedures which are translated into geometric forms with the aid of a computer. The supply of algorithmic elements is inexhaustibly large (a reflection of life and nature itself).

Fractals serve as a type of icon for the variegated and diffuse shapes that nature dances into being. Fractals, as distinct from Euclidean geometry, also enable us to interpret and comprehend our world, not as a series of inert, fixed objects, but as a moving, dynamic (changing) structure forever undergoing modification and transformation.

Fractals also provide us with deeper insight into the symmetrical shapes and contours of the created universe, reminding us once more of the symmetry which arises spontaneously in many dance forms, classical and popular.

THE MANDELBROT SET

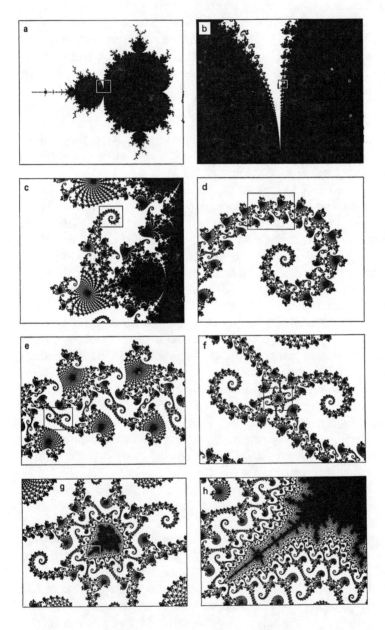

The Mandelbrot Set: If any region of the set is magnified, new and intricate detail appears as illustrated in the above sequence. *Source:* H. O. Peitgen and D. Saupe, eds., *The Science of Fractal Images* (Heidelberg: Springer-Verlag, 1987), p. 202, © H. O. Peitgen, H. Jürgens, and D. Saupe.

The Symmetry Within

"Symmetry" is one of the most frequently recurring words in contemporary scientific literature. The fact that space is the same in all directions (isotropic) and in all places (homogeneous) is an example of symmetry. The fact that time is homogeneous is another example. Something is symmetrical if certain aspects of it remain the same under varying conditions, e.g., a cannonball falling in accordance with the law of gravity, over a long distance, remains a cannonball. Symmetry relates to harmony and simplicity of form and is manifested in many aspects of nature. A snowflake displays a remarkable hexagonal symmetry; crystals exhibit characteristic geometrical shapes; the rain droplet is a perfect sphere, and when frozen, as a series of accretions of water from the air, becomes a spherical ice ball we call a hailstone.

Nature exhibits a vast stock of symmetries, acclaimed by poets and mystics. Scientists, on the other hand, tend to probe the underlying rotations and reflections, which they frequently detect in the course of their research. Sometimes new and unexpected symmetries are discovered by physicists while exploring the mathematical description of a physical system. With the aid of mathematics, scientists can decode the symmetries of nature, unearthing a symbolic content that is not readily apparent to someone observing the physical system itself. By manipulating the symbols in their equations, physicists can try to discover the full range of symmetries, including those that cannot be visualized. In recent years, the symmetry bonanza has proved so fruitful that it has taken over the thinking in many fields of contemporary research. (More on this topic in Pagels, 1985; Stewart and Golubitsky, 1992).

Music as a Pulse of Creation

When we dance, we follow the rhythm of music. Music is a form of sound, a harmonic rhapsody that elevates our spirits, awakens our hearts, and often transports us to either the heights of ecstasy or the depths of estrangement. Learning music is often perceived to be tedious and repetitious. Many young people never take it beyond second level, especially when the exam pressure of a "more serious" subject takes precedence. Where are our true values?

Twenty thousand years ago our ancient ancestors were already highly skilled in flute music. For thousands of years previously, instruments such as the drum (see Swimme and Berry, 1992, 44), rasp, rattle, and harp were used. In prehistoric times, music was considered to have magical qualities, facilitating communication with the gods, and capable of driving away evil forces. Music was used to induce altered states of consciousness in an attempt to realize in oneself and awaken in others (and in nature) the God-consciousness which pervades all life. According to some theorists (e.g., Hayes, 1994), music is based on notational structures which reflect the fundamental design of nature itself (e.g., the predominance of combinations of *three,* further explored in chapter 7).

Our ancient ancestors seem to have had an intuitive appreciation of music as a primordial, archetypal form of sound. And that sound was a creative energy — a vibration resonating through the instrumentation of created forms. Thus, the original power of creation is described in many religions as the power of sound, which in Judaism and Christianity we refer to as the "Word." As already indicated, the Aramaic *dabhar* does not mean "word" as understood linguistically, but rather an irresistible creative energy exploding into voluptuous and prodigious creativity (see Fox, 1984, 35–40).

Music, song, incantation, droning all embody this primordial, creative potential which animates the created order. It is not by accident, therefore, that contemporary physicists are rediscovering the musical undercurrent to our creative universe. Echoes can be detected in the fascination and controversy engendered by *superstring theory,* which postulates that the fundamental energy that enlivens everything in the universe may be compared to the vibrating energy that occurs when we move the bow over a musical string, the music being the "voiced" language of the silent energy. Swimme and Berry (1992) make liberal use of the music metaphor and in a rather inspirational passage (p. 40) describe humanity's role as a sounding board for a universe that is essentially melodious in nature.

For science and theology alike, I believe we are touching here on a truth of great depth and originality. The medium of scientific research can no longer be constrained by classical categories nor by traditional methods of observation and measurement. We can conceive of a universe in which the spheres themselves are dancing, and from the musical vibrations we are beginning to glimpse a whole new sense of what the universal life is about. In the poetic words of Davidson (1989, 402), we are invited to dance "according to some higher strings."

The energy that animates and enlivens all life may well be supersonically melodious, and the life force itself may be something more akin to an orchestra than to any spiral of subatomic particles. These considerations enable us to formulate our first principle of quantum theology:

> *There is more to our world than what can be perceived by the human senses or envisaged by the human imagination. Life is sustained by a creative energy, fundamentally benign in nature, with a tendency to manifest and express itself in movement, rhythm, and pattern. Creation is sustained by a superhuman, pulsating restlessness, a type of resonance vibrating throughout time and eternity.*

The God Question

Theologians in general are not likely to quibble with these ideas, but those of more orthodox leaning will question our starting point, which is not God, but rather our experience of the world as perceived with the quantum imagination. Even in the specific terms of quantum mechanics, the universe is fundamentally mysterious. We can break down its constituent parts and reassemble them. No problem there! When we try to understand how the parts interact and function for the sake of the whole, then the mystery begins to unfold, and we confront questions of ultimate meaning that concern theological discourse. At the heart of that mystery is the sense of a superhuman, creative restlessness.

The reader will notice that I refrain from using the word "God." I do so for a number of reasons:

a. Traditionally, theology began with God and the divine revelation as disclosed through the "deposit of faith" as contained in sacred writings (the Bible) and their interpretation by lawful (church) authorities. In that context, only those who believed in God (as described by formal religion) could be theologians. Quantum theology seeks to dismantle this exclusivity and open up the theological exploration to everybody, to all who are prepared to engage with their lived experience of the universe as a quantum reality.[11]

b. In traditional theology, there tends to be an emphasis on the God who creates from nothing (*ex nihilo*), and is therefore superior and external to the created order. Even in an incarnational religion like Christianity — with the focus on the God who becomes human in the midst of creation — the God "up above" often takes priority over the God who is immanent in the world of our experience.

In quantum theology, the creative potential emerges (evolves) from *within* the cosmos. "God" co-creates in conjunction with the evolutionary process. Questions of the "beginning" or "end" of creation are considered to be anthropomorphic speculations (i.e., human constructs) that distract from the immediacy and challenge of how we *experience* our world as participants in its emerging evolution.

c. Traditional theology is characterized by a strong fear of pantheism, the notion that God becomes so identified with the created order that (s)he has no identity apart from it. Scholars like the late J. A. T. Robinson adopted the notion of "panentheism" — God is present in all aspects of creation but not confined to it — to offset that fear. Quantum theology wishes to transcend the dualistic (either/or) undercurrents that lead in the first place to the perception that God must be either inside or outside the created order. As we shall see in later chapters, quantum theology seeks to demolish all dualisms, on the conviction that life is fundamentally one, that there is no inside or outside, that the divine energy operates as an open-ended, creative vibration, full of surprises, probabilities, unpredictabilities. Pantheism may be of concern to us humans, but it is unlikely to be of any consequence to the creative life force which impregnates and enlivens our world with prodigious resourcefulness.

d. For quantum theology, idolatry and blasphemy are among the great sins of traditional theology. By attempting to state clearly, logically, rationally, and philosophically the attributes and nature of God, traditional theology begets an *ideology* (blind, irrational, and irrevocable convictions) rather than a *theology*, of God. It has generated images of God largely made in the image and likeness of man(kind). It has stripped God of the splendor, elegance, and intimacy of the divine co-creativity.

Quantum theology seeks to recapture the mystery of God without in any way diminishing the incarnational aspect (cherished by Christianity). In conjunction with Buddhism, it refrains from confining the divine power to religious categories. It opts for more dynamic namings like the creative energy, the ultimate life force, the source of being, rather than the word "God," which is perceived to be loaded with idolatrous and ideological connotations. In conjunction with Islam, it seeks to uphold a sense of reverence, awe, and respect for the divinity, and with the great Eastern religions advocates deep silence as a primary mode of connecting with the divine wellspring of pure possibility.

Quantum theology abhors the human tendency to attribute literal significance to the sacred writings of the various religions. It acknowledges that the sacred texts of all the religions may be divinely inspired, but that inspiration has been, and continues to be, mediated through the human mind and imagination and is committed to human language which is always conditioned by the particular influences and nuances of specific cultures. Language is a human invention, a symbolic system which seeks to convey meaning in local cultural settings. It can never be absolutized to communicate the depth or totality of the divine intent.

e. Finally, quantum theology radically challenges the cosmology (worldview) of traditional theology. Although mainstream theology has changed many of its views on the world — quite profoundly in some cases — it has not made the quantum leap of acknowledging the evolving world as the arena for the drama of divine revelation; this marks the starting point for quantum theology.

Although the quantum theory highlights the illusive and transitory nature of the observable world, its primary concern is the pervading and permanent sense of reality that both underwrites and transcends that transitoriness. In the quantum view, the reality of our world does not need an external supernatural raison d'être or explanation to uncover what is really real. No, the ultimate rationale is within the creative, evolving process itself. Our world is not devoid of, nor lacking in, reality; its potential is vast, largely unmanifest in the creative dance of energy that will unfold — perhaps forever — certainly for billions of years into the open, unlimited future.

The dance and its vibrating music are key metaphors for this new theological vision. They help to uncover that sense of dynamism and movement which characterizes the divine unfolding within the evolutionary process. There are other dimensions to this dynamic for which the metaphor of the *holon* is frequently used. We'll explore its meaning in the next chapter.

_____ *Chapter 5* _____

Wholes and Parts

Through the action of the quantum potential, the whole system is undergoing a coordinated movement more like a ballet dance than like a crowd of unorganized people.

—DAVID BOHM

Our consciousness has the character of unbroken wholeness. It hangs together and allows our experience to do so.

—DANAH ZOHAR

You don't see something until you have the right metaphor to perceive it.

—ROBERT SHAW

The philosopher-scientist Arthur Koestler (1978, 57) suggested that we call each whole thing within nature a "holon," a whole made of its own parts, yet itself part of a larger whole. Each holon has two opposite tendencies: a self-assertive desire to preserve its individual autonomy (for which terms like interiority or autopoiesis are used occasionally), and an integrative tendency to function as part of the larger whole (hence, the notion of communion). In a biological or social system, each holon must assert its individuality in order to maintain the system's stratified order, but it must also submit to the demands of the whole in order to sustain the viability of the system. A human being, a nation, an ecosystem are all holons.

No living creature or open system can ever be entirely independent. It is a holon within a larger holon, depending for its very life on its environment, which *is* its larger holon. The interdependence, demanding a complementary interaction of dependence and independence, is known as "holonomy." An individual person, for example, must transcend simple self-rule and integrate himself or herself with the rules of society, while human society must transcend its autonomy and integrate itself with the holonomy imposed by the larger life form, Planet Earth.

Beyond the Mechanistic Metaphor

Along with being a word used to describe a state of mutual interdependence, the holon serves as a powerful metaphor for imaging reality anew. The philosopher Thomas Kuhn (1970) has outlined the notion of a paradigm shift, in which one dominant mode of understanding yields pride of place to another. A major paradigm or model tends to evoke certain images which often carry a deep symbolic significance. The dominant image emerging from the Industrial Revolution, and used as the subconscious model to understand life at a range of different levels is the "machine."[12] As a cultural metaphor, it is still widely adopted — especially in science and medicine — but it is gradually being superseded by the "holon" as the dominant image for understanding the processes of life in our world today.

Every major shift in human culture throws up new symbols, metaphors, ideas, and possibilities. The Industrial Revolution, allied with the intellectual skills of Newtonian science (along with the religious dogmatism of the post-Reformation Era), adopted — subconsciously rather than consciously — the *machine* as the basic metaphor for understanding life. Within this conceptual framework, the universe was presumed to work like a mechanical clock, predetermined, predictable, and totally comprehensible in terms of a set number of parts comprising the whole. In the world of classical science, *everything,* from the cosmos, to Planet Earth, to the human body right down to the kitchen toaster, was understood and considered to be a machine. Even to this day, orthodox medicine retains this metaphor for modeling the human body, and for dictating the quality and quantity of medical intervention designed to address the diagnosis that has been made.

With the machine as its basic metaphor, industrialization, and the vast global, technological culture it produced, brought immense benefits to humankind, and still makes an important contribution. But from the beginning it was seriously flawed, because it looked on everything as an autonomous, isolated, independent *object.* It read the world as if the dance was not going on. It chose to ignore the connectivity, the interaction, and the interdependence that make life possible. It betrayed the notion of an "alive" universe — dominant in the Middle Ages — for a "more scientific" understanding of life as dead, inert matter.

By viewing all life's processes as mechanical interactions, objects relating autonomously alongside other objects, it progressively lost touch with the subjectivity — the feeling, intuition, sensitivity, and mutual interaction — that is so central to life and basic to the dance of mutual (biological) cooperation. In time, the mechanical dream began to turn sour: exploitation, pollution, depletion of natural resources, armaments build-up, and the general ravaging of Planet Earth created a universal sense of alienation and revulsion. The machine, with so much power and promise, had outlived its usefulness. A new paradigm and a new metaphor were needed.

The universal alienation was already quite potent in the early decades of the twentieth century and, in large measure, contributed to two world wars, but the typical autocratic power that accompanies the mechanistic consciousness ensured that the alienation was suppressed for as long as possible. Church authorities and their theologians colluded, thus becoming (inadvertently) primary agents in the process of repression. Some are still doing it. But in the early 1960s the flood gates burst open, and, quite literally, all hell broke loose (as in the student revolts of 1968). Custom and convention were overthrown, especially by rebellious youth. The angry voices of the Third World, at last, were heard in the West. Young folk opted out of all sorts of official institutions — including the church. The machine was being dismantled, and we had not yet named the new metaphor.

Wholes and Parts

The *holon* began to emerge as the new cultural metaphor. Most people in the official institutions of state and church do not yet accept this new metaphor; many have not even heard of it. Meanwhile, a radically new principle demands our attention and evokes our response. For the mechanistic mindset, *the whole equals the sum of the parts.* The machine is nothing more and nothing less than the sum of its constituent parts; if something goes wrong it has to be in one or other of the individual parts. With the holon, a new principle comes into vogue: *the whole is greater than the sum of its parts.* Rectifying faulty parts will not necessarily improve the whole; in fact, we may have to heal the whole in order to get the parts to function appropriately. We are dealing with a totally new way of perceiving and understanding reality.

In fact, it is not entirely new. The great mystics of all creeds and cultures have always been advocating this vision. Preindustrial European culture operated largely on this vision, unconsciously rather than consciously. But most important for the present work, the great scientific developments of the twentieth century — particularly the quantum theory — quite openly adopted this wholistic principle.

The dance takes on a new meaning now. Yes, many of us have had the experience — especially in circle dancing — of being carried along by the rhythm and beat of the music. Pray, who is the dancer and who the dance? Often it is more a case of we being danced rather than we controlling our movements and moods. And this is no fanciful feat of a wild imagination. We are encountering the power to interconnect within the larger pattern of universal life in a world that thrives on the principle of the whole being greater than the sum of its parts, a principle that often defies human rationality by the magnificence and complexity of its overall grandeur.

Within the liberating momentum of the dance, metaphor begets metaphor. After the holon, along comes the *hologram,* which chronologically existed before it, but in a world where time has become a dimension of the space-time continuum, notions like "before" and "after" have no ultimate significance.

The notion of the hologram was introduced initially in 1947 by the mathematician Dennis Gabor. It took almost twenty years (1965) before Emmett Leith and Juris Upatnicks constructed the first hologram with the aid of the newly invented laser beam. A hologram is a special type of optical storage system that is best explained by an example: If you take a holographic photo, say, of a dog, and cut out one section of it, e.g., the dog's leg, and then enlarge that section to the original size, you will get, not an enlarged leg, but a picture of the whole dog. We are dealing with a method of lensless photography in which the wave field of light scattered by an object is recorded on a plate as an interference pattern. If we look at it with our ordinary eyesight, we see a meaningless pattern of swirls. But when the photographic record — the hologram — is placed in a coherent light beam like a laser, the original wave pattern is regenerated; a three dimensional image appears, and any piece of the hologram will reconstruct the entire image.

The hologram provides a concrete illustration of the principle: "The whole is greater than the sum of the parts," but there is added a new and intriguing dimension which states: the whole is contained in each of the parts. We call it the science of holography.

In 1969, Karl Pribram, a neurophysiologist at Stanford University, proposed that the human brain functions like a hologram, interpreting bioelectric frequencies, not at individual centers, but throughout the brain. Memory, therefore — which was Pribram's main concern — may not be stored at specific local points, but spread throughout in wavelike frequency patterns, along a network of fine fibers on the nerve cells. The implications of this proposal for medicine, psychology, and education are still poorly understood and scarcely investigated. With good reason scholars such as Lockwood (1989, 240–60) can raise the question: could the brain function as a quantum computer, adopting but also transcending the inclusive principles of holography?

Our Holographic Universe

In 1971, David Bohm of London University who had worked with Einstein, proposed that the universe itself is a hologram. All that unfolds before our eyes is merely an external, fragmentary manifestation of an underlying unbroken wholeness. In the early 1940s, at Berkeley Radiation Laboratory, Bohm began what was to become his landmark work on plasmas. A plasma comprises a high density of electrons and positive ions. To his amazement, he found that once they were in a plasma, electrons ceased operating like individuals and started behaving as if they were part of a larger and interconnected whole.

In 1947, Bohm accepted an assistant professorship at Princeton University, and extended his Berkeley research to the study of electrons in metals. Once again, he was struck by the sense of self-organization — in this case, trillions of electrons — within a large whole. These collective movements of electrons he called "plasmons," and their discovery established his reputation as a physicist of world renown.

Bohm's next breakthrough was in outlining his concept of the "quantum potential," a new field that, like gravity, pervaded all of space. This was an attempt to extend the potential of the quantum theory's ability to predict phenomena and provide a new way of conceiving the basic structure of reality.

Bohm's passionate concern was the *whole* rather than the *parts* that comprise it. Wholeness was, in some way, the primary reality. It was equally powerful everywhere. It did not diminish with distance. It expressed something of the identity of reality that could never be understood by studying the individual, "localized" parts.

This universal property is now known as "nonlocality" (or action at a distance). It claims that matter, instead of being static, moves through space, which is itself an unbroken web of creative possibility.

In quantum mechanics, two subatomic particles can interact locally and then move very far apart. But the rules of quantum physics are such that even if the particles end up on opposite sides of the universe, they must be treated as an indivisible whole. This was ably demonstrated in Aspect's experiment of 1982 (see Davies, 1984, 46–47), when two identical photons were emitted by a calcium atom in opposite directions. It was noted that if certain influences were brought to bear on one of the photons, then the second is also affected, although the latter may be on the other side of the moon.

Bohm's next step was to grapple with the relationship of order and randomness in the world. This led to the piece of work for which he is best known, his theory of the implicate/explicate order (Bohm, 1980; Bohm and Peat, 1988). Our primary reality, he suggests, is the unbroken wholeness, or implicate order. Although inaccessible to the human senses, this is the subtle and universal reservoir of all life, the wellspring of all possibility, and the source of all meaning (similar to the notion of the "collective unconscious" in Jungian psychology). The explicit, unfolded order, which is visible and discernible, is the product of the former. The primary reality, therefore, is not the external, visible, sensory world, but the invisible enfolded realm of potential and possibility.

One of the disturbing consequences of this discovery is that the tangible realm of our everyday lives is understood to be a kind of illusion (what the Buddhists call *maya*). It is the deeper realm of existence, the implicate order, that gives birth to all the objects and appearances of our physical world in much the same way that a piece of holographic film can manifest the entire holographic picture.

At the unmanifest level, what the human senses cannot perceive, what only the *heart* can *intuit,* the landscape is one massive, restless flow of energy. My environment consists of minute particles, forever changing and fluctuating in wavelike patterns. And according to quantum theory, we cannot say when one particular particle ceases to exist and another comes into being; we can only speak of the *virtual* existence of such realities which are operative not in isolation but in relationship with associate particles and in cooperation with the environment (on virtual reality, see Helsel and Roth, 1991).

What I perceive, therefore, is not a landscape of facts or objects, but one of *events,* of process, movement, and energy. In this creative flow, past, present, and future are indistinguishable. Every creation of matter, influenced as it is by consciousness, is a recapitulation of all past creation and carries an inherent propensity to become something more than it is at any present moment. For this continuous, creative movement, Bohm coined the term "holomovement."

Everything in the cosmos is made out of the seamless, holographic fabric of the implicate order. An electron is not just an elementary particle; it is a name given to a certain aspect of the holomovement, one of the several dancers in the great cosmic sequence of movement and pattern. Despite the apparent separateness of things at the explicate level, everything is a seamless extension of everything else, and ultimately the implicate and explicate orders blend into each other. These considerations lead us to a second important tenet of quantum theology:

> *Wholeness, which is largely unmanifest and dynamic (not stable) in nature, is the wellspring of all possibility. In seeking to understand life, we begin with the whole, which is always greater than the sum of the parts; paradoxically, the whole is contained in each part, and yet no whole is complete in itself.*

The World as Subject

Traditional Christian theology, along with Judaism and Islam in particular, tends to focus on the parts rather than on the whole. Consequently, mainstream theology portrays quite an ambivalent attitude toward the *world*. All the major religions view the world as an object to be studied, analyzed, and dissected, not as a subject to be related to with love, respect, and admiration.

When we look on the world as object, we then tend to adopt toward it a confrontational, clinical attitude. We set ourselves up as the masters of nature and the conquerors of alien forces. Finally, we develop a notion of God as the supreme (masculine) controller — loving the world, yes, but from a safe distance. We retain the divisive, dualistic mode that begets fragmentation and destruction rather than growth and development.

Haught (in Birch et al., 1990, 171) reminds us that the perception of the universe as subject marks a return to a very ancient wisdom underpinning evolution itself. Our tendency to perceive and treat the cosmos as an object to be conquered and controlled has alienated us humans, not merely from the cosmos (especially from the earth), but from our very selves as relational creatures. Because everything in our universe is interdependent, evolutionary growth is fostered not by the competitive ability of the various life forms to outwit each other (as in the Darwinian-type survival of the fittest), but by the co-operative and concerted interaction, characterized by mutual respect and a communal commitment to the advancement of all. For us humans, to let go of our adversarial and arrogant stance, over against the universe and the earth, and learn instead to befriend universal life, as *subject* in relation to *subject,* is the unique and most urgent challenge of our time.

When we begin with the whole, of which we ourselves and everything around us is a particular aspect or manifestation, we are invited to engage with some fresh insights:

a. Our universe is so vastly complex and mysterious that no one species (no matter how enlightened) and no one religious system (no matter how sophisticated) could comprehend and understand its totality.

b. The creative energy which makes all things possible and keeps all things in being is *within* and not outside the cosmos. The notion of an external creator is a construct of the human mind, a projection initially adopted to assuage our fears of threat and possible annihilation. Creation is sustained from within, not from without.

c. The cosmos survives and grows amid continuous flow and change, in an evolutionary unfolding of great age, complexity, and destiny (developed at length in Part Three). In itself, the evolutionary process is the greatest "proof" of a divine creative energy at work in our world, a conviction that is beautifully illustrated by Swimme and Berry (1992) in their rendition of the universe's story.

d. As a human species, we grossly exaggerate our role within the evolutionary process. The monotheistic religions in particular — Judaism, Christianity, and Islam — consider ours to be the final and ultimate species to inhabit, not just the earth, but the entire universe. This is anthropomorphism of a dangerous and delusory type, leading not merely to a grossly inflated self-image, but also to a caricature of *our* God as the one and only true one.

e. And from our exaggerated anthropomorphism comes another misguided notion of our time, namely, "specieism," the tendency to set humans over against and superior to all other species, especially the animal and plant kingdoms. We humans seem so reluctant to acknowledge that we are an integral aspect of the cosmic whole, crucially important to the entire process, but ultimately no more or less valuable than the fishes of the sea or the birds of the air. Our true identity rests, not in lording it over other life forms, but in sharing life convivially and cooperatively with the great diversity of creatures that accompanies us in inhabiting Planet Earth.

Wholeness and Uniqueness

But what about our uniqueness as a human species and the special role, under God, which is ours? We are not unique because of what we can impose from outside the created order, but because we can participate from within it. And for that participation there is no blueprint — other than the cosmic dance itself, that matrix of energy and movement that enlivens the whole of life and animates all creatures within its nourishing and sustaining ambience. We belong to a greater whole from which we receive our very being and without which we have neither meaning, purpose, nor uniqueness in the great cosmic drama. We discover our true uniqueness not in isolated, competitive individualism, but in convivial cooperation with the great evolutionary unfolding of our planet and our universe. Apart from the greater whole, we are worth nothing!

The time is imminent for us to adopt a new cosmic spirituality, based on conviviality and cooperation rather than on patriarchal supremacy and planetary domination. The Judaeo-Christian conviction of mastering creation, whatever its appropriateness in the past, offers nothing of hope or meaning for the new age that is dawning upon our world. For this new global ambience, we need a fresh spiritual vision.

All the great spiritual traditions call their adherents to *conversion,* the need to change, not once, but frequently, to hear afresh the call to the fulness of life. At this time, all of us, whether of religious orientation or otherwise, need to heed Bohm's warning that the conceptual pigeonholes we use to parcel out the universe are of our own making. They do not exist "out there," for "out there" is only the indivisible totality, Brahman.

We need to let go of the monotheistic, patriarchal dogmas of our recent past. No matter how well they may have served us, they are no longer appropriate or adequate for the emerging world of our time. The wholistic consciousness, engaging the will and imagination of increasing numbers of people, calls us to new ways of being in the world, not in oppositional isolation or confrontation, but in convivial cooperation with our evolving universe leading us to fresh horizons of wholeness (holiness), hope, and possibility.

Part Three

The Relationship

The perception of relations precisely is what constitutes insight.

—ERROL E. HARRIS

_____ *Chapter 6* _____

The Horizon of Belonging

We are on an island, but it is getting wider.
                                    —WERNER HEISENBERG

The pivotal shift in spirituality's meaning for the twentieth century resides in the birth of a worldview of interdependence or relationality. In its broadest sense, ...spirituality is the relational component of lived experience.
                                    —KATHERINE ZAPPONE

The nature of fields is inevitably mysterious. According to modern physics, these entities are more fundamental than matter. Fields cannot be explained in terms of matter; rather matter is explained in terms of the energy within fields.
                                    —RUPERT SHELDRAKE

Eastern philosophy and religion frequently adopt the concept *maya* (meaning, illusion) to highlight our limited mode of human apprehension. We tend to view the external form and assume it to be reality in its true nature. Thus we form illusions, false assumptions, superficial perceptions. We fail to comprehend and appreciate the deeper, richer meaning of what we see, hear, feel, and touch.

One of the most damaging illusions of all is our tendency to view (and understand) things in isolation. In the Western worldview, everything is assumed to be independent, autonomous, and separate. Even when something is clearly dependent on something else for its growth and survival (e.g., how a human being is dependent on the environment), we still persist in treating the two as independent entities. We have been brainwashed in individualism and isolationism. We are victims of a cultural ego-trip into estrangement and alienation, the development of which is well described by Grey (1993, 67ff.).

At the heart of the quantum vision is the conviction that all life forces are interdependent and interrelated. In fact, we experience life, not in isolated entities, not in separate units, but in bundles of experience (quanta). Moreover, our human minds are tuned (designed) to receive life and the processing of our experience in *wholes* and not in isolated segments (see the example of the house cited on p. 31 above).

My perceptions are never isolated, nor can they be separated from the emotions and feelings that are inherent to my human and cosmic reality. Every human action, mental or otherwise, takes place in the context of relatedness. I am a participator in a quantum experience, characterized primarily by a capacity to relate, in which case, of course, the object of my perception is no longer an *object,* but a *subject* in a quantum dialogue, seeking or expressing connectedness.

Everything I do, everything I am, is the fruit of a relationship, not necessarily the result of a relationship in terms of cause and effect, because the quantum world does not operate in terms of cause and effect. The whole is not caused by the fact that all the parts function in unison. No, the whole is greater than the sum of the parts, yet, mysteriously, the whole is contained in each part (as in a hologram). Cause and effect make little sense in a world now understood to be fundamentally relational and interdependent in its essential nature.

Fields of Influence

The capacity to relate can be explored from a range of different angles. In our attempts to understand human bonding, we tend to use either attachment theory (for which John Bowlby is a leading name) or object relations theory (often associated with the work of Melanie Klein). In more recent times, the complex attraction and interaction that characterizes many relational modes suggests that all relationships happen within a system or network of influences (the systems approach). At an ecological and planetary level, the system within which the relationships emerge and grow is often referred to as the "field." In quantum terms, it is the wellspring from which all relationships emanate.

The concept of "fields" was initially invoked in physics by Michael Faraday and James Clerk Maxwell in the nineteenth century, and by biologists Paul Weiss, C. H. Waddington, and Rene Thom in the twentieth. In contemporary physics, there are four main fields, usually referred to as "gravity," "electromagnetism," "strong," and "weak."[13] Although it has been extensively explored and studied, scientists vary greatly in adopting the field theory, and some are reluctant to employ it at all. There also prevails a long-standing debate between physicists and biologists on how field forces are to be understood. Throughout this book, I tend to follow the biological and sociological understanding, with particular reference to the work of the British biologist Rupert Sheldrake.

Sheldrake (1988, 97) offers a comprehensive description of what field activity is about: Fields are nonmaterial regions of influence. The earth's gravitational field, for example, is all around us. We cannot see it; it is not a material object, but it is nonetheless real. It gives things weight and makes things fall. It is holding us down to earth at this moment; without it we would be floating. The moon moves around the earth because of the curvature of the earth's gravitational field; the earth and all other planets move around the sun because of the curvature of the sun's field. In fact, the gravitational field pervades the entire universe, curving around all matter within it.

There are also electromagnetic fields. They are integral to the organization of all material systems, from atoms to galaxies. They undergird the functioning of our brains and bodies. They are essential to the operation of all our electric machinery. The mental process by which I can see and read this book is a function of electromagnetic influence, in which the vibratory energy of light is traveling. Fields are the medium of "action at a distance," and through them actions can affect each other even though they are not in material contact.

Fields are endowed with an unbroken, wholistic quality and are not confined to time and space as traditionally understood. Fields are not bounded, but extend infinitely; each part of the electromagnetic world is, in principle, capable of specifying our whole material world. In this sense it is like a hologram of the material world. And the power of field influence has a pervasive, indestructible quality to it. If a magnet is cut in half, the original field is not divided, with each new part possessing only half the original power. No, each half becomes a whole magnet unto itself, surrounded by a complete magnetic field.

What is the origin or cause of fields? They seem to have emerged at a very early stage in evolution, perhaps within the first few milliseconds of the Big Bang. Their purpose seems to be primarily one of self-organization, potential sources of creativity. Mystically, we can envisage fields as the macrocosm which complements the microcosm of the wave-particle duality. The latter is the smallest energy force we know; the field is the largest. Life needs both.

Fields can be understood as *horizons of belonging*, creating a relational matrix for creative possibilities. The gravitational field provides a safe and, dare we say, loving environment which provides the balance and movement to undergird creative potential. A field is a realm of belonging in which like feels at home with like, yet the potential for variety is unlimited. We can imagine a field of influence that governs the behavior of sheep. Around the world sheep behave in a broadly similar manner according to their specific biological and etiological make-up. The field of influence creates a sense of uniformity and belonging, but not a conformity that rules out diversity or individual uniqueness.

Fields are endowed with an innate potential for self-organization. The biologist Paul Weiss uses the intriguing example of human conception. A new life is conceived, not simply because of sexual interaction of male and female (the cause and effect explanation), but because the field of influence governing procreativity provides the typical organization and specific conditions that enable fertilization to take place. Put rather simply, the procreators take the initiative and the field takes over from there. On two scores, this is a facile analogy that underscores the elegance and sense of mystery. First, the mutual interaction of the procreators themselves is itself the influence of a field — that which draws creatures into mutuality; and, second, the procreators participate in the field's activity rather than provide it with the original "raw material."

It would also be an oversimplification to allude to an internal and external agent. Dualistic distinctions have no place in the realm of fields. There is in fact no external agent; everything is internal, in the sense of being inherent to the horizon of belonging. Even the concept of an agent is inappropriate. It smacks of masculine manipulation and interference. It's not a case of one thing acting upon another; everything is designed to act together, to cooperate. Cooperation and co-creation are the energetic forces of all fields.

Fields do not remain the same forever. They change and develop (hence the notion of "morphogenetic" fields, from the Greek *morphē* meaning form, and *geneo,* to become) contributing to new patterns and habits of behavior. What Darwin called "natural selection" may well be the result of field development. Life forms change and adapt to new environmental conditions under the influence of a creative, organizing energy (the field). The fields themselves change in the very process of making change possible for the life forms being influenced. It is fundamentally a process of becoming.

In the process of becoming there is both continuity and change. According to Sheldrake (1988, 10ff.), fields are endowed with a memory, in which the influence of the most common past types combines to increase the probability that such types will occur again. Thus, for example, the morphogenetic fields of the foxglove species are shaped by influences from previously existing foxgloves. They represent a kind of pooled or collective memory of the species. Each member of the species is molded by these species fields, and in turn contributes to them, influencing future members of the species.

In Relation to the Whole

How does the memory work? By the nonenergetic transfer of information — what Sheldrake calls "morphic resonance" — making possible new adaptations and developmental growth. The oft-cited example is that of the monkeys on Koshima Island in Southern Japan, where in 1954 the local group of monkeys initiated a new mode of potato eating, and by 1958 monkeys all over Japan had adopted the new behavior although there was no physical contact between the two groups. In other words, the new behavior was communicated through the field influence or through the field resonance.

Another relevant example is that of immunity to disease. The human immune system consists of certain cells which have the specified job of protecting the body against destructive foreign invaders. The immune system recognizes a foreign invader by its three-dimensional configuration of individual chemical molecules. These foreign molecules are called "antigens." Once these appear in the bloodstream, the immune system releases a range of "attacker" blood cells — macrophages, T-cell lymphocytes, lymphokines — which lead to the production of antibodies. Antibodies are chemicals made out of protein, and out in the bloodstream they adhere to the original antigens and coat them. Coated antigens attract other scavenger white blood cells called phagocytes, which consume the coated antigens.

Once a foreign substance — virus, bacteria, fungus, poison, parasite — has been identified by the immune system, the three-dimensional configuration is remembered for decades. The next time the invader enters the body, the entire sequence of "attack" is performed faster, and with greater force. The cells of the immune system in any one person remember what approximately *one million* antigens look like. At any one time, the immune system of a single body is dealing with an average of seventy viruses. In this way, the foreign invaders are cleared from the system and the body strengthens itself against further attack.[14]

The immune system may be compared to a field, with a memory, programed toward life and well-being. The programming is about the storage and transfer of information, which seems to be a primary function of the DNA cells. Commenting on this specific role of DNA, Chopra (1989, 87) informs us that the DNA never budges so much as a thousandth of a millimeter in its precise structure, because the genomes — the bits of information in DNA — remember where everything goes, all three billion of them. This fact makes us realize that memory must be more permanent than matter. Consequently, a cell may be described as memory that has built some matter around itself, forming a specific pattern. The carrier of information, therefore (and dare we add, *meaning*), is the memory rather than the matter.

Davidson (1989, 103), Von Baeyer (1992, 104ff.), and Zohar (1990, 132) are among several contemporary theorists who draw our attention to the vast, empty spaces of the universe, the so-called "vacuum state." It is a fulness rather than an emptiness, a subtle energy field, consisting of formative blueprints, which retain a memory of all past experiences and will govern patterns of future influence (more on this topic on p. 102). Our world appears to be a great thought and not a great machine!

In contemporary research, the impact of fields is felt across a widening spectrum of experience. For example, Nicola Tesla, at the beginning of the present century, and Glen Rein (1992), in recent times, have developed the notion of scalar fields in an attempt to measure the "neutral" energy that exists in the balance between two opposing magnetic fields. The concept of bio-fields and mind fields is being explored in contemporary psychology, while W. D. Schuman in 1952 discovered what is now known as the Schuman Resonance, a natural radio signal, resonating as a standing wave around the earth and beating with a sharp pulse at about 7.8 Hz.

Significantly, the dominant brain frequency of all vertebrates so far tested is close to the value of 7.8 Hz. Although the frequency in people of Western industrial culture is often higher, that of healers, shamans, and people of spiritual orientation tends to be closer to 7.8 Hz. Following on this discovery, the Schuman Simulator has now become standard equipment for astronauts. Although this earth-pulse is widely considered to be an aspect of electromagnetism, in terms of the quantum worldview, its significance is probably far greater and as yet poorly understood.

The implications of field theory are far-reaching, not just for science and theology, but for every aspect of life. It provides a whole new perspective on how we understand life and the influences that bring about change. Applications of this vision in daily life include Group Dynamics (Yalom, 1985; Pines, 1992), which studies the attraction of groups for, and their influence on, various aspects of human behavior. Groups have a far greater impact on our lives than our individualistic culture is prepared to acknowledge. Systems theory (Von Bertalanffy, 1968; Miller, 1978; Wiener, 1965) highlights the role that systems play in the way we organize our lived experience. The theory also explores how systems that begin in a fluid and flexible manner often become staid, rigid institutions, exerting an inflexible hold over people and their freedom and reminding us how intricate and difficult it is to activate and initiate change from within social and structural systems.

Family therapy (see Satir, 1964; Burnham, 1986) is an application of field theory, alerting us to the complex dynamics that go on within a family unit, with serious implications for every constituent member. For example, we can choose to view an alcoholic father as a person with a disease that is his individual problem and for which he himself is ultimately responsible. But in family therapy, we seek to understand the alcoholic condition as a possible symptom, not of a sick person, but of a sick (i.e., dysfunctional) family that has subconsciously loaded the problem on to one of its vulnerable members (a process often referred to as "scapegoating"). As a therapeutic approach, family/group/systems therapy throws a great deal of light on many of the personal, interpersonal, and social problems of our time. It also endorses the perception and claim of liberation theology (see above pp. 14–15) that *structural,* rather than *personal* sin should be our primary context for addressing the outstanding evils in the world today.

Field and group theory alert us to the powerful impact of the whole, the larger reality, over and above the individual parts, whether we are considering nation-states or individual people. But most importantly for the purposes of this book, it evokes a profound conversion experience, inviting us to abandon our traditional adversarial stance whereby we treat creation as an object to be controlled and mastered. Instead we must learn to befriend our universe as a subject with whom we *relate,* a living organism within which we live, and move, and have our being, and without which we have neither meaning nor purpose in our daily lives.

Our universe is a sphere of belonging; Planet Earth is home to the human species and to all other life forms too (see especially, McFague, 1993, 103–29). It is our sense of "cosmic homelessness" (Haught in Birch et al., 1990) that alienates us, not just from life around us but also from our true inner selves. We are largely out of tune with the creative energies that form and mold us, that sustain and engender our growth, that nurture and enliven our inner being. We are not the masters and controllers of our own destiny; we are not the ultimate species. We belong to something bigger and greater than ourselves which is forever unfolding and evolving, and within that dynamic, creative process we rediscover, again and again, the meaning and purpose of what life is about.

Whither Revelation?

Our considerations of field theory and the sense of our universe as a realm of belonging invite us to address the major theological issue of *revelation.* This is a distinctly Christian notion and a central focus in the dialogue taking place between the major religions (see Hick and Knitter, 1988; Tracy, 1990). Although specifically a Christian concept, all the religions express a sense of divine disclosure. God has "spoken" through specific persons, writings, or experiences, and each religion considers its version to be superior to any other. The Christian church goes further, claiming that what it has inherited from the divine disclosure (contained in the Bible) is *unique* and embodies the *fulness* of revealed truth, not merely for Christians but for people of all creeds. Therefore, from a Christian viewpoint, the revealed truth of other religions is *valid* but not *complete;* only the Christian version is complete.

Not all Christian theologians would be as dogmatic as that; increasingly they appreciate that this understanding of revelation is constricted (and constricting). It arises from an isolated, adversarial view of Christianity and religion in general. It fails to acknowledge the spiritual evolution of the human species over thousands of years before formal religion ever came into being.

In prehistoric times, people acknowledged and responded to the divine disclosure from an innate, primordial sense of the sacred. The divine "spark" within sensed a divine energy without. This led to a wide range of prereligious rituals ranging from animism (based on the notion that everything has a soul), to nature worship, totemism, magic, etc. No longer do we consider these to be infantile, prelogical, primitive, pagan rites; they were appropriate for our ancestors at their stages of evolutionary development. More significantly, they embody primal and primordial aspirations that are fundamental to our human condition and have been largely subverted by modern, formalized religion.

The primitive urge to connect spiritually is innate to our human nature and, from a quantum viewpoint, it is also considered to be an intrinsic feature of universal life, manifested in the attraction and repulsion of subatomic particles. There is in all things a "within" forever yearning to connect with a "without" which in fact, is itself a larger "within," already described as a realm of belonging. According to Rahner (1969, 16), human beings are essentially and always listeners for a possible revelation from God, because innately we are disposed to fuller life and truth.

Our consciousness does not need to be informed by formal religious awareness in order to be disposed and receptive to the divine disclosure. Our very nature as human beings is to be open and porous to deeper meaning. And the spiritual story of humankind, unfolding over the millennia, suggests that the divine life force (God) reveals itself with a prodigious generosity of presence, power, and cultural expression.

That we can be blind to the divine disclosure, that we can block or hinder its impact on our lives, that we can resist the challenge to change and become whole (conversion), is a painful truth that millions vehemently deny today. To a degree, the religions themselves are culpable for this recalcitrant attitude. Not infrequently, the very system that was intended to mediate divine life and create a climate of openness and receptivity, has been the one that has alienated seeking souls from the wellsprings of hope and truth.

Religious dogma often assumes ideological significance because it fails to acknowledge the initial, experiential context. This applies particularly to the manner in which revelation is portrayed in the various religions. The emergence of formal religion, about five thousand years ago, undoubtedly marks a new stage in human and planetary evolution. But there is a shadow side to this, as there is to every major cultural development. As already stated, formal religion emerged from within the culture and context of the Agricultural Revolution and assumed many of the positive and negative qualities of that development.

Today we focus a great deal on the pros and cons of the Industrial Revolution, to such a degree that we tend to underestimate the enormous impact of the Agricultural Revolution. Culturally, it was a supreme moment of breakthrough, but also one of long-term negative and destructive repercussions. For the first time in history, we humans carved up and fragmented our world, imposing divisions and categories that in time became the basis for separate tribes, cultures, nations, and religions. The dominant patriarchal orientation was to divide and conquer, and hence the introduction of the deadliest divisive force of all: warfare. The idea of *man* being master of creation emerged at this time and became ingrained in the formal religious creeds of subsequent centuries.

The fact that each religion sought individual autonomy and integrity, setting itself in opposition to all others, *with its own unique body of revealed truth,* confirms the "divide and conquer" mentality of the Agricultural Revolution. Today we are rediscovering our sense of *one* world, an essential unity, that we choose to divide and fragment at a terrible price. This creates a new agenda for politics, economics, education, and also for our understanding of religion as a global, cultural reality. It is not the uniqueness of each part that matters anymore, but the uniqueness of the whole, which is fluid and open-ended, an unfolding matrix of possibilities, unlocking the mysterious divine potential as it impregnates creation with hope and meaning.

Consequently, we are invited to move toward a new revelatory horizon. It is new in terms of recent theological reflection, but very old in terms of our human, spiritual unfolding. It suggests that the creation itself is the *primary* revelation (Collins, 1995, 11–12, 219, 224; La Chance, 1991, 79; Swimme and Berry, 1992, 243, 255), of which the various disclosures of the major religions are particular expressions offered in the specific context of a certain historical and cultural milieu.

Two important considerations emerge here:

a. The creative process itself — with its beauty and elegance, but also with its pain and destructibility — is our primary, tangible source for experiencing the divine energy. In this way we have had access to the "divine power" for possibly a hundred thousand years, whereas the formal religions, with their official perceptions and interpretations of divine disclosure, are no more than five thousand years old. To reclaim the sacred nature of the cosmos — and of Planet Earth in particular — is one of the outstanding spiritual challenges of our time. It has also within it the potential for a whole new sense of what theology is about.

b. If revelation is mediated primarily through the creative processes of our universe, then our primary call is to be listeners at the heart of our world (and not just in the context of the church). Our human responsibility as one voice among so many throughout the universe is to develop our capacities to listen as incessantly as the hovering hydrogen atoms, as profoundly as our primal ancestors and their faithful descendants in today's indigenous peoples. In the words of Swimme and Berry (1992, 44), the adventure of the universe depends upon our capacity to listen (see also Grey, 1993, 89–92).

There is nothing particularly revolutionary or heretical about these ideas, because it is exactly what we humans had been doing for thousands of years before formal religions emerged in the wake of the Agricultural Revolution. The role of the church, therefore, is to keep us focused on the world and on the divine unfolding forever emerging therefrom. This is essentially what Jesus was suggesting when he spoke of the New Reign of God (the Kingdom), for which there are over 140 references in the Gospels, with only three allusions to the church (more on this topic on p. 115 below). Contrary to the dominant asceticism of the past few thousand years, Christianity is a world-loving religion, and not one based on dismissing, fleeing, or distancing itself from the world. A church which claims to be opposed to the world is fundamentally alienating itself from God's prodigious creativity at the heart of creation. Little wonder that many people today are abandoning the church.

When we suggest that the world is the arena of divine disclosure, we need to outgrow our dualistic tendency to attribute all goodness to God and all evil to Satan (whom we perceive to be the opposite of all that God stands for). In a quantum universe, dualisms of this nature make no sense. Very negative and destructive experiences may also be deeply enlightening, particularly as we humans co-create (or fail to do so) in conjunction with the creative divine energy. Fresh questions also arise on how we understand the divine energy and whether or not we can develop a sufficiently inclusive orientation whereby we include (rather than split off) our negative perceptions and projections.

Along with the creation-centered focus for the divine disclosure, there is always a historical context that can be liberating or restrictive, perhaps both at different times. According to Boff (1987, 62), revelation is historical and uses the sociohistorical context to communicate its call and challenge. Its forms are influenced by the particulars of a place and time. It is important then always to discern the transient historical expression from God's permanent communication. History and revelation are always intermingled, but the revelatory call will always embrace larger vision than that embodied in any one historical or cultural context.

It is this expanded understanding of God's disclosure that engages the quantum theologian. It evokes a whole new way of doing theology and grounds the theological enterprise in the heart of creation itself.

For quantum theology, therefore, *the expanding horizon of divine belonging is the context in which revelation takes place; all creatures are invited to respond, to engage in the co-creative task of being and becoming. All life forms have unique roles in this process, the primary focus of which is creation itself rather than formal religion.*

So where does this leave formal religion? In responding to this question, it may be helpful to return to the field theory. On a universal scale, there is the field experience of spiritual emergence in which the whole of life, animate and inanimate, participates. How the animate and inanimate forms experience this probably constitutes separate but overlapping fields. Within the field of human spirituality, we may consider the various religions to be subfields with a particular cultural realm of influence. For example, Hinduism clearly explores and articulates the Indian subculture (without being necessarily confined to India) in a manner that Christianity cannot do. In this context, the religions have a cultural relevance and may retain their relevance, but it will have to be *within* the horizon of belonging that we call *spirituality*. If the religions can accept and integrate this new challenge, then their self-understanding, along with their cultural and historical relevance, is likely to change significantly. Without that change, religion will fail to have any significant meaning in our quantum universe.

Undoubtedly, some religions will fade into oblivion. That is also appropriate. In a quantum universe, birth-death-rebirth is an unceasing process. And with the death of a religion comes the end of a particular God-concept, which by that stage has probably become an idolatrous burden and hence a barrier to fresh spiritual growth. The life-giving ferment is in the spiritual unfolding, not in formal religious adherence. Quantum theology seeks to safeguard the primacy of spiritual growth rather than the promotion of formal religion.

Spiritual unfolding is a universal field of influence and belonging. We all inhabit it and are inhabited by it. It constitutes a central aspect of our being and becoming and unites us indelibly with the tapestry of creation itself. It stretches far beyond the realm and influence of religion, which for many people is synonymous with spirituality. And this is one of the great misconceptions of our time, one that leaves the spiritual potential of many people dormant, underdeveloped, and often repressed. More than anything else, our world today and its peoples need to be spiritually liberated.

Reclaiming our spiritual identity is not a case of becoming religious again, going to church on Sunday, following the rules and laws of a particular faith, reading the Bible or Koran everyday. No, it goes much deeper than any of this. As many of the great faiths suggest (but poorly implement) spirituality is about *enlightenment* and *liberation*. The spiritual journey is about opening up new horizons of love and understanding, not by ignoring or bypassing the darkness and pain of life, but precisely through experiencing and integrating them. Through this process we are liberated from the confines, restrictions, and limitations imposed on us frequently by our own personal ignorance, but also by the collective oppression of our man-made institutions.

Our spiritual enlightenment is above all else a journey into the mystery of belonging where all is one, and the patriarchal dualisms and distinctions are seen for what they really are: destructive, controlling devices that fragment and alienate. Although we are surrounded by *interconnectedness* (which for Grey [1993] is the core element in the contemporary theology of revelation), we can spend a whole lifetime in the enclaves of our cultural darkness and fail to comprehend or appreciate the mystery of belonging, within which we are all intractably united. And that universal call to unity manifests itself particularly in *relationships* which are the embryonic web of all life forms. And there are quantum ramifications to all our relationships, which we'll explore in the next chapter.

_____ *Chapter 7* _____

Beyond Our Isolation

*Science cannot solve the ultimate mystery of nature.
And it is because, in the last analysis, we ourselves are
part of the mystery we are trying to solve.*

— MAX PLANCK

*I realize I am a maverick, for I can settle for nothing
less than the whole.*

— RENEE WEBER

*Gravitation binds everything so closely that alienation
is a cosmological impossibility.*

— THOMAS BERRY

The suggestion that our world is an interconnected web of relationships was initially voiced by the physicist Werner Heisenberg. It is a notion that no serious quantum scientist is likely to dispute.

When J. J. Thompson succeeded in splitting the atom in the 1890s, little did he think that he was opening up a mysterious horizon of belonging and interrelatedness. His intention and dream were exactly the opposite: the discovery of the ultimate building blocks, out of which everything is made, a reductionistic pursuit of the tiny units of matter, the bits and pieces, that make up the fabric of universal life. In pursuing the elementary particles, which we presumed (and many still do) to be *isolated and independent,* we continued to split the subatomic particles. We then proceeded to bash them to pieces in powerful particle accelerators of which CERN near Geneva and Fermilab near Chicago are among the better known. By 1960, we had already identified over a hundred different types of particles, without as yet any clear sense on how they related to each other.

In the early 1960s, scientists identified a new set of subatomic particles, about which they became immensely excited. They named them "quarks" (and proceeded to call their opposites "leptons"). At the time everything suggested that these might well be the ultimate building blocks, the final units of matter out of which everything else was made. It took over thirty years to identify and assemble the total quark repertoire; the sixth and final quark was discovered in March 1995 at Fermilab. The elegance and beauty of the quark world has led to such namings as "strange," "charm," and "truth." (On the discovery of the quarks, see Riordan, 1987; see also the special supplement in *New Scientist,* July 10, 1993.)

The excitement was eminently appropriate, yet it dissipated rapidly when the quarks refused to fit the mechanistic expectations. In experimental conditions quarks cannot be isolated. The hadron within which they are embodied cannot be split nor bashed into smaller units. Nature refuses to reveal her truths in the form of isolated, independent quarks (hence the oft-quoted quip of the 1960s: "Nature seems to abhor naked quarks"). Perhaps nature can't do that; maybe she has never done it!

For the physicists, this was not good news. It posed a threat to the subconscious desire to conquer and control. The quarks were proving to be highly elusive, making sense only in groupings of *two* or *three,* displaying an elegant versatility to manifest their existence only in *relationships.* The capacity to relate seems to be at the heart of the quark world!

And this was not all! Quarks insisted on playing to the quantum dance of the particle-wave duality. Whether it manifested itself as a particle or as a wave, no one could ever be sure. All one could be certain of was that the energetic force was operative, but it was elusive, strange, and yet so attractively elegant, it continued to command attention and fascination. All of this suggests that in the final analysis, nature is made up of *patterns of energy interrelating,* and not of isolated building blocks.

Physicists were becoming impatient with this uncertainty, despite the relatively wide acceptance of Heisenberg's uncertainty principle (which states that we can never be certain of a particle's velocity and position at the same time; certainty in regard to one automatically means uncertainty regarding the other). So the scientific community has agreed to spend billions of dollars building bigger and more powerful accelerators that, it hopes, will eventually provide the experimental conditions to crack open the quarks into smaller isolated, independent units of matter.

Perhaps they'll succeed, but many are skeptical. The quarks might well be the end of the particle line. We may have discovered the "ultimate building blocks," and we are left with the mysterious, paradoxical dilemma that they are not "blocks" with which we can build a Newtonian edifice. But perhaps they are bundles of experience (quanta) which will enable us to engage more meaningfully in the dance of life and understand afresh the creative energy at the heart of our quantum universe.

Trinitarian Relatedness

While the scientific community continues on the (misguided) task of trying to split the quarks into the hoped-for ultimate building blocks, their very discovery raises urgent theological questions which will occupy our attention for the rest of this chapter. The quarks demonstrate in a compelling and exquisite way that life in our universe thrives not on *isolationism* but on *the capacity to relate*. Zohar (1990, 206; 1993, 190ff.) goes even further and suggests that bosons as the basic glue in the particle world should be described as "particles in relationship." Everything is created out of relatedness, sustained through relationships, and thrives on interdependence.

This is an ancient wisdom, long known to mystics and sages and courageously reclaimed by many feminist theologians today (e.g., Heyward, 1982; King, 1989; Zappone, 1991; Brock, 1992; Grey, 1993). It is also a fundamental, archetypal conviction underpinning all the great religions known to humankind. Over the centuries, that basic, pristine truth has been couched in sacred dogmas which, paradoxically, have often camouflaged rather than disclosed deeper meaning. I refer to what Christianity calls the mystery of the *Trinity*.

In the early centuries of Christendom, theologians grappled with the mystery of the Godhead and concluded that God is fundamentally a unity (hence, monotheism) but one within which there coexist, in total equality, three separate persons, Father, Son, and Holy Spirit. What the councils of the early church understood by "person" continues to be debated even to this day. Seemingly, the intention was to offer an understanding of God as deeply personal, taking personhood (as then understood) to be the supreme mode of meaningful existence. The dogma of the Trinity retains this deep, personal connotation in its description of how the Trinity functions. The Father begets the Son in a manner that includes biological procreation but far exceeds it, and the Holy Spirit is born of the loving union that exists between Father and Son; the Spirit is that bond, but also a "person" in his or her own right.

Belief in the triune nature of God is considered essential to the Christian faith. Most Christians don't comprehend the "mystery," nor does it have any real significance for them in their daily lives. Nor indeed do the heavy patriarchal overtones make it a credible or attractive notion for a world yearning for more wholistic and inclusive modes of perception and action (see Brock, 1992, 4, 54–55; Kimel, 1992).

At this juncture we note that many of the major religions have a similar notion in their belief systems. Examples that spring to mind include: (*a*) the triune figures of Vishnu, Shiva, and Shakti in Hinduism; (*b*) the Buddhist doctrine of the three bodies (manifestations) of the Buddha, namely, the dharma-kaya (eternal dimension), nirmana-kaya (appearance body), and sambhoga-kaya (bliss body); (*c*) the Zoroastrian triplicate of Zurvan, the mighty god of time, and his two sons, Ahriman (active force) and Ormazd (passive force); (*d*) the Egyptian cult of Isis, Serapis, and the divine child, Horus; (*e*) the Neoplatonic triplicate of the Good, the Intelligence, and the World Soul. Traces of this triune relationship also occur in the literature on the Great Mother Goddess worshiped by humans for some thirty thousand years in prehistoric times, echoes of which occur in one of the most unexpected of sources — an early version of the Islamic Koran (see Hayes, 1994, 165ff.). We are dealing with something that is not unique to Christianity, but an archetypal phenomenon that transcends all the religions, a key ingredient of universal life and culture.

Greenstein (1988) and Barrow and Tippler (1986) also allude to this trinitarian aspect of universal life. They note that the three-dimensional nature of space is an inherent quality of cosmic interdependence, on the one hand, necessary to maintain appropriate distances of space between the various planets to facilitate their orbital trajectories and, on the other hand, essential to the proper functioning of the human nervous system and the flow of blood in the human body. In two-dimensional space, objects settle down to rest or to stable orbits, whereas those interacting in three dimensions show a unique complexity and a potential for novel behavior as they weave in and around each other. Of the entire range of conceivable dimensions only one number — three — is amenable to life. Any choices above three make it impossible for planets to remain at proper distances from their suns. Anything below three scrambles the orderly communication so crucial to living beings. For gods and creatures alike, *three* seems to be a number of immense cosmic significance.

The Dutch theologian Van Beeck (1979) claims that theology thrives on overstatement. In regard to the doctrine of the Trinity, the problem may be that we Christians explain it (or explain it away) by understatement. By inventing a type of theological jigsaw puzzle, trying to fit the three into one, we have created a rather mechanistic paradigm for the Godhead that makes little sense in a wholistic age.

For orthodox theology and mainstream religion, dogmas serve as landmarks for guidance and certainty. In a quantum world, they serve a different purpose: they are pointers to a deeper truth, the totality (whole) of which is never fully grasped and demands fresh reformulation in each new cultural epoch. I suggest that the doctrine of the Trinity is an attempted expression of the fact that the essential nature of God is about relatedness and the capacity to relate, that the propensity and power to relate is, in fact, the very essence of God.[15] God's individual identity is of no real consequence (as Buddhists claim). God becomes meaningful in the very process of relating. God's revelation or self-disclosure is, in essence, an invitation to mutuality (see the pioneering work of La Cugna, 1991). In the plain but profound language of the Christian Bible: God is love!

Judaism, Christianity, and Islam pride themselves in being monotheistic religions. They promote and safeguard the oneness and unity of God (particularly, Islam). But historically, monotheism is based on a very spurious polemic. It is very much the product of the political and religious aftermath of the Agricultural Revolution when the planet was divided into continents, religions, tribes, and races. Monotheism became a powerful ideology to suppress and overthrow prehistoric belief systems in which a polytheistic faith (in numerous gods) was widespread, a notion that has been retained in Hinduism, the oldest of the major religions.

The development of the monotheistic religions (as in Judaism, Christianity, and Islam) is often portrayed as a maturation of an inchoate, disparate, primitive set of beliefs, incorporating the notion of many gods rather than one. But that is a perception born out of a particular mode of consciousness, appropriate (perhaps) to humans at a certain time in our cultural and evolutionary development but today inappropriate and irrelevant for our emerging, wholistic (quantum) consciousness.

The real issue for our time is not whether God is monotheistic or polytheistic, a distinction with dualistic overtones of bygone days. What science — for long the perceived enemy of religion — reveals and confirms is what many belief systems have been struggling to articulate in their trinitarian doctrines: God is first and foremost a propensity and power for relatedness, and the divine imprint is nowhere more apparent than in nature's own fundamental desire (exemplified in the quarks) to relate — interdependently and inter-connectedly. The earthly, the human, and the divine are in harmony in their fundamental natures, in their common propensity to relate and to enjoy interdependent coexistence.

Questions arise which become immensely disturbing for orthodox theologians. "Does God, then, have no independent existence?" "Is God somehow dependent on evolution?" (a misgiving often voiced against process theologians). "Doesn't your argument about related-ness slide into pantheism?" These questions — and many others — arise from a human need to couch the God-question in specific, man-made theological categories. They arise from a certain mode of patriarchal consciousness, characteristic of our mechanistic age, needing certainty, precision, and authoritative clarity. They are valid questions, but of no real interest to a quantum theologian, who is happy to live with unanswered questions and wishes to refrain from casting profound, evolving truths into too neat a set of human constructs.

For the quantum theologian, the doctrine of the Trinity takes on a very vibrant meaning, intensifying the call to relate, in love and jus-tice, to all life on Planet Earth and beyond. This in turn calls into question the tendency in traditional Christian theology to uphold the dignity of the *individual* person as a special duty. The notion of individual uniqueness is a relatively recent one in human evolu-tion. Indeed, it is very much a byproduct of industrial society when personal competence and the ability to compete became core values. Around these expectations, covert rather than overt, there grew up an array of cultural systems — educational, medical, ecclesiastical — with the focus on the robust individual, independent and alone. Thus for much of the twentieth century, indeed ever since the time of the Reformation in the sixteenth century, the salvation of the individual soul was considered to be the ultimate goal of the Christian faith.

In prehistoric societies, and in many parts of today's world (es-pecially Africa, Latin America, and Asia), the individual's value and worth are esteemed relative to the person's role within and contri-bution to the common good. Cooperation rather than competition is the guiding value. But something much deeper is at stake, a con-viction that is resurfacing in the emerging consciousness of our time, namely, *we are our relationships*. What we are as individuals, and what we will become in the future, is determined by the quality of our interdependence on others — humans and nonhumans alike.

Our very being as persons is dependent initially on the procreative act of two people. The quality of our life, health, and well-being very much depends on the depth of love and intimacy that led to that original procreative act. Today we realize that prenatal development — all that happens in the interdependent life of the womb, influenced as we are by so many other factors — has a significant impact on the type of people we become in later life. Even before we are born, we are already embedded in a web of relationships, which remains the primary context of our lives until the day we die (and, indeed, after that too).

Even the person who tries to become a Robinson Crusoe on a remote island is acting out of a context of relationship. That person may be trying to escape from stifling and stultifying human relationships, and that in itself is a powerful statement about the impact of human intimacy. And to survive on the remote island, the lone ranger will quickly adopt new behaviors in order to relate meaningfully with the novel surroundings. Our very constitution as human beings is our capacity to relate, and in our struggle to do so authentically we reveal to the world that we are made in the image and likeness of the Originating Mystery, whose essential trinitarian nature is also that of relatedness.

Individual Uniqueness

Cultural and moral implications ensue, evoking the concern of the quantum theologian. In a world designed for relatedness, in which we depend on human relationships for our very survival, *individualism* (exalting the individual above all other considerations — sometimes described as "ego-inflation") becomes a serious moral transgression. No less culpable, however, is the concept of *individuality,* employed to highlight the dignity and priority of the individual above and beyond the collective. Statements like "the person is all that matters," "human beings come first," "people are more important than things," all belong to this category.

Individualism — usually characterized by selfish preoccupation and arrogant self-inflation — is readily recognizable and distasteful to many people, whereas individuality, characterized by a strong sense of self-worth, achievement, and prowess is admired and affirmed. Behind these two concepts are undercurrents which need to be exposed and explored. Individualism is often a response (or rather, a reaction) to an oppressive regime whereby freedom has been curtailed and creativity subverted. People who are hurting inside (for whatever reason) cling on desperately to any bit of self-power they can attain. Behind the overt behavior of the manipulator and hoarder is often a dependent, lonely subpersonality. A type of infantile dependency accompanies individualism. If the person can be empowered to face the inner reality, then the tendency toward individualism can be transformed into a life orientation of greater scope and openness.

The focus on individuality is much more difficult to shift, buttressed as it is by powerful political, economic, social, and even religious agendas of our dominant Western culture. In the West, particularly, the individual is deemed to be supreme, just as the individual God is supreme over creation. Western democracies pride themselves in safeguarding individuality and individual rights; so do the multinational corporations! What initially seems to be a very coherent and humane concept can easily become devious and destructive. It is this form of personal arrogance that underpins a great deal of the environmental and ecological exploitation currently posing such a serious threat to human and earthly life. Individuality largely diminishes the emphasis on relatedness and almost totally erodes the sense of interdependence that should exist between humans and other life forms.

Individuation Process and Need Satisfaction

STAGE/EXPERIENCE	DOMINANT NEEDS
Individualism	Survival and safety "I need to be loved ... " Gratification Control Self-determination
Individuality	Esteem by self and others "I will do the loving ... " Dominance Achievement Self-actualization
Individuation	Interrelatedness/Interdependence "I am lovable and capable of loving" Cosmic centeredness Transcendence Intimacy

As individualism is closely related to unhealthy dependency, so individuality is strongly linked to exaggerated independence, a kind of craving for power. But the call of our times — and indeed the authentic journey for every person — is to outgrow, as far as we can, both our dependency and independence as we are invited to become more and more *interdependent.* Accompanying these stages is the evolution from individualism toward individuality, and beyond that into the process of *individuation* (see Goldbrunner, 1955).

Individuation is a concept borrowed from Jungian psychology where initially it denoted a process of personal growth aimed at integrating the conscious and unconscious elements of human experience, an undertaking which Jung attributes to the second half of life (usually) and is often the byproduct of a major trauma, serious illness, or nervous breakdown. A key feature of individuation — which is not a once-and-for-all experience, but usually a lifelong process — is the openness and receptivity to a larger reality: social, ecological, spiritual, cosmic. In its most highly developed stages, it merges with mysticism, and the boundaries of "me" and "not me" begin to melt away.

This is a radically new way of understanding humanity and comprehending the mystery of our existence. It is neither pantheism (being absorbed into God) nor creationism (being absorbed by creation). We lose nothing of our uniqueness, dignity, or personal worth. In fact, we rediscover them anew and continue doing so every day of our lives. The urge to control and manipulate is gradually abandoned, while the care and cultivation of life takes on a fresh sense of urgency. We begin to feel a sense of oneness with our universe.

Individuation breaks down barriers and walls which the ego has erected between itself and the surrounding world. We begin to realize that everybody and everything need each other, not in a competitive and manipulative way, but in an orchestrated interaction which seeks to extrapolate and utilize the best which each person and each reality has to give for the benefit of the whole.

The Search for Community

We now turn our attention to a notion much in vogue in the emerging consciousness of our time: the search for community, often pioneered by people grappling with the challenges of the individuation process. We use the word with a range of different meanings. We speak of "the community of nations," "the human community," "the community of faith," "the community of the church," a rural/ urban community, the local community.

While often not knowing what precisely we mean, it seems clear that a fundamental aspiration of humankind is being articulated: the desire to relate more closely and more intimately with a wider circle of people. Even people who enjoy the love and support of a family, a residential household, the satisfaction, achievement, and camaraderie of a closely knit work-group, or even a very intimate couple-partnership still yearn for communion within a wider and larger ambience. The circle of human compassion, the propensity for relatedness, is a deep-seated archetypal yearning, a divinely bestowed aspiration that forever seeks the paradoxical paradise of something very intimate and, simultaneously, something that will open us up to the realms of total possibility.

Many organizations, including the religions and formal churches, claim to offer their adherents the experience of community (*oikoumene*). But the (often unconscious) institutionalization of community destroys the very possibility of being in communion. The more we try to invent community along specific lines — cultural, social, or religious — the more we endanger the very possibility of its meaningful existence. As already indicated, only people who have internalized some sense of individuated growth can accept both the challenge and paradox of being in communion, an experience which at one and the same time includes the desire to be in close relationship with significant others in a specific, local context while also fulfilling global aspirations for peace, justice, and a sense of universal harmony. And the local context of today may not meet the new needs and aspirations of one or five years from now. The search for community, therefore, can be a lifelong pilgrimage which for many culminates only in the banquet-feast of eternal life.

The theology of church in the Christian context takes the creation of community as its central raison d'être (Hoffman, 1988). The church (*ecclesia*) convokes the gathering of the people to celebrate the bond that already exists — through their shared, common baptism — but also to build up the "body of believers," to be a sign and sacrament of communion for the world. But the weight of tradition, along with religious exclusivity, has all but eroded the communal base of the official churches. People in general do not experience community through their churches, and consequently increasing numbers look elsewhere for that experience. Only a church de-institutionalized, de-legalized, and de-clericalized can hope to recapture this central concept without which its existence is largely a charade.

The Christian churches have also developed a sacramental system, with — in some cases — quite an elaborate ritual (as in the Orthodox churches) to celebrate, communally, the living out of their faith. Baptism and Eucharist are two of the more widely practiced sacraments (with interesting parallels in other major religions). Baptism celebrates the welcome and formal admission into the Christian community, while Eucharist provides a sacred, ritual meal in which members of the community reenact the breaking of bread and sharing the cup, as a celebration of new life bestowed on them by Jesus, their Savior.

Sacraments are intended to serve a purpose similar to rites of passage in other cultures. The participants move into a different mode of being, not to escape from the realities of life, but to reenter, renewed and refreshed for the ongoing task of human, planetary, and cosmic regeneration. A sacramental experience is a distinctly social, communal event; it awakens a desire for communion and confirms the sense of community that already exists. Sacraments in their pristine meaning were never intended to be ritualistic acts designed to set the *individual* at rights with God, and insofar as they have evolved along these lines (as has largely happened in the Catholic tradition) then, proportionately, they have lost their power to be communal and transformative experiences. They have become insipid rituals instead of life-giving experiences.

Donovan (1989) is one of a number of modern theologians who provide a timely critique on how we celebrate sacraments in the Christian tradition and offer creative alternatives, encouraging a relocation of sacramental celebration from the cloister-like, anti-worldly atmosphere of many of our ecclesiastical buildings to the heart of real-life experience. He suggests that in our celebration of Eucharist we try to rediscover the original tradition of the *sacred meal* — celebrated initially in people's homes (a custom still retained by the Jews in the weekly shabat) — and develop a contemporary context in which the celebration of Eucharist becomes a real experience of life around the sacredness and sharing of food.

Ritual and sacraments are not merely inventions of formal religion. We humans are essentially creatures of symbol and ritual. We use symbolic behavior to express and communicate some of our deepest relational intentions, e.g., in the act of sexual intimacy where the physical aspect is transcended into a deeply tender "mystical"

experience. In our contemporary culture, our capacity to relate sym-
bolically and imaginatively is poorly developed; we have become
too individualistic, literalist, rational, logical, and clinical. We have
largely lost our capacity to dream, to imagine, to be playful, to celebrate, to ritualize, and being thus impoverished, we have lost our
capacity to *relate* wholistically. A rediscovery of meaningful ritual
and inspirational sacrament is one of the more urgent needs of our
time, a prerequisite for rediscovering an authentic sense of human,
planetary, and global community.

The search for community is not merely a pursuit of security
and intimacy to obviate our loneliness in an anonymous and im-
personal world. It is much more than that. It is the expression —
however haphazardly and imperfectly made — of a yearning from
deep within the created order itself, a groaning arising from the heart
of creation (to paraphrase St. Paul), seeking reciprocity and mutuality. The very fabric of creation and the very nature of God sing
in unison a song of love. According to Plato, love is the pursuit of
the whole. Our broken, fragmented world yearns to be whole again.
We humans imbibe this longing and, on behalf of creation, we give
it conscious expression, particularly in our desire and efforts to re-
create a sense of the earthly and cosmic community (see Swimme
and Berry, 1992, 257).

Thus the quantum theologian is concerned with church at the
heart of the world rather than with church over against the world.
And church is, first and foremost, community gathered around the
exploration and articulation of a deep, spiritual yearning. To engage with that yearning, we commune through rituals and sacred
rites, in which we become present to one another in a quality of
relatedness that often transcends words. In the depth of that sacred
experience, we encounter the trinitarian relatedness of the Godhead
itself. At some deep, mysterious level, we know in the depth of our
hearts that we are in touch with the Whole, the source of all we are
and have.

From these reflections we offer another central element of quantum theology: *Because the capacity to relate is itself the primary
divine energy impregnating creation, we humans need authentic ecclesial and sacramental experiences to explore and articulate our
innate vocation to be people in relationship.*

Humanity today hungers for genuine love, the ability to interrelate and interconnect. We yearn to realign the disparate parts and
outgrow our man-made, competitive, and destructive isolation. The
future toward which we are evolving, the call to participate in the

new world order, demands the demolition of many barriers, distinctions, and boundaries. We'll get to the future in each other's arms — across all the divides of race, creed, and culture — or otherwise we may not get there at all!

Part Four

The Story

As long as the stories of person and God remain exclusive accounts of separated entities, reality is inevitably split and all energies are spent on building bridges over gulfs that do not exist rather than exploring relationships which do exist.

—JOHN SHEA

Chapter 8

In the Beginning

The nature of the universe was from the beginning such that it would come alive however and wherever possible.

—ELIZABET SAHTOURIS

Only now can we see with clarity that we live not so much in a cosmos as in a cosmogenesis, a cosmogenesis best presented in narrative; scientific in its data, mythic in its form.

—BRIAN SWIMME AND THOMAS BERRY

Every child, and the child in every one of us, is ready to plead: Tell me a story. For the role of stories is to explain life, and the good stories, in their very substance and in the structure of their language, become revelation.

—ANDREW M. GREELEY

In the beginning, the energy of silence rested over an infinite horizon of pure nothingness. The silence lasted for billions of years, stretching across aeons the human mind cannot even remotely comprehend. Out of the silence arose the first ripples of sound, vibrations of pure energy from the nothingness of the creative vacuum. The stillness became restless and tiny bubbles of ether emanated from the space of infinite emptiness, the featureless ferment of quantum possibility.

And a mighty sound ruptured the tranquil stillness as a single point of raw potential, bearing all matter, all dimension, all energy, and all time, exploding like a massive fireball. The temperature exceeded 1,000,000,000,000 degrees centigrade, so hot that even elementary particles like electrons and protons could not exist. The time, according to human reckoning, was somewhere between fifteen and twenty billion years ago. From that time on, the silence begets the dance and the dance explodes into story.

It was the greatest explosion of all time. An irruption of infinite energy danced into being. It had a wild and joyful freedom about it, and like all dance it was richly endowed with coherence, elegance, and creativity. The earth is still so radioactive from this initial explosion that its core is kept hot by continuing nuclear reactions, and many atoms all over its surface — in rocks and trees, even in our own bodies — are still exploding. In our own bodies, Sahtouris (1989, 35) estimates that three million potassium atoms explode every minute.

Current theories state that after one-thousandth of a second of the so-called Big Bang, the universe had cooled sufficiently (to 100,000,000,000 degrees centigrade) for elementary particles — electrons, protons, and neutrons — to form. Three minutes later, when the temperature had dropped to 900,000,000 degrees centigrade, neutrons and protons combined to form stable atomic nuclei, initially those of hydrogen and helium. The cosmic dance of interrelating and procreating was well underway.

The universe continued to expand and cool until after about seven hundred thousand years, when the temperature fell to about 4,000 degrees centigrade, which is roughly the temperature of our sun. At this stage, the first simple atoms came into being. Below 4,000 degrees, the force of gravitation joined the cosmic dance, and atoms began to clump together forming, over thousands of millions of years, into clusters (communities?) of primordial galaxies. Within these giant clouds, hydrogen and helium gases continued to gather into ever more condensed masses, eventually giving birth to the first stars about five billion years ago.

Many of these early stars were intensely hot. They flared up and exploded in brilliant supernovas, each as bright as an entire galaxy. The force of those explosions sent heavier elements spewing out into space, condensing over millions of years into new stars, of which our sun is probably a fourth generation progeny, dated at 4.5 billion years ago.

It was about this time also that our solar system was formed from a huge cloud of interstellar dust. Most of the cloud consisted of frozen hydrogen, helium, and ice, but Planet Earth was fortunate to condense out of a part of the cloud rich in a diversity of elements, including all those necessary for the evolution of carbon-based life.

Some four billion years ago, with the appearance of the first algae and bacteria, the dance of life reached a more complex level of integration. Molecules clustered together to form the first cells; it was the beginning of biological life as we know it today.

Fish began to inhabit the waters about four hundred million years ago, and two hundred million years later the first mammals appeared on earth. Mammal and animal evolution became more elaborate and sophisticated right up to the emergence of humankind, which today we can trace back to some 4.4 million years ago (preceded by primitive forms dating back possibly to 14 million years ago), with our species Homo sapiens sapiens emerging around 40,000 B.C.E.

Both religion and theology have largely lost the central significance of our human, planetary, and cosmic story. They have become preoccupied with *fact* and to a corresponding degree have lost touch with *mystery* and *myth*. In a universe which is actually expanding (Hubble's theory of the 1920s) and will continue doing so for some millions of years yet to come, quantum theology calls for a more expansive understanding of the universe and of our role in it. The cosmic evolutionary saga is far from finished. In fact all indications are that this is a relatively young universe, which in evolutionary terms may still be growing through its adolescent phase (Sahtouris, 1989). And in the ensuing millennia or billennia, we humans will be outgrown by other species, as yet not even vaguely imagined in the universal Mind.

The evolutionary narrative is the membrane for every story ever told. It is a quantum story of unlimited potential and indescribable elegance. It is a story without beginning or end, an epic of ceaseless becoming. It embraces all the dreams and aspirations, pains and contradictions, that ever have been or ever will be. It is the context for all science and for all silence. It is the womb of creative vision.

The Potential for Self-Organization

Let's return to the story! As the explosive energy of the Big Bang began to cool — in those first microseconds of space-time — atoms began to form from subatomic particles, which themselves were produced from the cooling of energy. Other invisible forces, which today underpin all life in the universe — gravity, electromagnetism, the strong and weak forces (described in end note 13) — became operative. The universe was already displaying one of nature's most elegant and creative potentials: the power of self-organization.

The ability to self-organize seems to be a function of invisible fields (described in chapter 7), associated with all matter, from the tiniest subatomic particles to the most complex creatures, humans included. When atomic fields interact and join together, a molecular field is evoked; the interaction of molecular fields leads to the creation of a mega-molecular field, creating new patterns of interaction which become cells. Cells form several complex combinations — under field influence — to create organisms. Organism fields interact to form species fields. The fields of several species interact to form ecosystems. Ecosystems interrelate and thus create bio-regional fields, which are influenced by the planetary field of the earth itself. The earth, in turn, is influenced by the field of the solar system, which itself is affected by the field of the Milky Way galaxy. Galaxies interact gravitationally throughout the entire universe.

All visible organization arises out of invisible fields. Everything and everybody is the subject and beneficiary of field influence. All of us belong to a web of interrelationships, empowered by an intricate and mysterious life force. And it is the ability to self-organize, more than anything else, which promotes and enhances life in our universe.

The Gaia Hypothesis

In the past three to four hundred years, life itself has become something of an endangered species. The metaphor of the machine has modified our perceptions and understandings, which are quite alien to the realization of our deeper needs as human and planetary people. In our human compulsion to control, we have released forces of destruction which now threaten our very existence as a species. Ironically, it is in facing this grim reality that we are rediscovering the deeper truths of what life in our universe is all about (see Margulis and Sagan, 1995).

In the past twenty years, we have become much more enlightened about the fact that we live in an *alive universe*, a conviction which, as yet, is shared by only a minority of people in the Western world. With our linear, rational mode of thought, the concept of an alive universe is difficult to comprehend. The first question: "Is it alive in the sense that we humans are alive?" illustrates the nature of the problem. Why does the human sense of being "alive" have to be the norm for all other modes of aliveness? After all, we are not around very long in the evolutionary story of life, and the fact that we claim to be the most highly evolved species is based on *our own* inflated and misguided perception.

So what do we mean when we claim that the universe is *alive?* *We* don't need to make that claim; the universe itself, in its own evolutionary narrative, makes the claim much more cogently and convincingly than we humans ever could (see Swimme and Berry, 1992). We need to listen and be receptive to the evolutionary story itself. When we choose to listen, we begin to glimpse the deeper meaning, as it is manifested to us in that aspect of creation to which we humans are most closely connected, namely, Planet Earth itself.

Today we often refer to our planet as Mother Earth. In a world striving to be nonsexist, some feel uneasy about this description, while most dismiss the mother metaphor as a lot of sentimental dribble. There is, in fact, a profound wisdom in the notion of the earth as mother, challenging us to relate to the home planet, not as an object to be exploited and controlled, but as a subject who nurtures and sustains all her creatures and seeks a subject-to-subject relationship with all living beings.

Some members of the scientific community warmed toward the notion of the earth as mother after hearing the stories shared by cosmonauts throughout the 1960s and early 1970s (see Kelly, 1988). In describing their view of the earth from outer space, many related an experience of awe and wonder on beholding the planet, not as a lump of dead, inert matter but rather as an organism that resembled a living creature:

> The first thing that came to mind as I looked at Planet Earth floating in the vastness of space, was its incredible beauty, a blue and white jewel suspended against a velvet black sky.... The presence of divinity became almost palpable and I *knew* that life in the universe was not just an accident based on random processes. This knowledge came to me directly — noetically...an experiential cognition. (Words of Edgar D. Mitchell quoted by Murchie, 1979, 618)

> Looking outward to the blackness of space, sprinkled with the glory of a universe of lights, I saw majesty — but no welcome. Below was a welcoming planet. There, contained in the thin, moving, incredibly fragile shell of the biosphere is everything that is dear to you, all human drama and comedy. That's where life is; that's where all the good stuff is. (Words of Loren Acton, quoted in La Chance, 1991, 175)

> I really believe that if the political leaders of the world could see their planet from a distance, their outlook would be fundamentally changed....I think the view from 100,000 miles could be invaluable in getting people together to work out joint solu-

tions, by causing them to realize that the planet we share unites us in a way far more basic and far more important than differences in skin, color, religion or economic system.... If I could use only one word to describe the earth as seen from the moon, I would ignore both its size and color and search for a more elemental quality, that of fragility. The earth appears *fragile* above all else. I don't know why, but it does. (Collins, 1974, 470, 471)

In fact, the astronauts were not the first to receive such privileged insight. The Scottish scientist James Hutton, often considered to be the father of geology, suggested in 1785 that the earth should be regarded as a superorganism and went on to propose that its proper field of study should be physiology. In the late nineteenth century, the Russian scientist Ivanovitch Vernadsky put forward the notion that life is a geochemical process of the earth. The biologist G. E. Hutchinson took up this idea in the early part of the twentieth century, but not until the early 1970s, when James Lovelock (1979, 1988), in conjunction with Lynn Margulis, developed what we now call the Gaia hypothesis, did the scientific community exhibit any degree of openness to these novel ideas.

For Lovelock, Planet Earth is not merely the product of past geological processes, but also an ongoing process of co-creation. Living organisms continually renew and regulate the chemical balance of air, water, and soil in ways that ensure their continued growth. Life creates and maintains precise environmental conditions favorable to its existence, a frequently cited example being the oxygen level in the atmosphere delicately poised at approximately 21 percent: a little more and fires would start all over the planet, even in wet grass; a little less, and we, along with all other air-breathing creatures, would die. In a similar vein, Fell and Liss (1993) have noted that algae contribute to the temperature homeostasis of the planet.

Considering the earth as an alive organism requires us to view the whole universe as being alive also, because the earth, in all its functioning, is interdependent within the larger creation, particularly in the context of the solar system. According to the proponents of the Gaia hypothesis, the earth is a planet of the right size, orbiting a star of the right kind, enveloped by an atmosphere with the right composition, and with a hydrosphere unique among the solar planets. It harbors elements and compounds with extraordinary properties, all propitious and most of them indispensable for the propagation and maintenance of life.

Russell (1992, 213ff.) outlines a series of coincidences, minute in

detail and for long presumed to be insignificant, but now considered to be crucial to the evolution of life and even to the existence
of the universe itself. For example, why was the number of particles
at the Big Bang slightly greater than the number of anti-particles?
Had it not been for this initial imbalance, the material universe —
with its galaxies, stars, and planets — simply would not exist. The
number of particles left over, about 10^{80} also seems critical, determining the pace of gravitational forces that allowed the universe
to evolve with the multiplicity of life forms that exists today. Once
again, the sense of mystery and purpose seem most compelling at the
minute, unmanifest level. The mass of the neutron, the particle that
together with the proton forms the nucleus of the atom, is so finely
constituted that a decrease of 0.2 percent in its actual value would
cause the proton to decay (into a neutron) and atoms, the basis of
existence, would never have formed.

The strength of the nuclear force also seems to be finely tuned,
allowing for the complex evolution of hydrogen into helium and,
consequently, into carbon, oxygen, and nitrogen. These latter elements also demand that the proton functions at a very specific
charge. The forces of gravity and electromagnetism, aspects of life we
take so much for granted, operate at very specific strengths, clearly
designed to create optimum conditions for the evolution of stars, su-
pernova, and all life forms (including ourselves) that ensue thereafter.
According to Thompson (1990, 217), the odds against getting the
cosmic balance right has been estimated as 10^{60}, that is, one followed
by sixty zeros.

Finally, there is the fascinating story of carbon, initially synthe-
sized in stars and forming the basis upon which all the proteins,
amino acids, vitamins, fats, and carbohydrates of the human body
are built. But the creation of carbon itself is something of a miracle, based on the very rare combination of three helium atoms made
possible by a phenomenon called nuclear resonance. If the nuclear
resonance level for carbon was not exactly the value it is, virtually
no carbon would have formed inside stars, and life as we know it
would never have evolved.

And that is not all! A fourth helium nucleus combines with the
carbon atom to form oxygen. Once again, the combining agent is a
nuclear resonant, but on this occasion, its value lies just below the
critical point.

The sense of purpose is all-pervasive and deeply ingrained in the
fabric of the universe. Even the curvature of space itself is delicately
poised — between the demise of collapse into a massive black hole,

had the initial curvature been a fraction larger, or an explosion into a scattering of lifeless particles, had it been a fraction smaller. Indeed, it is only on a universal scale — at the quantum level — that we can perceive and appreciate the multiple intricacies of the cosmic tapestry. Only when we realize that we humans are totally dependent on the material of stars (carbon) for our existence, and that the very creation of that substance is something of a cosmic miracle, can we begin to contemplate *purpose,* not in terms of a final outcome, but in the very process and nature of evolution itself. (For further elucidation, see Greenstein, 1988; Sahtouris, 1989; Swimme and Berry, 1992).

These conditions are all interdependent. Nothing is brought about by our ability to discover it. It is not because we are here that the world comes to be so disposed, but rather the opposite. The planet survived — and thrived — for billions of years without our aid; and long after we have outlived our usefulness as a planetary species, the earth will continue its evolutionary unfolding.

Propensity for Self-Regulation

At the heart of the Gaia hypothesis is the controversial claim that earth, like all living organisms, functions as a self-creating, self-regulating, autopoietic system. The function of *autopoiesis* (from the Greek for "self-production") occupies a special place in the earth's story (see Jantsch, 1980). The concept was introduced in the early 1970s by the Chilean biologist Humberto Maturana (along with Francisco Varela). A system is autopoietic when its function is primarily geared to self-renewal. Whereas a machine is geared to the output of a specific product, a biological cell is primarily concerned with renewing itself. Upgrading (anabolic) and downgrading (catabolic) processes run simultaneously. Not only the evolution of a system but also its existence in a specific structure becomes dissolved into *process.* In the domain of the living, there is little that is solid and rigid.

It is in this capacity for self-organization and self-renewal that the earth story manifests its uniqueness. Throughout its evolutionary history, the earth has endured and survived several major catastrophes, many of global, universal proportion. Because these often resulted in large-scale extinction, we know relatively little about them. The nineteenth-century French geologist Georges Curvier claimed that in its long evolutionary history, Planet Earth has experienced *twenty-*

seven major transitions. Many of these were cataclysmic in nature, involving severe climate changes, widespread volcanic eruptions, and meteorite impacts over large segments of the earth (see Russell, 1992, 184ff.; also Verschuur, 1978).

And yet Planet Earth not merely survives, but thrives. Perhaps one of the most fascinating examples of autopoietic, self-regulatory action was about three billion years ago when photosynthesis (the use of light in the manufacture of food) began, and the first algae and bacteria evolved. Some of these were known as blue-greens (because of their color). By assimilating the energy of light and hydrogen from the seas, they grew and thrived. But all growth is at a price, in this case, the release of a deadly poison caused by the utilization of hydrogen. "Oxygen" was the name of the poisonous substance.

We think of oxygen as good and necessary, a life-giving and life-saving gas that is essential to the maintenance of life. But for the first living creatures it was lethal; in fact, it was more destructive than ultraviolet. If the atmosphere then became full of oxygen, as it now is, the large molecules could never have formed, and life would have ceased to exist. But Mother Earth, ever inventive, and apparently never to be outdone, made an ingenious intervention.

The free oxygen combined harmlessly with dissolved rock minerals, such as iron, and while it was absorbed in this way, it remained safe. About a billion years later, however, all the iron had been turned to rust, and the oxygen began to accumulate in the atmosphere.

Initially, some bacteria responded by burying themselves in the mud where the poisonous oxygen could not get at them; the bacterial agent which today facilitates the digestion of hay in cow's stomachs is believed to be the product of this ancient self-regulatory behavior. Blue-greens invented enzymes which neutralized the oxygen's harmful effects. Others solved the problem by living together in thick colonies where those of the outer layer were burned to death and thus formed a protective cover for those underneath. The blue-greens, while creating food molecules, learned how to use the waste oxygen to burn those same molecules and thus create energy. Today we call this process "respiration." It is a classic example of how Planet Earth converts a potential threat into a resource that not only saved the world from extinction, but made possible the vast array of life forms that have evolved since then.

There is a final chapter to the oxygen story which further illustrates the extravagance of Gaia's creativity. In order to escape the poisonous effects of oxygen, the early bacteria veered more toward the sunlight and in the process were destroyed by the radiation. A new planetary crisis was imminent, until the extra oxygen combined to form what we now call the "ozone layer" in the upper atmosphere, thus warding off the damaging effects of ultraviolet light. In Lovelock's words, a murderous intruder was turned into a powerful friend!

The story of Planet Earth is a not a descriptive tale about some object out there in space, dependent on us humans for its survival and growth. The true narrative is not about life *on* earth, but about the life that *is* earth. Could it be that we are dealing with a life form more sophisticated, creative, resilient, and integrated than our human mode, perhaps even more enduring than all the known life forms combined? Could it be that our ancient ancestors in identifying the earth with the Great Mother Goddess were in fact unraveling the mystery of our existence with a degree of wisdom and intuition which the rational mind of our time is unable to attain? The answers to these questions are likely to emanate from the planetary story itself. The unfolding narrative of evolution is a wellspring of profound wisdom.

The Creative Vacuum

As the story unfolds, the interdependent nature of planetary and cosmic life becomes all too apparent. A vital clue to the planet's relationship to other planets and stars is the nature of space itself. According to Greenstein (1988), the emptiness and vastness of space is essential to planetary existence and presumably to stellar interaction also. Our cosmos seems to need a vast amount of empty space if it is to be cool enough to generate and maintain the diversity of its life forms. Greenstein suggests that we imagine the earth as a marble, then the sun could be modeled as a medicine ball and would sit three hundred yards away. But the star Alpha Centauri would be a full 49,000 miles away and, in terms of our planet, that is considered to be the closest star.

The vastness of space is not just to accommodate the dance of life. It is an aspect of the dance itself, in fact, a very critical dimension. It is grossly misleading to suggest that it is "empty." Its fulness is a reservoir of prolific energy, which Davidson (1989) very rightly calls the "creative vacuum," and which the great scientist Max Planck once described in these words:

As a man who has devoted his whole life to the most clear-headed science, to the study of matter, I can tell, as a result of my research about the atoms, this much: *there is no matter as such*. All matter originates and exists only by virtue of a force which brings the particles of an atom to vibration and holds the most minute solar system of the atom together.... We must assume behind this force that existence of a conscious and intelligent Mind. This Mind is the matrix of all matter. (Quoted in Davidson, 1989, 128)

In probing the nature of the vacuum, Davidson reclaims the notion that (a)ether is the fundamental stuff of "empty" space. Underpinning the ether — or perhaps inherent to it — are the various field energies, formative blueprints, a creative memory holding original impressions which, over time, become manifested in the external forms of creation. But for Davidson (1989, 125), there is an even deeper reservoir, namely, consciousness, to which he attributes divine origin and describes it as a vast holographically structured mega-computer where the primal power or undifferentiated energy is wrapped around with pattern, vibration, or form, giving rise to the laws of polarity or causality. It is the architect of cosmic justice, a mechanism which never fails since its power comes from the supreme consciousness of God.

The Gaia story focuses on how earth is alive from within; the vacuum is a reservoir pregnant with unlimited possibility. To describe the world as "teeming with life" sounds exhilarating, but in the light of our evolving story it may even be an understatement. The potential for life is so overwhelming, pervasive, and mysterious, it almost defies human comprehension.

Yet, we continue to analyze, rationalize, and interfere. We have created an anthropomorphism that is as deadly as it is irrelevant. We set ourselves up as the masters, not merely of Planet Earth, but of the entire universe and, in the infamous words of Francis Bacon, we ruthlessly set out to torture nature until she reveals her last secrets to us.

The Anthropic Principle

We have scarcely begun to address our insatiable compulsion toward self-inflation. This addictive drive, with its sinister undercurrents of control and manipulation, undermines the wholeness and vitality of the quantum vision which is at the heart of our planet's story. Instead of addressing the whole, we go part of the way and end up with what seems a praiseworthy "enterprise," but in effect it is flawed in its fundamental logic. One such enterprise is what scientists have named the cosmological anthropic principle.

In 1974, the British physicist Brandon Carter coined the term "anthropic principle," which basically states that if some features of the natural world are required for our existence, then the world doesn't make sense without us. Another formulation focuses on the conviction that the universe would have no meaning unless we were here to give it meaning: the only things that can be known are those compatible with the existence of knowers.

Here we touch on one of the great unresolved debates of the quantum theory. According to the Copenhagen School (Neils Bohr and associates), reality does not exist until we observe it. Therefore, our observation creates the world with which we interact or, to use Wheeler's language, the universe in which we *participate*. The alternative, many-worlds view, suggests that our world, even if created by our observation/perception, is only one of many worlds and, consequently, apart from our observations, an objective world exists out there that can be measured and analyzed *objectively*.

In my opinion, both arguments are flawed and the consequent dualism (the either/or) becomes unavoidable. The major weakness in both arguments is the assumption that we humans, at this stage in our evolution, can pronounce the final word on how things are in the universe. There is no higher wisdom than ours — we implicitly (and often explicitly) claim — and we seem to add, subconsciously, that there never can be. This anthropomorphic strain is one of the major pitfalls of classical science and, sadly, permeates many of the scientific breakthroughs of the twentieth century.

The anthropic principle is the icing on the cake of this misguided anthropocentric drive. It brings into consciousness and validates (or tries to) what for long has been an unquestioned assumption. Now that the issue has been exposed, we can examine more openly what it attempts to state.

Barrow and Tippler (1986) provide a comprehensive overview of the anthropic principle. There are four dominant variations, offering ranging degrees of emphasis on the underlying conviction which claims that the highest, possible levels of intelligence, information, and consciousness are those developed, or due to be developed, by human beings, *in their presently evolved state*. But we humans, *in our presently evolved state*, are not the final goal of evolution. We are not the ultimate, nor even the penultimate, chapter of the story; in fact there may be no such thing as a *final* chapter. Homo sapiens will evolve into a more highly developed creature who will view, observe, and relate to the planet (and to the universe) in a more sophisticated and enlightened way than we are capable of doing.

Yes, our universe is an intelligent organism, with an infinite capacity for enlightened, autopoietic growth and renewal. In the billions of years of future evolution, we humans will be surpassed by other more highly developed creatures. The time has come to acknowledge this fact, and to reevaluate, soberly, honestly, and humbly, our role in the grand evolutionary story.

From the beginning of time until now, every creature and species has contributed to the intelligent unfolding of life. The process of photosynthesis, which began billions of years ago, is intelligent altruistic behavior of an alive planet where all the parts cooperate under the influence of a higher intelligence which is greater than the sum of the parts. The delicate and intricate interaction of subatomic particles — along with their mysteriously poised measurements (to minute degrees of 1 percent, as in the case of the neutron outweighing the proton, or in the ability of the strong force to hold the deutron together) — illustrates a profound and elegant wisdom.

Humans and Gaia

Theologians may be quick to suggest that this is living proof of divine creation; proponents of the anthropic principle will argue that it's all in place for the sake of intelligent (human) life. But the quantum theologian (e.g., Ruether, 1992) tends to opt for a more wholistic stance and will plead that we:

- refrain from the analysis for a while and simply behold (contemplate) the sheer wonder of it all;

- open up our limited intelligence to the universal Mind, whose resourcefulness far outstretches what we humans have ever achieved;

- at least entertain the idea that the planet we inhabit is endowed with a quality of "aliveness" that supersedes our human form and may be more elaborate and dynamic than all the life forms known to us;

- open our hearts to the "call to conversion," the letting go
  we need to do if we really wish to be participants in the
  evolutionary letting-be.

Both Lovelock (1979, 1988) and Sahtouris (1989) in their explorations of the Gaia hypothesis present a grim future for us
humans if we don't learn to refrain from our exploitation of planetary life and choose to continue on our ego-inflationary route of
self-aggrandizement and deleterious interference. In the evolutionary story — ours and that of Planet Earth — the planet *always*
wins out. Mother Earth has an amazing resilience, a very profound
intelligence, and can be quite ruthless in maintaining her integrity.

In Gaian terms, we are just another species, neither the owners nor
the stewards of the planet. Our future depends much more on a right
relationship with Gaia than on enforcing our self-righteous claim to
be masters of creation. Gaia is not purposefully anti-human, but so
long as we continue to change the global environment against her
preferences, we encourage our replacement with a more environmen-
tally benevolent species. We are also discerning that Gaia's incredible
complexity makes her tougher and more resourceful than we are. We
are far more likely to obliterate our own species by destroying our
environment than we are to kill Gaia. We would be wise to remind
ourselves often that Gaia's dance will continue with or without us.

We humans have become a cosmic anomaly. We rape and pollute
the very womb that nurtures and sustains. We have become a dysfunctional family, blind to our own addictions, heading headlong for
self-destruction (see Wilson-Schaef, 1987; La Chance, 1991). As we
approach the end of the twentieth century, time seems to be running
out for Homo sapiens. The wisdom that begot the Agricultural, Industrial, and Information Revolutions is largely a spent force. Our
achievements have become our atrocities. Only an honest confrontation without helplessness or hopelessness can in any way bring us to
our senses. That is unlikely to happen — but what we can't do for
ourselves, Gaia will do on our behalf; therein lies some semblance
of hope for the future! We'll return to this subject in subsequent
chapters.

Theological Implications

It is only in the past twenty years that theology has given serious
thought to evolution, and as yet few theologians put cosmology

center stage. Meanwhile, cosmologists and philosophers grapple unceasingly with the imponderables of how it all began, particularly who or what caused the Big Bang and what, if anything, was there before it. Did God have to create and to what degree does God's creation inhibit or enhance human freedom?

These questions recur many times in the story of orthodox theology. They take on a fresh significance today, because they arise within a whole new cosmological context. The context is new precisely in its invitation to seek meaning from *within* rather than from *without*. Even those theologians who adopt an evolutionary perspective tend to image God as an *external* agent directing the evolutionary unfolding. On the other hand, process theologians (Whitehead, 1979; Cobb and Boswell, 1982) claim that God *co-creates* in conjunction with the evolutionary process, which often sounds as if the pace and course of evolution dictates the mode and degree of God's creative power.

To these profound and intricate questions, quantum theology wishes to bring some fresh considerations:

a. Since the whole is greater than the sum of its parts, then the "whole" of the evolutionary/creative process will always outstretch our human, scientific, and theological speculations. The evolutionary/creative process is a subject for contemplation and mystical comprehension rather than for theological discourse or scientific analysis.

b. Quantum theology asserts that the greater "whole" of the evolutionary/creative process is empowered and animated by a supernatural life force. However, it considers that life force to be inherent to the creative process rather than external to it.

c. Quantum theology is not particularly concerned about the nature of God. Since any quantum vision has to accept and integrate unanswerables and imponderables, quantum theology happily accepts the dictum: Let God be God! Orthodox theology often seems to collude with mainstream religion in subconsciously trying to "conquer" God by discovering and knowing everything about the divine reality. The outcome is nearly always an idolatrous one — with notorious validations of war and manipulation in the name of one or other omniscient, omnipotent God.

d. These reflections on the Godhead demand novel perceptions on humanity's role in the co-creative process. Since "God" is not into conquering or controlling the world, nor the evolutionary process, neither should we humans be. We are not in charge of the universe; we are participators in its growth and development. We *belong* to the universe and to its unfolding process. Our lives have no meaning apart from the universe. The universe is not an object set over against us, the subjects. No, it is the great Subject, with whom we are invited into a subjective interrelationship (explored in chapter 7).

So what is our role in the grand, evolutionary process? Perhaps we are intended to be the nervous system of Planet Earth, or as increasing numbers of scientists and philosophers are intimating, the *conscious* dimension of the universe — in the sense that reflective consciousness (the ability to reflect on the fact that we can reflect) seems to be unique to us humans. In the mechanistic worldview, we assume that we have been endowed with consciousness in order to subdue all other, "inferior" life forms. In the quantum worldview, we are invited to use this gift in the service of the universe, becoming more conscious, since consciousness is perceived to be embedded in all creation and seems to be awaiting a fuller sense of awakening; hence, Zohar's provocative and perceptive insight that we ourselves might be thoughts (excitations) in the mind of God (Zohar, 1990, 212). Perhaps the fullness of evolution itself is the conscious universe fully alive!

Beyond these speculations and reflections, the quantum vision invites us to a new theological threshold. Since all theology is about the *logos,* the Word and the wording of ultimate reality (God), then the quantum horizon becomes an energy for storytelling. In quantum terms, our theological role as human beings may well be that of narrators of the sacred, cosmological story. Beyond the academic pursuit of ultimate building blocks and the intellectual search for convincing ("provable") answers is the creative, contemplative exploration of the evolutionary story itself, where divine initiative and human response blend into one. Only when we enter deeply into that story, feel its meaning in the depth of our hearts, have we really understood what life is about. We won't have conquered the world, but we will have understood; we will have seen the Light! Then, and only then, can we be truly at peace — with ourselves and with the whole of life.

We conclude with another key principle employed by the quantum theologian: *Our passionate desire to understand in depth will not be attained by intellectual prowess or technological achievement, but by immersing ourselves in the divine, evolutionary story and committing ourselves to the contemplation and narration of that story in each new epoch.*

Chapter 9

Stories Generate Meaning

*The most expressive metaphor for what science finds in
nature today is no longer law, but story.*
—HOLMES ROLSTON

*Stories are designed to force us to consider possibilities.
Stories hint that our taken-for-granted daily realities
may, in fact, be fraught with surprise.*
—WILLIAM J. BAUSCH

*It's all a question of story. We are in trouble just now
because we are in between stories.*
—THOMAS BERRY

Once upon a time, there was a cat...destined for notoriety in the
world of quantum mechanics. And there was a scientist called Erwin,
who in a moment of desperation decided to experiment with the cat,
in the hope of making some sense out of a crazy phenomenon called
the quantum theory.

So Erwin took the cat to his laboratory. He built a solid, opaque
box, into which he inserted a diabolical apparatus which, when activated, had a 50/50 chance of releasing a poisonous gas. In goes the
reluctant cat — with the 50/50 chance of coming out alive.

The lid is sealed and the gadget is activated. Something has happened. Either the poison has been released and the cat is now dead,
or it hasn't been released and the cat is still alive. But Erwin can't see
what's happening inside the box, so he's left in a dilemma, wondering
whether the cat is alive or dead!

The thought-experiment of Schrodinger's cat is a landmark in
twentieth-century science (see Gribbin, 1988). In fact, the story is as
bizarre as the experiment itself, and yet both seem to have assumed
an enduring attraction. According to classical science, the outcome of
the experiment is clear from the moment the apparatus has been ac-

tivated: the cat is either dead or alive; you open the box and discover what has actually happened.

According to many quantum theorists, *our* observation determines the outcome (the so-called Copenhagen interpretation of quantum theory). Applying this criterion to the cat experiment means that whether the cat is dead or alive after the experiment depends upon *our observation*. In some strange bizarre sense, our opening the box and looking in causes (or contributes to) the cat being dead or alive.

The argument flies totally in the face of common sense and highlights only one of several "incomprehensibles" of the quantum theory. Indeed, many scientists who support and advocate the quantum vision don't find the experiment either helpful or enlightening. Nor is the entire scientific community convinced that the Copenhagen interpretation is central to the quantum theory in its various scientific and cosmological applications.

Stories Stretch the Imagination

From a theological point of view, I am fascinated by the *story,* rather than by the mechanics of the experiment. It has a ring of truth similar to the parables of the Christian Bible, or to some of the sacred epics in the other great religions. As a story it grips one's attention and imagination. It articulates a desire to move beyond the neat, rational, dualistic outcome of either "dead" or "alive." It invites us to contemplate other possibilities beyond our simplistic dualisms.

As we listen to the story and try to comprehend the scientists' subconscious world, we sense a desire to break out of old (mechanistic) molds, to befriend uncertainty, and to entertain paradox. The neat classical world of either/or is too simple to be true to life. Meaning forces us toward fresh horizons. The edges become frayed and the man-made boundaries collapse. Truth is bigger than all our inventions and outgrows all our observations.

The point I wish to highlight here — which is also the concluding observation of the previous chapter — is that story is the most dynamic and versatile tool available to us humans for the exploration of meaning and mystery. Every body of knowledge and research creates its repertoire of stories (usually at a subconscious level). Although science is portrayed as a field of observation and experimentation and theology is depicted as a body of irrefutable dogma, both science and theology are primarily the product of story. Obviously, this is more apparent in the case of theology. Even the very name, with its focus on *logos,* conjures up narrative impact.

In the scientific literature, we occasionally catch glimpses of the narrative infrastructure. Examples that spring to mind include Einstein's rigid allegiance to the God of mechanistic science, illustrated in the oft-quoted words, "God does not play dice with the universe"; Bohr's sense of shock at the incomprehensibility of the quantum theory: "Those who are not shocked when they first come across quantum theory, cannot possibly have understood it"; Heisenberg's somber and reflective mood when he narrated: "I remember discussions with Bohr (1927) which went through many hours until very late at night, and ended almost in despair. . . . I went for a walk in the neighboring park and repeated to myself again and again the question: Can nature possibly be as absurd as it seemed to us in these atomic experiments?"; Feynman's poetic quip: "To do science you've got to have taste"; or Hawking's cryptic remark: "Every time I hear about Schrodinger's cat, I want to reach for my gun." Finally, there is the story of Einstein's humble sense of humor that when a newspaper announced: "One hundred scientists prove Einstein wrong," his reply was: "It would only have taken one."

In all these "throwaway" phrases, and a host of others which sporadically turn up in the scientific literature, we get unfiltered access into the struggles, the meanderings, the imaginings, and the questions of the scientific mind. But more than that, we begin to get a feel for the scientific "heart," searching and seeking out the ultimate meanings — those unattainable insights that baffle the seeker to the point of despair, but never culminate in intellectual or spiritual paralysis.

Norman O. Brown one time claimed that meaning is not in things but in between. It's not in events, nor in objects, nor even in proven discoveries that ultimate truth lies, but in the process of seeking, searching, experimenting, and discovering. Behind the external activities is an internal process which manifests itself in the unpredictable moments of surprise, humor, jest, and storytelling. The narrative infrastructure of any science reveals a depth of truth and meaning which no laboratory experiment, no matter how thorough, can convey or communicate. The deeper meaning is embedded in the story, not in the verifiable facts.

Consequently, story and the narrative process are the primary contextual framework, a type of primordial laboratory for the scientific pursuit, for the wisdom and discovery that comprises scientific exploration. Without the underlying story, science becomes a mechanistic ideology, compulsively bent on domination and manipulation, juxtaposed to other branches of wisdom and exploration, and both alienated from and alienating to the wholeness that comprises universal life.

Not only is story at the heart of scientific pursuit, but science itself, in common with all other forms of wisdom, is born out of story. It is very much the product of humankind's need to make sense and meaning out of life. But it goes even deeper: the scientific story is also a statement of the universe's own potential and desire to give expression to its inherent creativity, to narrate its evolutionary unfolding in the various manifest forms that comprise the visible and tangible world around us. When we learn to let go of our anthropomorphic stance over against the universe (as subject vs. object), and re-vision our role as co-creators within the evolutionary process, then and only then will we grasp the deeper meaning, which for science and theology alike is in the story and its narrating and not in irrefutable dogmas or in objective verification.

The Word as Story

Theology has not entirely abandoned its rootedness in story (see, for example, Shea, 1978, 1980; Wright, 1988). Christian theology claims to spring from the revealed word of God in the scriptural story of the Old and New Testaments. But as Fox (1984) astutely remarks, our theology is so focused on words that it has largely betrayed the *Word* (in its original Aramaic, *dabhar*, meaning creative energy). In our attempts to get to the theological building blocks (in what sense was Jesus God and/or man? How do you fit three persons into one Trinity? What precisely makes a sacrament a sacrament?), we have often lost sight of the story which sustains and nourishes theological discourse. And because we have neglected the *story as story*, we have, over the centuries, turned it into an ideological statement giving literal significance to something that was never meant to be taken literally (e.g., the Genesis creation story, the Virgin birth story, the parables).

Over time, facts and dogmas tend to assume ideological proportions. Truths that initially offered liberation, hope, and new life often become millstones, burdens that stifle and stultify. All the major religions today — and theology in general — suffer from narrative deprivation. Even when original myths (beginnings and endings) are still narrated, they are over stylized and couched in legalistic and devotional categories that inhibit, and frequently prevent, the story from being retold in *today's* context, and not in that of hundreds or thousands of years ago.

Readers of this book, whether Christian or not, will have some contact with dominant Christian stories such as the Virgin Birth of Jesus, the resurrection from the dead, the miracle stories, and such well known parables as the Prodigal Son (Father) and the Good Samaritan. I wish to submit that the entire Bible, along with the sacred texts of other religions, is first and foremost a *story,* and not a record of definite facts and events. In terms of faith, what brings meaning and integration to one's experience, the facts are quite secondary. It's the story (and not the facts) that grips the imagination, impregnates the heart, and animates the spirit within (the spiritual core).

Whether or not there was an empty tomb, whether or not anybody actually saw the Risen Jesus, is not of primary significance. If through modern archaeological research we were to rediscover the remains of Jesus, thus establishing that he never rose physically from the grave, that discovery would not undermine the faith of a genuine believer. It would create immense doubt and confusion for millions who follow a dogmatic creed rather than a spirituality of the heart. (It could also be a catalyst for a profound conversion experience.)

Theologians in general and guardians of orthodox religion will find the above comments quite disturbing; some will consider them to be blatantly heretical. I invite such people to explore the pedagogy used by Jesus and by all the great teachers of the various religious traditions. Jesus did not theologize, legalize, or preach in any formal sense. Jesus *told stories,* the best known being the *parables.* Catechists and religious educators often portray the parables as simple stories to illustrate important truths. Often the parables are reinterpreted, in preaching and teaching alike, in terms of immediate daily and personal experience. A sense is conveyed that everybody and anybody can apply the parables to contemporary experience and get the full impact of the original message.

This is a reductionistic approach, with the accompanying risks of oversimplification, misinterpretation, and narrative deprivation. Often the original context is not appropriately acknowledged. Scant attention is given to the hermeneutical task of translating ideas, concepts, and language from one culture to another. Consequently, the narrative impact, along with the inherent call to change and conversion, is often negated.

The parables of the Christian story, and corresponding narratives in other faith systems, bear an archetypal, primordial significance.

They are not just ordinary stories; in fact, there is no such thing as an "ordinary" story. Their original context and impact is one of a newly emerging culture engaging with an established, orthodox one and confronting it with its inevitable demise. The parables in the New Testament largely belong to the vein of prophetic discourse in the Old Testament, where the old order is crumbling and a new vision is struggling to be born. The parables are transitional stories that are intended to disturb and challenge the hearers, and motivate them to move into a radically new way of engaging with the world and the call of the times.

Bausch (1984, 117–37) delineates six characteristics of the New Testament parables:

- They uncover our competitiveness and envy and invite us to brotherhood and sisterhood instead.

- They uncover our wrong centering and invite us to a right centering.

- They uncover our need to hoard and exclude and invite us to share and include.

- They uncover our assumptions and challenge us to turn them around.

- They uncover our timidity and invite us to risk all for the sake of God's Kingdom.

- They uncover our self-centered despair and distrust and invite us to hope.

The Central Myth of the Christian Story

In the Christian context, the parables serve as subplots in an even more embracing story, which the Gospel writers invariably call the "Kingdom of God" or, as in Matthew's Gospel, the "Kingdom of Heaven." This is the central myth of the New Testament, the core message of Jesus for humanity and for the world. It is the archetypal truth that underpins all that Christianity stands for, the fundamental norm that makes Christianity unique, not in the sense of being apart from, but in what it has to share with the other great religions and with all people who embark on the spiritual journey of life.

What Jesus meant by the "Kingdom" (what others prefer to call the "New Reign of God" or, in feminist terms, the "Kindom") is difficult to describe concretely (see the comprehensive studies by Fuellenbach, 1995, and Sheehan, 1986). Remember, we are dealing with a *story*, not with a dogma. But the story of God's New Reign, activated for Christians in and through Jesus, has a particular orientation which we can describe as follows: It is the invitation to work for a new world order, marked by right relationships of justice, love, peace, and liberation. It is new in its essential nature, global in ambience (not just for Christians), and practical in its application. It includes but also transcends the religious dreams and hopes of all humankind.

The church — which is rarely mentioned in the Gospels — is intended to be the servant and herald of the New Reign of God in the world. The major problem facing the Christian churches today is that they have lost touch with the Kin(g)dom agenda. The churches have largely betrayed the raison d'être of their existence. The major crisis facing the Christian churches is not the drop in numbers, the shortage of clergy, credibility in the eyes of the world, failure to organize, etc. No, above and beyond all these problems is the church's failure to acknowledge the reason for its existence, to be at the service of a higher, more universal call and not to be concerned about its own status and survival, with which it is largely preoccupied at the present time.

Because many theologians are affiliated with, and accountable to, churches they tend to fall prey to the morass and confusion of a church that has lost its way. Although genuinely trying to be enlightened and informed, they unconsciously, and often consciously, convey a "churchiness" that undermines the authenticity of their message and alienates their potential clientele. Even the very language used by theologians often belongs to a religious environment that simply doesn't resonate with the hopes and aspirations of our emerging culture. While theologians may offer reassurance to those who draw nourishment from past traditions, rarely do they offer real hope to those who struggle to bring about a better world characterized by the Kin(g)dom values of justice, love, peace, and liberation.

Theology needs to reconnect at two levels: (*a*) with the emerging world of our time, and, in the case of Christianity, (*b*) with the original myth of the New Reign of God in the world. In fact, these are two dimensions of the one reality, because the New Reign of God can be activated only in the world, not outside it. And the Kin(g)dom has a relevance for each new cultural epoch which can be discovered only by exploring the biblical story in the context of our contemporary planetary and cosmic narrative. The world is the arena for the historical realization of the Kin(g)dom. In other words, the New Reign of God unfolds in the world, or it does not happen at all. Such is the co-creative challenge which Christians inherit; such is the privilege and call to be a Kin(g)dom person.

These considerations enable us to formulate another principle of quantum theology: *Ultimate meaning is embedded in story, not in facts. All particular religious stories belong to a larger story which includes, but also transcends, the particular religious traditions of any one historical or cultural epoch.*

Every body of wisdom — scientific, religious, or otherwise — has its repertoire of stories. The stories are reservoirs of meaning and of the pursuit of an intelligent universe arising from the tendency toward intelligence (information) which is inherent to the universe itself (see Barrow, 1990, 193–99; Davies, 1992, 162ff., 200–205). Consequently, the telling of stories is always more than a personal or interpersonal experience. Both narrator and listener — who are really participators — are absorbed into a more global, universal ethos. The personal and collective unconscious intermingle; person and planet fuse into one.

At this level, the distinction between science and religion breaks down, as do all traditional dualisms, and the new spiritual awareness that may ensue will not be easily integrated into old religious categories. The quantum sense of the whole being greater than the sum of the parts is initially experienced, at both the personal and interpersonal levels, as a jarring, disquieting experience. Old certainties collapse, old securities crumble; nothing seems clear anymore. Yet, something much more powerful and meaningful is calling us forth into new, adventurous territory. Whether to take the risk or not becomes the heart-rending discernment.

Interpreting Sacred Texts

In the light of these observations, how does the theologian engage with sacred texts? Inspired writings such as the Bible, the Koran, the Bhagavagita do seem to embody enduring truths, but today many people acknowledge that these same truths cannot be fully expressed, articulated, or explained in the language of any one culture or epoch. Moreover, the truths themselves convey a depth that cannot be explored or experienced through the medium of the spoken word alone. Archetypal meanings and mythic values veer toward metaphoric, symbolic, and ritual expression before being capable of formulation in either the written or spoken word.

Verbal language can be quite limited in its ability to articulate deeper meanings. In pursuing the journey of the heart, whether in a spiritual, psychic, or psychotherapeutic process, people frequently resort to the nonverbal mode (e.g., art, movement, music) to express what is going on within. In the evolutionary story of our time, many people seem to be transcending the literalist and rational dimensions of the verbal or written forms. Perhaps we are reclaiming something of our prehistoric experience, prior to the era of the spoken word (since about 100,000 B.C.E.), when we communicated and related nonverbally for at least *four million* years.

Our inherited sacred texts also embody elements of that ancient experience and, in all probability, contain a great deal more that is deeply symbolic and archetypal, rather than an orientation toward meaning that can be comprehended primarily at the rational, academic level. Engaging, therefore, with sacred texts is a challenge which calls forth not just intellectual prowess (which only the chosen few possess, leaving the rest of us feeling spiritually inferior), but an attitude and orientation of listening, understanding, openness to be surprised, receptivity not to one but to several meanings (often depending on how we question the text), and readiness to engage with the complexity inherent in the message.

When we touch into archetypal meaning, we are dealing not merely with the past, but encountering an enduring will-to-meaning that draws on the past to impact upon the present and project us into the open-ended future. In archetypal terms, past, present, and future are dimensions of the one unbroken web of life. Sacred texts, therefore, may project us into an unexpected sense of the future, often inviting us to places we would rather not go. Consequently, to use sacred texts in order to preserve a monolithic sense of the past may undermine the deeper meaning of the text itself, while also jeopardizing the human engagement with the message and power of the narrative. For the quantum theologian, therefore, ongoing reinterpretation of sacred texts is considered both normative and essential. It safeguards against the stultification of language and the anthropocentric imposition of cultural forms and challenges us to examine continuously the academic and political imperialism within which we humans tend to couch religious dogma.

The process of reinterpretation also helps to maintain our gaze on the future: open to the changing and diverse nature of human culture and universal life, necessitating fresh interpretations, new discoveries, and unexpected insights. And for the quantum theologian, there will always remain the incompleteness of the task and the open-endedness of the all-encompassing mystery which ever beckons us on to new and unchartered horizons. At best, therefore, sacred texts serve as approximations, pointing to deeper truths that belong to the realm of the ever old and ever new, the wellspring of ultimate meaning, which we humans seek to captivate in linguistic and literary forms. But the mystery of truth we engage with is greater than all our scholarly creations and forever eludes and transcends our human urge to conquer and control. The freedom and challenge to reinterpret is precisely what saves us from literary idolatry.

Story in Peril?

I wish to conclude this chapter with some pastoral considerations. At the personal and interpersonal levels, there often exists a gaping vacuum: To whom do I tell my story? Will they understand? Can they hear me through? This is where disillusionment and disenchantment with church and formal religion often begins. There is a nauseating suspicion that the institution has nothing of substance to offer anymore; perhaps I have outgrown the need for it and how do I share or explore that feeling? A moralistic script from the past is likely to intrude: "How arrogant! Can you be sure you are right?" This often leads to a guilt trip, by which time the seeker — in desperation — may either return to the insipid institution or seek false security in a sect or a cult; alternatively, one may abandon faith all together, thus opting for a spiritual vacuum, a space which in today's world is grossly overpopulated.

As a human species, we have become creatures without a common story, actors without a script. We compensate by indulging in verbose rhetoric out of which the media accumulates wealth and power. We have become narcissistic and addicted to the banal as a means of escaping the pain of our meaninglessness. Ours is a culture in confusion, in a deep state of crisis. We have become too lethargic, on the one hand, and too obsessive (addicted) on the other, either to listen to or narrate our story. Amid the plethora of outdated myths (including many formal religious and scientific ones) is a narrative in fragments, a story that one time served us well, but has now grown archaic, irrelevant, and insipid.

The contemporary arts — music, art, sculpture, poetry, drama — illustrate our cultural death-wish (see Shlain, 1991). Walk into any

modern art gallery and you see it all: imagery absorbed in the nihilism and bawdiness of our time, symbolic constructs incapable of
projecting us to a higher level of meaning. The arts serve us well in
portraying our "lostness," aimlessness, and confusion, but when the
arts themselves (and religion) succumb to the morbidity and inertia
of a dwindling culture, then what is left to project us toward new
meaning? This is the heart of our crisis today. The medium itself has
been highjacked. The storyteller has no story to tell and doesn't even
know where to begin the new one (see Trussell, 1989–90; O'Murchu,
1988, 30–35).

It is at the level of the imagination that contemporary life is weak-
est. With two-thirds of humanity struggling to meet basic survival
needs and the other third largely preoccupied with accumulating and
hoarding wealth, the human capacity for reflection, intuition, and
the development of the imagination is at an all-time low. Rational
thought, buttressed by our utilitarian, stereotyped educational system (especially in the West), has all but usurped the artist within us.
Ours is a body without a soul, dispirited by uninspired architects,
bent on conquering and controlling the objective world.

Some are striving to tell the story anew. It is an uphill struggle
against the forces of apathy, ignorance, and cynicism. The apathetic
won't even listen; perhaps they don't known how to listen amid the
din and confusion of our time. The ignorant choose not to listen;
why bother? What's the point? Perhaps the greatest fear in the ignorant is that the story might disturb and challenge them. And the
cynic already knows that it is dangerous to listen to the new stories
of our time, because they do disturb and challenge, and then one
has to confront choices and options — many with uncomfortable
consequences.

Somehow or other, the story continues to be told; evolution itself
guarantees that! It may be at a low ebb right now, but the narrative infrastructure — a key element in the search for meaning — is
intact. Totalitarian regimes of both past and present try to erode the
power of the imagination, but never with final success. The storyteller is unassailable, and when we "rediscover fire" in the many new
stirrings of our time, then the storyteller will emerge again "to save
those who have no imagination." (George Bernard Shaw).

Part Five

The Shadow

Love winter when the plant says nothing.
—THOMAS MERTON

Chapter 10

Embracing the Dark

Nothingness spreads around us, but in this nothing we find what we did not know existed.

— SUSAN GRIFFIN

Indeed, chaos is just a special but very interesting form of self-organization in which there is an overload of order.

— PETER COVENEY

The possibility that humanity may not pass the test that Life has set cannot be overlooked.

— PETER RUSSELL

This book, like any book ever written, is a story unto itself. Thus far, our narrative is like a tapestry in the making: pattern forming and unfolding; different aspects interconnecting as various bits relate to each other; and finally, the overall story begins to emerge. And then, perhaps quite unexpectedly, something goes wrong; the flow is disrupted. Sometimes one problem leads to another and everything seems to be in turmoil. We become frustrated, angry, and may begin to dislodge our tension onto a whole range of scapegoats. What for long was a manageable project now poses a threat and tends to become a nightmare.

A perennial danger is that, in our exasperation, we are no longer energized by what we have achieved thus far. The cumulative goodness to date seems to have evaporated in a cloud of doubt and confusion, all because of one or a few recent errors. What, in fact, is happening is that we have succumbed to the old divisive enemy of the *dualistic mindset*.

What we perceived to be a disruption to the flow may actually be part of the flow itself. We come down with flu and have to spend time off work, not just because we have picked up the "bug," but perhaps because the body needs to rest, and this is nature's way of caring for her own needs. So the evil of the flu may, in fact, be a blessing; the disruption is effectively a process of realignment.

The disruption we describe has many aspects within the spectrum of our personal/planetary lives. It may be the 101 daily frustrations which we all experience. It may be personal sickness, pain, suffering, tragedy, or loss. It may be family struggle or trauma of one type or another. It may be the more generalized pain and suffering of the world, the "forces of evil" at work, the negative impact of economic recession or the horrible injustices that fragment and divide our planet. In evolutionary terms, it may be the great dark ages, sometimes covering millions of years, in which species were obliterated and global catastrophes of one type or another occurred.

These are the forces of darkness that concern us in this chapter. What are they all about? What do they mean? Where do they fit into our quantum worldview, and, theologically, what can we say about them that hasn't been said or written before?

Darkness is a concept that tends to evoke negative reactions. Many people feel uncomfortable in the dark; it has connotations of ignorance, lifelessness, oppression, a sense of being lost. Darkness is something to be conquered, controlled, and, if possible, eliminated.

And yet, many beautiful things happen in the dark. Seeds germinate and strike root. Most creatures rest during the hours of darkness. Passionate sexual intimacy often occurs in the dark. Many of our body functions operate during the rest of night. Life seems to need the realm of darkness to realize its full meaning and potential. Even at the cosmic level, the forces of darkness seem to play a crucial role.

Perhaps most intriguing of all is the recent discovery that, despite all our advances in science and learning, we know relatively little about the composition of universal life. So much is still in the dark, and appropriately we call it "dark matter," referring to those huge nebulous superclusters that populate the far reaches of space and are believed to comprise at least 90 percent of all matter in the universe (more on this topic, p. 182 below). Engaging with the dark has mystical and poetic overtones, but today it is probably the single greatest challenge confronting the scientific and theological communities.

Black Holes

In contemporary physics, black holes serve as a type of symbol or metaphor for the powers of darkness at work in our universe. The

term was coined by John Wheeler in 1969, although the phenomenon itself has been known for at least two hundred years. We are
describing black voids in space completely dominated by the power
of gravity.

The name is somewhat misleading. Black holes are the result of
stars collapsing in on themselves due to the depletion of hydrogen
and other gases. But they are not *black;* in fact, they are *white hot.*
They produce a form of energy known as Hawking radiation, which
is manifested (we think) as a feeble glow. But from the matter absorbed, most black holes produce vast quantities of X-rays, a very
powerful form of energy on the strength of which one black hole
could run ten large power stations — if only we could harness its
power.[16] The physicist Stephen Hawking estimates that 100 billion
black holes exist in our galaxy alone. This exceeds the estimated
number of visible stars. Consequently, the cumulative effect of black
holes may be the major force determining why our galaxy rotates at
the rate it does. To put it philosophically, the forces of death may be
driving the forces of life.

Despite the massive number of black holes, none has ever been
sighted and very few have been detected. Astronomers are generally agreed that an object in that part of our galaxy known as
Cygnus X-1 must be a black hole (see Powell, 1993). It is also widely
accepted that Magellanic Clouds are black holes.

Black holes are like cosmic vacuum cleaners that suck up everything they encounter. And once the object is sucked in, there is no
escape. There is a sharp edge to the black hole called the event horizon, inside of which everything is trapped, outside of which an object
may escape the gravitational pull-in, if it has enough speed. When an
object does escape, it is often distorted in shape or size due to the
gravitational force that acts upon it.

It is this aspect of the black hole, the event horizon, that is of real
significance for contemporary physicists, of whom Stephen Hawking
(1988, 1993) is a leading authority. Hawking suggests that in the final stages of collapse, a star arrives at the point of pure energy (a
singularity) similar to what must have been the content and density
of energy prior to the Big Bang, from which our universe evolved. If
we can gain access to this singularity, then we will obtain vital information about the conditions prevailing in the earliest milli-seconds of
time. But our only hope of obtaining this information is at the verge
of the black hole (known as the event horizon); at any point beyond
that our "instruments" (whether they be ourselves or our tools of
investigation) are sucked into the hole and lost forever.

So how do we get sufficiently close to obtain the crucial information without getting sucked into the depths of no return? Hawking's response is highly speculative but, nonetheless, commands the respect and credibility of many scientists. In quantum terms, empty space is never really empty. It is always active and cluttered. Pairs of elementary particles like electrons and their anti-matter opposites (positrons) exist for a fraction of a second before annihilating each other. At an event horizon, it is conceivable that, prior to annihilation, one particle gets caught in the grasp of gravity, but the other escapes back into universal space. To an observer, it would look as if the second particle had just popped out of the black hole. In fact, the escapee has become a new particle in its own right having assimilated some of the properties of the black hole.

Let us assume that this process is happening on a large scale with perhaps millions of particles impinging upon the event horizon. What in fact is transpiring, in Hawking's opinion, is that the black hole is gradually "evaporating" as it explodes more and more "new" particles into the universe. In time, over millions or billions of years, the orderliness of the universe will absorb the disorder of the black hole.

Quite an amount of research and exploration centers on the black hole phenomenon, briefly but comprehensively surveyed by Powell (1993). What is progressively emerging is that black holes are not as destructive as we once assumed. Indeed, evidence to the contrary is accumulating, suggesting that they may be reservoirs of enormously creative energy.

The black hole is a metaphor of profound scientific and religious significance. It has a Bermuda triangle connotation of mysterious alien power from the clutches of which nothing can escape. And yet, if Hawking and other scientists are right, it possesses crucial information on the origin, meaning, and creativity of our world. But more than that, its power to captivate and destroy may not be as definitive as we have long assumed.

If our present universe began with the explosion of a *singularity,* as is widely believed, and that singularity was itself the product of black hole activity, which would normally be the case, — then our universe originated from a black hole. Such speculation has led scientists like Hawking (1993) to suggest that our cosmos may consist of many universes, born from the mysterious forces which defy human intelligence but continue to fascinate the human imagination. According to these speculations, the black hole produces a worm tunnel in space-time, and whatever disappears down its singularity exists somewhere else at another time through a reciprocal *white hole* (an object from which matter and radiation escape, but nothing falls in). There may well exist an intriguing interplay of order and disorder where the forces of life do not merely win out, but stretch the will-to-live to proportions our feeble brains have not as yet even vaguely comprehended. (More on worm holes in Boslough, 1992, 189–91, 206–9).

What is worth noting at this juncture is that we humans have little or no control over the quantum behavior at the heart (singularity) or at the verge of the black hole (although the Copenhagen school would claim that whatever is happening there is caused by our perception or observation of it). The electrons and positrons are doing their own dance on the periphery where the forces of life and death interact in fascinating ways. Perhaps it is one of the few situations where we humans can do little other than stand still, contemplate, and behold the wonder inherent in the creative process itself.

There is a paradoxical quality to black holes, whereby their destructive power of absorption seems to be a precondition for their life-giving power of "evaporation." The particles that escape may be endowed with information about the black hole, obtained from its counterpart that has been sucked into the black hole; in this way we may obtain access to a profound cosmic wisdom which, otherwise, remains trapped within the entropy of the black hole. Perhaps here we have on a grand cosmic scale an insight known to mystics for centuries: abnegation is a precondition for fulfillment; struggle is a pathway to happiness; sickness is the shadow side of health; failure is success in disguise; Calvary precedes resurrection; darkness gives way to light.

The Theory of Chaos

What the black hole represents as a quantum phenomenon stretches the human imagination to its absolute limits. We are only at the earliest stages of this fascinating and enormous exploration. Not at all unrelated to these considerations is the theory of chaos, also of recent discovery and far more comprehensible (but no less mysterious) than the black hole phenomenon. Readers are likely to be familiar with the notion of chaos from the popular work of James Gleick (1987).

Now that science is looking, chaos seems to be everywhere, and it provides the crucial link to interpret and comprehend aspects of universal life that heretofore tended to be regarded as deviations. Because it is a science of the global nature of systems, it has brought together thinkers from widely diverse fields of study. In fact, many scientists now believe that the theory of chaos may be as central to twentieth-century exploration as relativity and quantum mechanics.

In classical science, chaos was attributed to randomness, a freak of nature that science might one day understand and control. Classical examples of chaotic behavior include the dripping of a water tap, the turbulence of a river, the design of snowflakes, the unpredictability of weather, the fibrillation of the human heart. Now that chaotic systems are being mathematically modeled, we are discovering hidden patterns of order and beauty embedded in the chaos — the approach adopted by Gleick (1987), Stewart (1989), Feigenbaum (1978, 1979), Mandelbrot (1977), and Wilson (1983) in his development of renormalization. There is an alternative approach, developed primarily by Prigogine and Stengers (1984), suggesting that chaos is a precondition or stimulant for activating the self-organizing creativity inherent in all living systems. These two approaches may be considered complementary rather than opposed to each other.

What in fact is happening is this: advocates of many scientific disciplines are acknowledging that our universe, at all levels of existence, has a strange and amazing propensity that often comes to light most elegantly in dealing with irregularities and chaotic behavior. Feigenbaum Constants, named after the American physicist Mitchell Feigenbaum (1978, 1979), offer an intriguing example. In attempting to calculate movement in irregular or chaotic systems such as dripping taps or pulsating stars, researchers tend to encounter period-doubling, where the solution curve breaks into two directions, known as a bifurcation. On this first break, the curve can take on two values and for some time it will oscillate between the two. Further on, more bifurcations occur leading to what is known as a bifurcation tree. The rate of dividing or branching gets faster until an infinity of possible branches is reached. This point is often described as the onset of chaos.

In numerical terms, the critical value at which chaotic behavior begins is calculated to be 3.5699. The gaps between successive branchings become closer and closer; one finds that each gap is slightly less than one-quarter of the previous one, a ratio that tends to have the fixed value of 1/4.669201. Feigenbaum also noticed that the rate of shrinkage between the prongs on the bifurcation tree is also close to a standard two-fifths of the previous one and calculated to the numerical value of 1/2.5029. We are describing a phenomenon known as scale-invariance: as we examine the detailed nature of the bifurcation tree, we discover within the detailed (deep) structure patterns which enable us to comprehend and understand the whole.

Feigenbaum initially came across the curious magic numbers 4.669201 and 2.5029 by accident while toying with a small calculator. The significance of these numbers lies not in their values but in the fact that they recur, again and again, in completely different contexts. It seems that chaos has universal features and that Feigenbaum's numbers are fundamental constants of nature. Thus, although chaotic behavior is by definition dauntingly difficult to model, there is still some underlying order in its manifestation, and we now have mathematical models that enable us to understand the principles that govern this particular form of complexity.

The theory of chaos draws together many strands of research on the complexities and irregularities inherent in nature. Gone are the days when the isolated building blocks were the main target of research and exploration. We now acknowledge that our universe cannot be broken down into a few simple elementary units of matter. Not only is that ultimate simplicity based on false assumptions, but it undermines the very creativity of life which requires *complexity* as an essential dimension of all living systems.[17]

Today chaos has become big business. Peters (1991), Wheatley (1992), and Chorafas (1994) are all specialists of the commercial, business world who are encouraging their colleagues in commerce and finance to explore the possibilities for growth presented by a fluctuating, chaotic market. Arbuckle (1988) suggests that contemporary transitions within church life need to be understood and interpreted in a way that accommodates (rather than denies) chaotic dimensions. Hayles (1991) provides a fascinating and comprehensive review of how contemporary literature explores the metaphor of chaos. Around the world, mainstream institutions — political, economic, social, and religious — are scarcely able to hold together the chaotic forces that seem to threaten the very fabric of our "civilized" society. Chaos is all around us. Chaos abounds! (For a recent survey on chaos theory in a quantum context, see Gutzwiller, 1992).

The major problem confronting us is not the chaos itself but our attitudes toward it. By and large, we *deny* its very existence, because we are scared of its impact. Why? Because we perceive and interpret its significance within an old paradigmatic context. Within the old paradigm, chaos was considered to be evil, disruptive, dangerous; it threatened the status quo of our patriarchal value system, and threatened our power as the managers of a hierarchical, orderly system. Within this paradigm, there was no room for deviation, differences, disagreements. The shadow side was totally suppressed. Our linear mindset was neat and orderly, but so much out of touch with personal and planetary reality.

Denial, more than anything else, is what we use to subvert the potential creativity of chaos. We pretend not to see what is so glaringly obvious: old institutions and their accompanying values are fraying at the seams. But we continue to plaster over the fissures, hoping that some day the storm will abate and we'll return to "normality": full employment, proper balance of payments, elimination of crime, diminution of poverty, strong religious allegiance! No, we live in a different era; the old world order is collapsing, and as we approach a new evolutionary threshold, the chaotic forces are likely to intensify before they abate. Chaos will be around for a long time to come!

But, of course, is there ever a time in which chaos is not around? Perhaps chaos is as integral to order as conflict is to harmony and darkness is to light. Life is not about the dualistic either/or, but the integrative both and. We are more aware of chaotic forces at the present time for two main reasons:

  a. Our species and our planet seem to be undergoing a major evolutionary shift, and movements of this nature have never been smooth or easy, as is convincingly illustrated by Swimme and Berry (1992).

  b. We are emerging from a protracted era of masculine domination and control in which negative experiences like chaos tended to be suppressed. Consequently, we are now having to endure the massive eruption of repressed and submerged feelings, long subdued by repressive forces.

Learning to embrace the chaos, acknowledging its cultural and personal impact, and striving to integrate its effect on our lives, personally and collectively, are among the major challenges of our time. What makes the task so daunting is that most of the main institutions (of church and state) to which we look for guidance and support are unable to assist us in this endeavor. The institutions for the greater part are playing the old games of *denial* and *resistance*. Only when the changing consciousness reaches a more critical mass can we hope to (co)create institutions that will enhance rather than inhibit our evolutionary development.

In today's world, traditional scientific values such as determinism and predictability yield pride of place to openness and creativity. Instead of equilibrium, we seek movement and imbalance as being "normal" states of being. Instead of trying to conquer and eliminate the negative, we try to comprehend and appreciate its complementary role for the positive. Finally, instead of the second law of thermodynamics, which predicts that everything in the universe is declining in a progressive, entropic deterioration, toward the ultimate destruction of a heat-death, we now realize that our universe is an open, creative system, capable of self-regeneration over and over again (which, in fact, may be consistent with other interpretations of the second law; see Pagels, 1985). Once more, we encounter the inescapable paradox: in destruction life is redesigned; in chaos it is reformed; in death life flourishes anew!

Being and Nothingness

Starhawk (see Fox, 1984, 135) describes the dark as "all that we are afraid of, all that we don't want to see — fear, anger, sex, grief, death and the unknown." We dread the dark and we fear the chaos. In the Western world, we tend to suppress pain and we shudder at the thought of death. We are scared of being alone. We have largely lost touch with our human vulnerability and, to a corresponding degree, with our planetary home, the earth.

We surround ourselves with all types of gadgetry and material acquisition to numb our senses against the reality of life. We seek to drown out our alienation with alcohol, drugs, sex, and hedonism. We try to keep life as *full* as possible, totally cluttered on the outside but, alas, a lonely empty shell within.

Contemporary writers such as Wilson-Schaef (1987) and La Chance (1991) vividly portray the addictive trap which we humans have created in our world. Its central feature is an illusion of power and control which has become progressively compulsive, acquisitive, manipulative, and self-destructive. According to Wilson-Schaef (7–8), this cultural/global addiction is based on a fourfold myth:

a. The White Male System is the only thing that exists.

b. The White Male System is innately superior.

c. The White Male System knows and understands everything.

d. It is possible to be totally logical, rational, and objective.

In our addictive commitment to power, we ourselves have become quite powerless, but like all addicts we vehemently deny and disown that fact. We have become a dysfunctional species, codependent on forces that alienate us from them and from ourselves, because we ourselves have created and sustained that alienation. The very resources of life, intended to nourish and sustain us, are poisoning us through our cultural intoxication (see La Chance, 1991, 46). By polluting our water, we pollute our own unconscious. We do the same when we cough industrial filth into the air. The destruction of the soil community is the destruction of the community of which we are all members. When we eliminate a species, as we do by the thousand yearly, we diminish the vocabulary of our own unconscious. Because we are the conscious phase of the earth's process, everything we flush into the earth washes back to intoxicate us.

We are caught up in a spiral of power and powerlessness; the more we try to control, the more everything gets out of control. The only way we can break that cycle is to admit our powerlessness, but that would mean the collapse of the great Western empire that we have fabricated — and it is highly unlikely we'll agree to that. We are then left with the grim option of species self-destruction, which is manifested in behaviors ranging from the chronic toxification of the planet to the elimination of so many life forms, to our rabid nationalism, to our several forms of addictive consumption. Each of these is progressive and potentially deadly to our spirit, to our culture, and even to our planet.

We live in a dark age, but, alas, nobody wishes to entertain that notion. We are unable to befriend the darkness because our addictiveness and compulsiveness keep us firmly rooted in *denial*. The whole thing is too painful to look at, so we choose to befriend our pathology rather than befriend its deeper truth. And our denial becomes even more convoluted when people who are striving for personal integrity realize that the social and political structures are themselves addictive. This is where the real sinfulness is embedded, where the darkness assumes demonic proportions, as we'll explore at greater length in the next chapter.

The reader is left bewildered, wondering what to do about it. Where does one begin? Even to allow or enable oneself to become more *aware* is a step toward befriending the dark, which is the critical response needed to break the addictive cycle.

We dread emptiness of any type, and we dare not even think of nothingness. Yet, most of the known universe is made up of empty space, total nothingness, in the Buddhist sense of no-thing-ness. Most humans take for granted the vastness and emptiness of open space. To our mechanized, pragmatic Western consciousness, it is neither of interest nor of concern. It doesn't earn us money, nor enable us to produce arms, oil, or motor cars. And yet, therein lies the paradoxical secret to much of life's meaning and purpose.

The emptiness is in fact a fulness from which everything emanates, what Coveney and Highfield (1991, 141–42) appropriately call "the seething vacuum." And the fulness is not a neat smooth accumulation of life forces, but a boiling, chaotic conundrum of raw potential. When matter and anti-matter meet, physicists talk of "annihilation." Actually, it is not annihilation, but a process of "transformation," bringing into being a totally new reality (see Zohar, 1990, 207).

But let's not diminish the painful, destructive force; the transformation is a diminution, a dying, a dissolution, for the sake of something else, for the benefit of new life. There could be no "newness" without a painful termination of the old. Such is the mysterious interplay of life and death, chance and necessity, rest and activity, emptiness and fulness.

Salvation and Redemption

Many of the issues explored in this chapter tend to be treated in a fragmentary and partial fashion in orthodox theology. Notions such as "original sin," "salvation," and "redemption" explain away rather than explain the encapsulating mystery. Quantum theology offers a very different set of insights.

1. Creation is an unbroken whole, a totality within which everything — including darkness, chaos, pain, and suffering — plays an interdependent role.

2. Creation is essentially *good* and not *evil*. Original blessing rather than original sin characterizes life in its fundamental essence. Negative forces such as suffering, pain, and chaos ensue from the free, indeterminate nature of evolution itself. In Teilhardian terms, suffering may be understood to be the byproduct of an open and free creative process (e.g., the "waste" created in making a suit of clothes).

3. Much of the meaningless pain and suffering is directly, and often deliberately, caused by human beings. Daly (1988, 167) claims that the greatest and most meaningless sufferings ensue from human behavior, intensified by the conscious or unconscious desire to inflict pain on others. Nonhuman violence, devoid of this conscious malice, is more easily tolerated and integrated. If the human contribution to the world's pain was eliminated, or at least diminished significantly,

the meaning, relevance, and necessity of suffering would be a great deal more apparent. We humans are the great enigma in the cosmic, evolutionary drama.

4. Dualistic thought patterns, and the major institutions which thrive on dualistic value systems, exacerbate the meaninglessness of pain and suffering in our world. Instead of striving to befriend the dark, we continuously split it off, counteract it in antagonistic fashion, and empower its destructive impact. We have so alienated negative forces that we eventually personalized them into a supreme, divine evil force, called Satan, the Devil, or Lucifer (which, ironically, means bearer of light). We have invented yet another false god to idolize the very thing we are called upon to diminish by befriending it.

The befriending referred to here is no mere sentimental, apathetic tolerance. It is, in fact, a heightened sense of concern and imagination and includes the prophetic qualities of moral outrage, righteous anger, verbal (poetic) denunciation, protest, and defiance. It is characterized by a passion for justice and solidarity for all who are poor and oppressed. Befriending the dark of our world involves the castigation not of one, but of many oppressive and ideological forces. (On the notion of redemption as power toward right relationships, see Heyward, 1982; Grey, 1993; and also a unique contribution to this discourse from the physicist Danah Zohar, 1990, 210ff.).

5. Throughout the centuries, the subject of sin and salvation has dominated Christian theology. How the passion and death of Jesus atoned for human sin, in a once-for-all manner, is a cherished though poorly understood tenet of Christian theology. Atonement doctrines tend to fall into one or other of these four categories:

a. through Jesus' death, the enemies of God are reconciled to each other;

b. humanity is under bondage to sin, requiring Jesus' death as ransom;

c. sin causes humanity to be at a deficit so Jesus' death pays the debt;

d. Jesus Christ is a propitiation, a pure sacrifice, who cleanses humanity of sin.

In all cases, people (and creation) are portrayed as hopelessly flawed and totally dependent on an external, superhuman agent if they are to be rescued and saved. By the same token, people are stripped of all accountability and responsibility for the deficiencies of the human and earthly condition. The negative is projected onto a divine, patriarchal scapegoat, thus creating a theological polemic which modern theologians, and feminists in particular, call into question.

Atonement christologies flow out of the belief that humans are born with a tragic flaw, traditionally called original sin. Therefore, we must be dependent upon the perfect father to show us the way to a restored relationship with God and with each other. The punishment of one perfect child has to occur before the father can forgive the rest of his children and love them. In more benign atonement forms, the father does not punish the son. Instead the father allows the son to suffer the consequences of evil created by his wayward creation. In this scenario, the father stands by in passive anguish as his most beloved son is killed, because the father refuses to interfere with human freedom. The sacrifice of this perfect son is the way to new life with the father for all those who, in their freedom, choose to believe someone else's suffering can atone for our defective nature. The emphasis is on the goodness and power of the father and the unworthiness and powerlessness of his children, so that the father's punishment is just, and the children are to blame. Little wonder child abuse has been so prevalent in some Christian circles! (See Brock, 1992, especially 53ff.)

The fall/redemption theology of the Christian faith reinforces rather than resolves the forces of evil. It turns evil into a type of divine, alien force and projects it onto a divine scapegoat. Although depicting a God of total and unstinting forgiveness, it fails to challenge the wrongdoers to mutual coresponsibility for *their* irresponsible behavior. Consequently, those who exploit, manipulate, and oppress learn to project their guilt on to the divine scapegoat, and not infrequently in the name of Christianity (or Islam, Judaism, Hinduism) they oppress and exploit others. Conquering the world for Christ, Yahweh, or Muhammad has led to the most outrageous atrocities of war and barbarity ever known in human history.

To befriend the dark we must engage with the truth that liberates, which is reflected in the *life* rather than in the *death* of Jesus. (The nature of his death — its quantum significance — reflects the prophetic nature of his lifestyle.) The truth of genuine engagement is a harsh one, which the many oppressive regimes of our world will attempt to subvert at any cost. This is the man-made hell that we disown, on the one hand, and, on the other, accommodate in a whole range of collusive behaviors. This is our great darkness, so urgently and desperately awaiting redemption, which we alone can activate, because it is *our* problem and not *God's.*

All the major religions highlight the salvific nature of pain and sacrifice, and many of the divine personifications are portrayed as enduring hardship for the sake of others or for ascetical purification. This polemic predates religion by millions of years. It is the paradoxical mystery of evolution itself whereby life unfolds from the death-like fermentation of new possibilities. To grapple with this mystery, to embrace it, personally and culturally, we can draw inspiration and hope from the religious traditions. But it is an inspiration that invites us into action and engagement — for the building of a better world — and not an excuse to abdicate the difficult and exciting challenge to be co-creative agents in the divine-human transformation.

Quantum theology seeks to befriend the pain and embrace the dark. It seeks to redeem the chaos, not by projecting it onto a divine scapegoat, whether it be the Christ once crucified on Calvary or those who endure a daily crucifixion to satiate the greed and selfishness of global power seekers. In embracing the chaos, all humans are invited to recognize the interdependent nature of light and darkness, sickness and health, death and rebirth. By learning to befriend the chaos of our world we interact with, and integrate, our personal chaos (sinfulness) in more authentic ways. Instead of seeking to escape from our pain by the addictive behaviors of denial and scapegoating, we begin to engage with it, listen to it, and learn from it. We become coresponsible for life in its totality, and not just in fragmented, dualistic ways.

In terms of quantum theology, *redemption is planetary (and global) as well as personal. Redemption is about reclaiming the darkness, nothingness, and chaos of our world, and celebrating the negative potential for new life and wholeness.* Consequently, concepts such as sin and salvation take on a whole new meaning, which we'll explore in the next chapter.

Chapter 11

Integrating the Shadow

*Pain destroys the illusions of false, that is, elitist plea-
sures. It burns from the inside out. It, therefore, sensi-
tizes us to what is truly beautiful in life.*

— MATTHEW FOX

*The day is not far distant when humanity will real-
ize that biologically it is faced with a choice between
suicide and adoration.*

— PIERRE TEILHARD DE CHARDIN

*Sooner or later, nuclear physics and the psychology of
the unconscious will draw closer together, as both of
them independently of one another and from opposite
directions, push forward into transcendental territory.*

— C. G. JUNG

In his book *Understanding Mysticism,* Richard Woods (1980, 7)
suggests that the task of the mystic is to rewaken the collective consciousness so that we can reclaim values and beliefs that have been
forgotten or submerged. It is not by accident that some contemporary physicists look to mysticism as the new arena for scientific
exploration. In fact, this strange partnership was boldly predicted by
the great psychologist C. G. Jung well over fifty years ago.

We are also indebted to Jung for unearthing aspects of the quantum theory that scientists treat only in a rather fleeting manner. I
refer to the realm of "consciousness." This is quite an ancient concept, popularized in our time by Freud, for whom there are basically
three conscious states: "conscious," what I am presently aware of;
"preconscious," what I can recall from the past; and "subconscious,"
the aggregate of instinctual feelings and emotions that I am not consciously aware of but that influences at least 70 percent of my daily
behavior as a human being.

Freud, and classical Freudians to this day, consider the power of the unconscious to be located in the *id* and thus emanating totally from within the individual person. It is, therefore, up to each individual to change and modify the instinctual forces by bringing them into consciousness under the guise and direct control of the ego. This was, and still is, considered to be the work of Freudian psychoanalysis.

Freud's influence on the culture of the twentieth century is largely underestimated. He is often depicted as a liberal thinker who brought sexual ghosts out of the closet of repression and encouraged us to ventilate our anger openly. Perhaps that was his intention, but what society extrapolated from Freud was his image of the sick, neurotic individual forever battling with the instinctual drives of passion and power. Proponents of original sin had a heyday with Freudian theory; so had all regimes which sought to justify oppressive measures of any type.

Jung never warmed to the Freudian image, and in fact spent his whole life striving to dismantle it. Even to this day, Jung is not taken with great seriousness — although scholars of many disciplines acknowledge the depth and profundity of his vision. Where Freud and Jung differ most radically is in their understanding of the human personality. For Freud, each person is a unique, independent phenomenon in his or her own right; the world is populated with *individual* (atomized, if you wish) beings. Underpinning the Freudian vision is the classical scientific claim that the whole equals the sum of the parts, and hence, the acceptability of Freud among mainstream scientists and theologians alike.

For Jung, people are unique, not in their own right, but in terms of the larger entities to which they belong. All of us are products of our relationships. Our very attempt to be independent is itself a statement of our mutual interdependence. And our interdependence is not merely interpersonal, but also planetary and cosmic, even in minute details. From this vision, Jung coined his notion of the "collective unconscious." He called it a *Grenzbegriff,* a concept used to describe something that feels very real but somehow beyond analysis or even description. (Kant used the same term to designate the concept of God.)

For Jung, the collective unconscious is a vital force permeating all creation; it contains both past and future, light and shadow, presently active in humans and in all created reality. It may be described as a type of ethereal energy, containing all the thoughts, feelings, and dreams of the past and all the hopes and aspirations of the future, even the evolutionary "aspirations" of the universe itself. It contains both good and evil, more as complementary rather than opposite poles, and its attraction or magnetism is toward growth and integration.

According to Jung, the reality of the unconscious represents the mysterious, suprarational within humanity and within creation, and this for Jung is as real, and merits as much attention, as the rational and observable. It is at this juncture that many colleagues of orthodox psychiatry and academic psychology part company with Jung, considering his taste for the spiritual and mystical to be unscientific, misleading, and even dangerous.

What I wish to adopt from the Jungian vision for the purposes of the present study is:

a. the commitment to the greater totality (the quantum) as being the more authentic reality;

b. the rejection of dualistic thinking and dualistic value systems, because dualisms misrepresent reality in its deeper meaning.

The Power of Dualisms

Dualisms are so attractive, and yet so lethal! They enable us to divide things up into neat constructs of opposing forces. Obviously, we all favor what we perceive to be good, and we begin to develop mental constructs, attitudes, values, educational systems, and political regimes which set us so defiantly on the pursuit of the good that we, unconsciously, adopt all sorts of strategies to eradicate the "bad." Every now and again, something reminds us that the negative is also part and parcel of life, which usually provokes us to activate yet another set of culturally learned reactions (defenses), first to *deny* what we perceived and, second, to *bury* it even more deeply in the personal unconscious. Unknowingly, we are driving ourselves mad, in a world that is already largely insane. Why? Because it has chosen to cut itself off from 50 percent of its essential nature.

Let's take the case (already cited) of an alcoholic, a person who, according to the medical/psychiatric textbook, is addicted to alcohol, a condition that cannot be cured, but can be remedied by eliminating the consumption of alcohol. We assume the condition to be an *individual* one and we label the condition "alcoholism." No matter how we try to understand the condition, the label takes on a negative, derogatory connotation. So do all labels ("schizophrenic," "manic-depressive," "homosexual"). Labels are also highly dangerous insofar as they provide a partial explanation of what is usually a complex condition, demanding not one, but several frames of reference.

The traditional treatment for alcoholism involved hospitalization (drying out) and counseling. Often the recovery was remarkable and lasted, perhaps, for the rest of one's life, but not always! On returning to the social context of one's family or workplace, the old habit commenced again, or if it didn't, it recurred elsewhere in the social system, e.g., the spouse or another family member began to drink heavily, and not infrequently the pattern recurred in a subsequent generation.

Today the focus of treatment has shifted significantly. Even in orthodox medical circles, it is generally recognized that alcoholism can have not just one, but a range of significant meanings. The biomedical model is perceived to be too individualistic and mechanistic. Systemic factors have become quite central, especially the family unit, for which the alcoholic person may be serving the unconscious role of scapegoat. In other words, it is the family as a system that is sick, and within the intriguing dynamics of the family system, a vulnerable member has been loaded with the unresolved pain of the sick system. Hence the popular but poignantly true statement: "They drove me to drink."

It is when we refuse to deal with the sickness within the system that the problem recurs in all sorts of unexpected places, especially in subsequent generations, and even in the partners we choose as significant others. Healing, therefore, is mediated by addressing, not just the individual problem (which may not even need address at an individual level), but the whole system, for which the individual problem serves as a symptom, as a classic example of scapegoating. Only by healing the "family tree" can we hope to bring healing to the individual person. Hence, the increasing popularity of family therapy and systems therapy to address addictive behavior today.

What we are witnessing here is another shift from the mechanistic to the wholistic worldview, from the atomized (individualistic) approach to the quantum (whole) one. It makes so much sense, and yet meets with enormous resistance — for a range of reasons:

a. Our traditional mode of thinking is so deep-seated; we have turned individualism into such a heroic ideal that we shudder at the thought of destabilizing it.

b. In the systems approach, we are all called to be coresponsible and to carry the burden of our mutual deviation. That presents a totally unacceptable option for our patriarchal culture. Patriarchy of its very nature demands idols to be emulated and deviants that stand condemned. Patriarchy thrives on dualistic divisions; it would crumble to pieces if it didn't have scapegoats. (In former times, women were classic scapegoats for our predominantly patriarchal culture.)

c. Our mechanistic, patriarchal culture cannot stomach too much vulnerability. Feelings, emotions, woundedness — and even positive feelings of joy, exuberance, and imagination — must not become public property. They are relegated to the private domain of the clinic, the surgery, the psychiatric hospital, the confessional, to be sorted out before they become too public. Our dominant culture today is fundamentally alienating, deceptive, oppressive, and immoral.

d. The systems approach invites us to acknowledge and own our darkness as well as our light. It invites us to integrate our fundamental goodness, but also our fundamental self-destructiveness. This is enormously difficult and very threatening to a culture that from the cradle to the grave is being brainwashed, through advertising and patriarchal propaganda, but also through childrearing, education, and social influence, to strive for a perpetual high of achievement and success. Little wonder we live in such an addictive society.

e. The systems approach seeks to confront our subtle (and at times very open) tendency to collude with evil rather than engage meaningfully with it. Western political systems and mainstream religious organizations are notorious for duplicity and collusion. Both Christianity and Islam morally endorse modern warfare (the just war and jihad theories). The British government proudly displays its National Health Service, which is effectively a National *Sickness* Service, with the national quality of health deteriorating all the time while annual health costs continue to rise. Governments all over the world give assent to helping Third World nations and add injury to insult by spending approximately ten times more on armaments than on food relief. Little wonder that our Western culture — along with its major institutions — is scared of systems analysis, wherein *all* are called to be accountable.

Integrating the Shadow

Jungian psychotherapy (and analysis) focuses very specifically on the integration of the shadow. Instead of splitting off the nasty bits of ourselves (and thus giving them power over us), we are invited to acknowledge and own those aspects of ourselves we would ordinarily prefer to ignore or deny. We tend to drive our demons "under the carpet." The more we tread upon them the more ferocious they tend to become.

Increasingly, we realize that integration of the shadow is not merely a *personal* challenge of our times, but also a *social/cultural* one. The collective unconscious influences social processes much more powerfully than it affects individual behavior. As indicated earlier, a great deal of individual activity is influenced, for weal or for woe, by social and cultural factors. In our interdependent world, we humans are much more influenced by global and cultural events than we are capable of influencing them. Our patriarchal mindset, so bent on power and control, is based on wildly exaggerated and delusory claims. Not only are the claims false (in the sense of being untruthful), they are also highly destructive, because the more we enter into battle with planetary life, the more "wounded" we ourselves become. By setting ourselves over against the planet (as object), we are in fact plunging ourselves deeper and deeper into meaningless oblivion. Ultimately, we ourselves become the first victims of our calamitous action, a global human catastrophe that could well befall us before the end of the twenty-first century.

We humans have become an endarkened species, trapped in the shadow of self-destructive power. And we delude ourselves to the point of assuming that the planet may be destroyed (as in a nuclear holocaust) but somehow we will manage to survive. This is the ultimate act of denial, because as we have seen elsewhere in this book, the planet has a resilience toward life that we humans do not possess. The planet survived for billions of years without us; it will do so again, irrespective of how we treat her. As Lovelock (1988, 212) reminds us, Mother Earth is not a doting creature tolerant of misdemeanors, nor is she some fragile and delicate damsel in danger from brutal humankind. She is stern and tough, always keeping the world warm and comfortable for those who obey the rules, but ruthless in her destruction of those who transgress.

Perhaps a first step in integrating our destructive shadow is to enlighten ourselves on the awesome and unconquerable will-to-life that underpins cosmic and planetary evolution. Much of our denial and destructiveness is reinforced by a series of cultural ideologies that we need to confront. Many of these are theological in nature and, traditionally, were accounted for in the Christian doctrine of sin, redemption, and salvation. Sin was, and continues to be, understood as a *personal* deviation from the laws of God (and of the church) as laid down in the Ten Commandments. Morality sought to provide the guidelines for behavior that would guarantee *personal* salvation. The focus was distinctly individualistic, and the power to respond was assumed to come from within the individual person — influenced by the redemptive grace of God or the negative temptations of the Evil One.

The social, cultural, and global dimensions were largely ignored. Indeed, the basic biblical connotation of the word "sin," which means "missing the mark," was given scant attention. "Missing the mark" indicates a process of searching and seeking rather than "mechanistic" acts which are deemed to be either right or wrong according to fairly rigid guidelines. "Missing the mark" implies that there are various ways and means to hit the target. There is an openness and flexibility in this notion that seems to be absent in much of mainstream Christian morality.

For quantum theology, morality is an issue of central concern, not in the traditional dualistic sense of right vs. wrong, nor in the need to draw up yet another moral code, but rather in its commitment to fundamental values without which planetary and personal life is deprived of its richness and vitality. The values in themselves are not fundamentally different from those of traditional morality — honesty, truth, peace, justice, love, liberty, etc. How these values are *contextualized,* how they are incarnated in human, social, and political structures, is what concerns the quantum theologian.

Morality, in the quantum context, attends first to the whole, and only secondarily to the parts comprising the whole. The integrity, dignity, and rights of every "part" (people included) can be promoted only within the relational context from which it emerges. Self-determination, a value much in vogue in the recent past, may lead to self-diminution, if not pursued within the larger, relational, and interdependent matrix from which all life unfolds and without which no person or system can hope to reach its full potential.

Quantum morality seeks to address the context, the system, the institution, the larger forces that affect and influence individual and interpersonal behavior. And every realm of life is called to moral accountability: religion stands accused every bit as much as international (or local) warfare. There is a shadow side to *all* of reality — even to our concepts of God! All life is wounded; all life forms (and ideas) need to be healed, and all have the potential to become whole again.

Sins of Our Time[18]

For the quantum theologian, the following are among the major sins of our time, needing urgent redress:

Biocide/Geocide

All the formal religions include suicide, homicide, and genocide among their major moral transgressions, with only scant or negligible attention to our destruction to, or neglect of, the earth itself and its various life forms. Legally and morally we seek to protect human beings, with legislation also intended to foster growth and development. Only in recent years have we begun to recognize that the resources of creation, on which we depend for life and meaning, also have a claim on our concern and protection. The political gestures made to date, particularly by the United Nations, on issues of environmental protection, fall well short of comprehensive moral responsibility; and in not a few cases Western governments ignore these guidelines to suit their individualistic self-aggrandizement.

On an international and global scale, the religions and churches are so anthropocentric in their moral teachings that environmental and ecological issues scarcely get a mention. We are still stuck in the anti-world polemic of being on the side of the sacred and, therefore, must not be contaminated by the affairs of the world. Such dualistic rationalization is untenable in the precarious world situation of the present time.

Specieism

Specieism is based on the conviction (rarely articulated) that we, the human species, have inalienable rights over the rest of creation and consequently can claim the right to manipulate and control universal life as *we* deem appropriate. We either ignore or deny the fact that Planet Earth herself — and the entire cosmos — is also endowed with life (of which we are an interdependent part). We also tend to ignore the fact that the cosmic evolutionary process predates our existence by billions of years and will outlive us by billions yet to come.

Specieism refers to the grossly exaggerated and highly destructive role we attribute to our human species. Implicit in this claim is the perception that we, *at this stage in our evolutionary unfolding,* comprise the highest possible form of creaturehood. In other words, we assume that *we* are the end of the evolutionary line, with no possibility of a better or more enlightened being evolving in the future.

This sin often manifests itself as *anthropomorphism:* the tendency to understand, interpret, and absolutize various aspects of life (e.g., our images of God) according to *our* limited understanding of the human condition (see Guthrie, 1993). A great deal of scientific modeling — which considers the human mind to be infallible and insurmountable in terms of future evolution — is affected by this immoral disorder. Even some theologians succumb to the anthropomorphic flaw, as indicated in the following quote from a contemporary, reputable theologian (Cupitt, 1988, 24, 26):

> The old objective theological drama of creation, judgement and redemption is now hominized. It has become the drama of our own responsibility for creating our own future. Our life and our death are in our own hands.... Salvation is full personal integration.

Dualisms

Dualisms are human fabrications of reality, designed to reinforce our human, addictive compulsion to conquer and control. Dualisms undermine the wholism and mystery of life; they present a false, divisive, and misleading picture. They encourage thwarted growth and development, always tending to project the "negative" on to an external scapegoat, and thus discouraging the integration of our personal, social, and cultural shadows.

Insularism

The sin of insularism has several familiar forms:

- personal individualism: always putting "me" first;

- tribal exclusivity: acting out of a false superiority in terms of family or business status;

- nationalism: rating my (our) national needs above those of the planet (and cosmos), and acting aggressively to defend my national "rights";

- time restriction: examples being our tendency to define civilization as a "post-Christian" phenomenon in a world at least fifteen billion years old, or our tendency to teach history in a manner that begets sectarianism, nationalism, and specieism;

- sexism and racism: two of the most obnoxious manifestations
  of the insular mindset, whereby we categorize and label people
  in order to exert destructive pressure or power over them.

Idolatry

Anything to which we are deeply committed can become a "god."
Money, power, possessions, pleasure, scientific certitude, religious
dogma are among the leading gods of our age. Insofar as none of
these can bring us ultimate happiness or fulfillment, they are false
idols. We worship them not out of love, but out of an unconscious
need for power.

Many of the gods of formal religion are also false, in the sense
that they are caricatures of our own perceptions. Even in the revealed
religions (Judaism, Christianity, and Islam) we use *human* language
and ideas to describe the Godhead, and then turn our humanized
image into a divine caricature in the name of which we often carry
out outrageously immoral acts of control and domination. The fact
that two mainstream religions, Christianity and Islam, morally justify war (the just war and jihad theories), is evidence of a perverted
religious ideology.

A recent Christian document, signed by Christians from various
parts of the Third World, describes idolatry as the denial of all
hope for the future. We become so locked into the religious/political/
scientific ideologies of the past, that we prevent ourselves and others
from addressing the pressing needs of the present and future. We
become blind to the real world. In fact, we become "gods" unto
ourselves.

Our world today is rampant with idolatry, specieism being one
of the most pervasive manifestations. All forms of idol worship tend
to be self-validating and self-perpetuating, resistant to change, and
consequently deaf to the call to conversion.

Militarism

Modern warfare is largely a byproduct of the Agricultural Revolution, commencing about 8000 B.C.E. Armies and the general
infrastructure of warfare claim to be the guardians of freedom and
democracy. In effect, they serve now in subtle and devious ways what
they set out to achieve at the dawn of the Agricultural Revolution:
to conquer and divide the planet, at the whim of male, insatiable
craving for power and domination.

Currently, the production, distribution, and use of arms absorbs more time, money, and energy than any other activity of the human species. As a species, we are engrossed — to an irrational degree — in lethal war games. Unconsciously, we are bent on self-destruction.

Today there is no justification whatsoever for warfare. It is an inheritance from bygone days that may have been appropriate then (that, too, is disputable), but in our wholistic era, it has neither sense nor meaning. Nor can we any longer ignore the grave moral and ecological side effects of modern weapons of destruction.

To reverse, or even diminish, our addiction to warfare is a huge moral challenge for the twenty-first century. It will take something of a miracle, probably a catastrophe, to bring about such a deep change of heart.

(Man)Power

The issue of power is closely related to warfare. Here I am referring to the use of power in a masculine, rational, competitive, and compulsive manner, leading to the subjugation of some people by others, and the notion that the earth (and cosmos) exists to be conquered and controlled according to human whim and fancy. In other words, human beings try to play God, assuming that in God's name, they will do what is best for all, thus failing to recognize that there is also a shadow side to the God-power, which often manifests itself in barbarity, crime, destruction, and warfare.

Injustice

The fact that our world is so blatantly divided between "haves" and "have-nots," the fact that the daily expenditure on armaments would feed the world's population for a whole year, that most Western nations give less than 1 percent of their GNP to developing countries are just a few of the flagrant structural sins of our time. Our world is riddled with injustices, and most of these are political and structural in nature, often initiated and sustained by greedy, insatiable Western multinationals.

The Christian churches, often caught in a collusive web with Western political oppressors, champion the cause of love, but rarely preach justice with comparable or compelling conviction. Love without justice, which is often the ambivalent message from the churches, is a charade which often leaves millions with neither love nor justice, care nor compassion, in their daily lives.

There is also an "eco-justice," or what Conlon (1990) calls "geo-justice," claiming our attention today: the painful reminder that we humans cannot live in dignity and freedom while we exploit and pollute our planetary home (see also Kroh, 1991). In the oft-quoted phrase of Theodore Roszak, we need to recall, again and again, that "the needs of the planet are the needs of the person and the rights of the person are the rights of the planet."

Blasphemy

Traditionally associated with taking God's name in vain, blasphemy today is evident in convoluted, pernicious activities, such as clergy blessing nuclear weapons before they are disseminated to bunkers around the world, or religious leaders, committed to simplicity and frugality of life, living in luxurious palaces. To invoke God's name to justify oppressive regimes is another example of this moral outrage.

Even in our largely nonreligious Western culture, we continue to invoke God's name (and blessing) on all sorts of politically and religiously deviant systems. It gives a veneer of respectability to what are fundamentally immoral or, at best, morally ambivalent consumerist and oppressive regimes.

These structural sins of our time create an immoral enigma of huge proportion, yet millions take them for granted and assume them to be inevitable consequences of "the way things are." While the major religions preach and admonish ethical and responsible behavior at a personal and interpersonal level, they largely ignore the massive structural and systemic caricature of gross immorality. How can people be expected to act and behave morally in a world so riddled with immoral incongruity? How can any of us hope to create a more just society when many of our major institutions (including religious ones) are riddled with injustice?

For quantum theology, morality is one of the most critical and engaging issues. Our value-free culture has largely become a value-less culture, or rather the values of insatiable power, manipulation, and hedonism prevail in ways that have become culturally acceptable (and often politically and religiously validated) but, nonetheless, potentially lethal for the future of life on earth. We pride ourselves in having drawn up an international charter for human rights, and in many parts of our world we have courts defending people's rights. Rarely do we emphasize the complementary value of *duty*. And without this complementary emphasis, our rights often become instruments for manipulation, to enhance our insular, anthropocentric concerns.

There is great urgency in drawing up a new international, global moral code, one that will strive to safeguard the interdependent nature of all life forces at the service of our evolving cosmos. It's not merely people who need moral values and guidelines. The planet also needs them and so does every institution and sociopolitical system that we humans invent. Without such guidelines, the shadow side of life (the tendency toward the irrational) is either ignored, i.e., denied, or reaps uncontrolled havoc, as is currently happening. In quantum terms, the purpose of morality is the integration of the shadow in all its various expressions, ranging from the personal to the global. Traditional morality often seemed to be unaware of the power of the shadow and alienated the darkness even further by labelling it as "evil."

Quantum theology believes that:

- the shadow is a real and powerful dimension of *all* life;

- we cannot eradicate or eliminate the shadow, and the more we try, the more power we give it over us;

- the shadow becomes a potential source for creativity precisely when we engage with it in a spirit of receptivity and dialogue, as we strive to integrate it into the rhythm and flow of life.

Consequently, quantum theology adopts as a key principle: *Structural and systemic sin abounds in our world, often provoking people to behave immorally. To integrate the global shadow, we need fresh moral and ethical guidelines to address the structural and systemic sinfulness of our time. The formulation of these guidelines is as much a political as a religious obligation.*

The morality called for in this chapter seeks to outgrow the dualistic distinction between church and state. All people and all institutions are coresponsible for a world order that enables and empowers people to live in a creative and responsible way with each other, with the planet, and with the cosmos. Morality is not the sole, nor even the primary concern of churches or religions. It is everybody's responsibility, mediated through all structures and systems that impinge upon our daily lives. Only cumulative good will on the part of all is likely to address adequately the moral vacuum that poses such a threat to our world today.

Our moral sensitivity is heightened and our moral consciousness is sharpened when we acknowledge our mutual sinfulness, when we learn to befriend the darkness that we all inhabit. In one degree or another, we are all tainted; in Christian language, we all have sinned. A precondition, therefore, for a more responsible and compassionate world is that we learn to *forgive,* beginning with ourselves and extending our forgiveness toward the many others we have hurt or used.

Many people today are disillusioned, some embittered, others apathetic, when they confront the plight of our world. We cannot undo or change the past; recrimination or bitterness is futile. Forgiveness is the only disposition whereby we can let the past be the past — in the deep, and often painful, awareness that it cannot be changed — and redirect our creative energy to a fresh future. Forgiveness is a liberating mode that promises hope and new life. We learn to trust once again and give of ourselves more fully to each other and to the universe.

Forgiveness opens up fresh possibilities. We begin to let go of old animosities. We acknowledge more readily our own limitations and those of others. We tolerate inconsistencies without becoming complacent or indifferent. And we are disposed to grow into that liberating and healing wisdom that respects the shadow side of life for what it really is: an essential incompleteness forever awaiting fulfillment, a fertile emptiness (a nothingness) out of which creativity yearns to explode. Such is the paradoxical nature of the great shadow, the ecstasy and pain of life which we are ever invited to embrace anew.

Part Six

The Light

What immortal hand or eye
dare frame thy fearful symmetry?
   —WILLIAM BLAKE (referring to the tiger)

Chapter 12

The Search for Enlightenment

For the rest of my life, I want to reflect on what light is.
— ALBERT EINSTEIN

All of nature is organized according to the activity of significance.
— DAVID BOHM

Christian civilization has proved hollow to a terrifying degree.... Too few people have experienced the divine image as the innermost possession of their own souls.
— C. G. JUNG

Four billion years ago the first cellular creatures appeared on earth. Today we refer to them as blue-green algae. These first simple cells did not breathe oxygen. On the contrary, they produced it through a process we now take so much for granted: *photosynthesis*.

For some four billion years, sunlight has been nurturing and ingratiating Planet Earth. This is the energy source that drives life's processes and empowers its cycles of carbon, nitrogen, hydrogen, water, and climatic movements around our planet. Without sunlight, life on earth would have ended in suicidal self-absorption millions of years ago.

Tiny prokaryotic cells, of 0.0025 millimeter in diameter, form the original complex pathway for the absorption of solar energy in the form of light. In photosynthesis, one or two photons (light particles) transfer part of their energy to an electron which is thereby excited, and in turn, invests its excess energy in the development of biochemical, life-giving processes. In this way, energy is stored in the end product, particularly in the glucose molecule, for later use or degradation.

The Light That Shines

Photosynthesis is another of those mysterious coincidences of our global, evolutionary story. The quantity of electric/light energy required to activate many biochemical procedures is in the region of one to two electronvolts, which is the energy typical of a photon in the visible spectrum. Short-wave ultraviolet light contains double that energy and destroys biochemical operations, whereas infrared (heat) radiation, with only half that energy, is sufficient to generate the life-giving processes. Sunlight itself is something of an evolutionary miracle.

And the dance of life and light takes on an even more intriguing twist. In the early stages, the blue-green algae absorbed the sunlight in an oxygen-dependent relationship, known as aerobic photosynthesis. It took a further two billion years (to approximately 2.2 billion years ago) before the aerobic partnership was supplemented by oxygen-free (anaerobic) photosynthesis. Bacteria became the new participants in the cosmic dance, and with them *respiration* became a survival kit for millions of species in the ensuing millennia.

Photosynthesis is a cosmic parable rather than merely a biochemical, scientific fact. It provides a powerful illustration of evolutionary grandeur, with light penetrating and impregnating the nebulous uninformed membrane of primeval life. Little wonder that all the great religions and philosophies consider light to be a supreme symbol of life and meaning. Little wonder that all the great scientists from Galileo to Einstein, and Hawking in our own time, are fascinated by the nature of light and spend a great deal of energy and enthusiasm trying to fathom its meaning.

Photosynthesis as a cosmic, luminous parable carries a deep archetypal significance, while also impinging upon our daily lives in very real and practical ways. No less powerful, although much less tangible, is the symbolic impact of starlight. To date, it has tended to be the fascination of astronomers and astrologers, but as more people realize that the carbon which makes possible all life on earth, including our own, is the product of stars, we begin to sense an amazing affinity with those distant objects (creatures?), millions of light years away. We are the same stuff as the stars themselves!

Light is also the medium through which we receive a great deal of information, much of which is conveyed by means of electromagnetic waves. And in our world today, where information and knowledge dictate so many values and strategies (see Toffler, 1990), a better understanding of the source of knowledge may well augment a more creative use of this human and cultural commodity.

However, as we move beyond electronic into the realm of photo-tonic technologies, we realize that light, as a symbol, is loaded with metaphorical intent. Information in itself does not enlighten. We cannot clarify what is *mis*-information, *dis*-information, or propaganda in our media-bombarded world. The more information accumulates the more we need to acquire enlightened perceptual and understanding skills to comprehend and internalize the deeper messages and meanings of our Information Age.

The emerging technology contains within itself vital clues for our future. We are fast approaching the moment when information will be stored, not in any kind of visible, tangible object, but in the realm of consciousness itself. It is estimated that by the year 2000 we will be using 0.1 micron superchip (five hundred times thinner than a human hair) to store massive libraries of information. As a human species we are much closer than we realize to the point wherein everything we think will *automatically* happen, and every problem we put into words will *automatically* be solved. An exciting but chilling prospect!

Perhaps the saving grace will be in the ramifications such enlightenment will have for our own self-understanding. Instead of being driven by our compulsive and addictive powers to conquer and control (currently, through the information rat race), we will come to realize that the power of light that enlivens the forces of nature is also the greatest untapped resource for our own well-being and prosperity. Nature's light-conversion skill of photosynthesis produces in plants the chloroplast cells used to convert photons into usable glycogen, hydrocarbons, and cellulose. When our own photovoltaic cells can match the performance of the chloroplast, a breakthrough of enormous human and planetary significance will have taken place. We will learn to befriend life in a sustainable, cooperative, and evolutionary mode. The conversion required will be more than many can cope with, but we have reason to hope that a sufficient number of people can rise to the challenge, creating the critical mass that will make possible a new evolutionary shift for humankind (see the seminal work of Henderson, 1981).

Light has been the subject of intense scientific pursuit for the past few hundred years. The ancient Greeks considered light to be a form of energy but did not speculate about its essential nature. Newton, at the beginning of the sixteenth century, claimed that light consists of small, corpuscular bodies which travel in straight lines, and that within the light spectrum, sensation of color is determined by wavelength. The wave nature of light was confirmed by Thomas Young at the beginning of the nineteenth century, through his well-known double-slit experiment. In what sense, therefore, can we talk of light particles? This became the new tantalizing question which was finally resolved (not to Einstein's satisfaction) by the quantum theory and its acknowledgment of the dual particle-wave nature of light.

More central to the quantum theory, however, is Max Planck's postulate that light is emitted in quanta (packets of energy) which at times is manifested as particles and at other times as waves, depending (possibly) on the perception/observation of the experimenter. Light (or heat) now takes on a different symbolic significance, revealing new information, not just about light itself, but about the very essence of life, particularly at the microscopic level. If light impacts upon us in "wholes," whose essential significance (meaning) is greater than its constituent parts, perhaps this is true of everything in the universe. Could it be that light has the secret that can truly enlighten us and disclose the ultimate meaning of life itself?

The Path to Enlightenment

Whether we draw inspiration from sunlight, moonlight, or starlight is largely dependent on how well we connect with the Light within. Mystics, sages, and philosophers of all ages and cultures have sought *enlightenment,* not just intellectual understanding or esoteric knowledge, but a deep intuitive sense of what life is about, an inexplicable conviction that, despite all the paradoxes and contradictions, it all does hang together. Light features dominantly in how people tend to describe their "mystical" experiences (Hardy, 1979). Some people spend an entire lifetime seeking enlightenment, whether it be in a scientific laboratory or a secluded monastery. And in the confused and misguided world of today, some hope to attain this deeper wisdom in the noncircuitous route of LSD or some other humanly invented utopia.

In recent years, there has been a revival of *meditation,* as a method or technique to attain enlightenment.[19] This has been mainly an Eastern development, but it has had a widespread influence in the West. People have learned to meditate for a whole range of reasons; some have gone off to India and lived with a guru for some time. Whether simply as a means of relaxation or as a pursuit of inner peace, whether for purely personal reasons or for lofty spiritual ones, meditation has caught on among millions in both East and West and seems to embody a deep cultural significance for our time. Meditation has been described as the art of *centering:* gathering together the diverse energies of attention so that I become grounded in the center of my being. It is a process that facilitates inward movement (*interiority* rather than *introspection*), a calming-down of sensations and feelings, a mental alertness, and an overall disposition of openness and receptivity.

Meditation is simply the name we put on whatever means we use in order to turn within and go from our conscious, through our unconscious, into the experience of pure truth or God. Frequently, we use the analogy of the icebergs in the ocean to explain the process of meditation. The conscious mind is like the one-eighth of an iceberg which appears above the surface. The seven-eighths not apparent to the naked eye is the subconscious. Beyond the subconscious is the collective unconscious, the noosphere, universal consciousness, or the total Godhead. This collective unconscious is like the ocean in which all the icebergs float. This ocean is not only the means of communication between all the icebergs, but it is the collection of total truth to which we, as individual icebergs, have access. Through meditation, we contact that total truth; we transcend our finite limitations and we communicate with each other.

Meditation is a type of tuning-up process, facilitating communication between my being and the "being" of life in the world around me (God, if you wish). In this way it becomes a transformative rather than a passive experience. I begin to see, feel, know, intuit in a different, more sensitive way, and this colors my attitudes and values along with the quality of my action. Meditation is neither action nor nonaction; it is a different state of being which includes both. It is religious in the full sense, yet transcends all our religious categories. It is the arena of pure mystery and the experience is one of reassurance that, in the final analysis, our relationship with mystery is benevolent.

Meditation may also be described as a state of enlightenment, providing the meditator with greater clarity of vision, a more open and receptive disposition, access to deeper wisdom, and a sense of being interconnected with the totality of life. A number of physiological studies have been carried out on meditators both during and after the experience of meditation. EEG findings indicate an increased state of synchronization throughout the entire cerebral cortex, suggesting brain activity of a holographic nature. It has been suggested that during meditation the encoded information about the universe

becomes holigraphically decoded, and the individual experiences a
state of unitive consciousness with the entire universe.

The potential to be more enlightened people and relate to life in a
more enlightened way seems to be largely unrealized. At this moment
of our human, evolutionary unfolding, our capacity and need to become more enlightened people is evoking new ways of connecting us
to the sources of universal wisdom. Meditation, of course, is an ancient wellspring of wisdom, but its popularity today among people
of such diverse cultural and spiritual backgrounds seems to suggest
that it is mediating something of immense significance for our times.

There are several methods or techniques of meditation. Following
the great mystical traditions of our world, we could say that it is
not we who meditate; rather, the divine life force meditates within
us. Meditation is very much a matter of letting go, releasing the
props, the attachments, the will to power and control, which has
so dominated our Western mind and psyche.

The mystical mode of meditation is that of disposing oneself, in
quietness and solitude, to the vibrations of inner power, especially
the inner resourcefulness we Christians call "grace." In the East
and West alike, there is a well-established tradition of *Centering
Prayer*, sometimes called mantric meditation; the Jesus Prayer of the
West and Transcendental Meditation from the East are among the
better known versions. In this approach, the emphasis is on gathering together our scattered energies so that we may use them in
a more creative and wholistic way. In the Buddhist tradition, there
is a strong emphasis on *concentration* (especially of the breath) in
order to bring the mind to the still point, whence enlightenment
begins.

Matthew Fox (1983, 188–200) devotes considerable attention to
the notion of meditation through *art,* a creative medium that un-
leashes repressed and unintegrated energies for novel use in more
integrated living. In Fox's outline, art may be that of music, sculpture, poetry, or movement (dance). Modern psychotherapy often
employs these approaches to help the client become more centered,
focused, and integrated in behavior.

Finally, we need to emphasize that meditation is a *natural birth-
right,* a potency awaiting realization within every human being.
There is a danger today that we perceive meditation as a highly spe-
cialized skill (especially for religious freaks) that we can buy with
money or learn from a textbook. We are in danger of trivializ-
ing this precious commodity which, although innate to the human
psyche, needs tender and careful nurturing by experienced medita-

tors, whether spiritual gurus, creative artists, mystics, or spiritual directors.

As a means of enlightenment, meditation breaks open new horizons of light, hope, beauty, and truth. It reconnects us to the fundamental goodness upon which life relishes and thrives. It challenges us to inflame the true Light which ignites, enlivens, purifies, and sanctifies. It helps us to make that quantum leap of mind and spirit that compels belief in, and commitment to, an unfolding evolutionary process that is benign in its fundamental orientation.

In all the great mystical and religious traditions, light is an enduring and predominant symbol. In the major religions it is the most frequently used word to describe the essence of God (*Noor* in Islam, *Jote* in Sikhism). It denotes ultimate yearning and fulfillment (as in the phrase: "may light perpetual shine upon them"), the resolution of pain and suffering ("light in our darkness"), the presence of the divine in our midst ("the light has come into the world"), the sure pathway to truth and ultimate happiness ("follow the light"). (For further examples, see Eliade, 1965.)

In orthodox theology, light is not a topic of serious consideration like salvation, sacrament, God, or sin. Theologians seem to allocate it to the realms of the spiritual life or the mystical journey, thus underestimating its more universal and generic significance. It is often contrasted with sin, evil, and the powers of darkness in a classical dualism whereby light denotes all that is good and dark all that is evil. As indicated in previous chapters, this simplistic dichotomy belies the rich complementary value of both concepts.

The Sacrament of Light

Why are people so fascinated by light? What is its deep, archetypal significance for our personal lives and for our universal culture? Might it point to some ultimate state of completion to which all life yearns for fulfillment? Perhaps the Omega point is a fulness of light!

Eastern mystics tend to identify *sound* as the primal energy of life. Sound is considered to be the original life force out of which all else unfolds. Hence the Christian and Jewish idea: in the beginning was the Word (*dabhar*), the energy of sound. Many Eastern meditation techniques use mantras, not for their theological or religious meaning, but for the sound quality of the words. They believe that the regular use of the mantra realigns the meditator with the original creative energy, not merely of one's own life, but of cosmic life in its totality.

If *sound* is a metaphor about our cosmic origins, might not *light* be the corresponding symbol for our ultimate destiny, as individuals and as a planetary/cosmic species? Light seems to have an overwhelming fascination for people of all ages, creeds, and cultures. It brings coherence, clarity, purpose, and vision into our perceptions, feelings, and actions. It inspires us to greater heights of achievement, wisdom (enlightenment), synchronicity, and wholeness.

As a religious/ritualistic symbol, light is universal. Every culture engenders and adopts rituals based on light (candles being the most frequently and universally used). In fact, the use of light in celebratory events transcends the man-made dualistic division between the sacred and the secular. By participating in rituals of light, everybody is drawn into a sense of the numinous; consciousness is raised; experience is transformed (in however small a way); we rub shoulders with the "divine," and we get a glimpse of eternity.

All the major religions create specific rites or rituals, some of which have evolved over centuries and millennia, to mark key moments in personal, interpersonal, or planetary life. In tribal cultures, we refer to these as "Rites of Passage"; in the formal religions, we call them "sacraments" (already referred to on p. 88 above). In the Christian tradition there are seven sacraments, five marking key moments of transition and growth in human life (baptism: birth; confirmation: reaching the maturity of young adulthood; marriage and/or priesthood: vocation in life; anointing of the sick: anticipation of death). Two sacraments relate to significant elements of daily experience: nourishment for health and wholeness (Eucharist); forgiveness for increased relatedness (penance, or reconciliation). In many of the formal religions, the celebration of sacraments has become excessively ritualized, overlegalized, and mechanistic. The ensuing experience is often that of a deadening ritualism rather than a sacred awakening; the participant often feels alienated from life rather than enthused for it or reconnected to it.

The sacramental experience, whether it be a rite of passage or a more formal religious ceremony, has a fundamental rootedness in light, and to this day the use of light is central to all these rituals. In its deeper meaning, the sacrament is a focal point for gathering scattered, fragmented energies. The recipient comes through the darkness (often symbolized in the use of clay and/or water) toward the light. Healing takes place and hope is awakened to assist the participant to become a more whole and enlightened person. The boundaries between the ritual light and the personal enlightenment merge into one. In the sacramental experience, "I" and "it" dissolve into a new fusion which in turn becomes the springboard for a fresh realignment with the wider world of daily experience.

The Sacramental Process

The Turners (1969) in outlining the ritual (sacramental) process describe three stages of *separation, participation* (initiation), and *re-integration* (return). Initially, the ritual act invites us to step aside from the "ordinariness" of daily life. This phase has many proto-typical examples in the lives of great religious leaders, saints, and mystics, whether it be the desert experience of the monk, the pil-grimage of the seeker, or the inner silence of the contemplative. It could be understood as our own innate collective wisdom reminding us that all action flows from in-action (being); words emerge from silence; "things" evolve from no-thing-ness; communion needs soli-tude as its complementary value. It's the paradox that defies logic and rational explanation, but it is the heart that holds together the apparently opposite pull of the energies of the Yin and the Yang.

The separation that the Turners refer to often involves a real (but temporary) absence from the context of daily life. It is still re-flected in our culture by adopting special modes of dress for religious services, or for occasions of special political, social, or diplomatic character. The separation is not about *escaping* from duty or respon-sibility. Quite the opposite! It is intended to liberate devotees from daily distractions and preoccupations so that they can enter as fully as possible into the ritualistic/sacramental state.

This is a deeply luminous, harmonious space, yet loaded with am-bivalence and ambiguity, what the Turners call a "liminal" space. Emotionally and spiritually, a transformation takes place (or is intended to), whereby the inner being is transported into a differ-ent modality. Feelings of bliss, intense happiness, reassurance can abound, but rarely without the accompanying sense of emptiness, transitoriness, or darkness. In the sacramental experience, the com-plementary values of life begin to interact in new ways; we become enlightened toward a new synthesis, one that is never complete and sometimes leaves us feeling very fragmented (torn apart), but always moving us on to deeper levels of self-awareness.

This is what authentic ritual should do; innately and subcon-sciously, this is what we want it to do for us. But because our culture has so mechanized and rationalized our symbolic world, this out-come is more the exception than the norm. One of the major tasks preoccupying the quantum theologian is the rediscovery and revival of authentic sacramental and ritual experiences.

The liminal, "in-between" space is characterized by unease and discomfort, often followed by a sense of challenge and, maybe, trauma. The participant awakens to a new sense of what life is about; the call to duty assumes a new impetus. Reintegration of val-ues and convictions takes place as the person returns to the world with a renewed sense of purpose and mission. In the experience of worship something quite new has taken place: the realization that I belong to the universe and that I owe it solemn obedience.

Christian theology considers sacraments to be special moments of encounter between the human and the divine. For much of the post-Reformation era, participation in the sacramental life of the church was deemed essential for redemption and salvation. Salvation was mediated primarily through the sacraments. Consequently, atten-dance at (as distinct from participation in) the sacraments assumed a legalistic and moralistic status of duty and obligation. In many cases, ritualism and legalism overshadowed the deeper meaning of the sacramental moment.

In quantum theology, the sacramental experience, incorporating the triple ritualistic dimension of separation, participation, and re-integration, involves a human-divine encounter, but in a much more wholistic way than previously envisaged. What sacraments seek to highlight and celebrate are the several divine-human encounters that mark our lives from birth to death, and even beyond these demar-cation lines. And that same encounter has planetary and cosmic dimensions that traditional sacramental praxis largely ignored.

The encounter, therefore, is multidimensional: with my own inner being, with my "community of faith," with my church (wider com-munity of faith), with my world in a range of different senses, and with "God" (however I understand the divine life force). It's a moment of constellating and crystallizing the diversity of my life and existence, of holding together amorphous and, at times, contradictory experiences, until some type of synthesis ensues.

In the here-and-now of the sacramental experience, the encounter is never complete. The person is changed, if only subconsciously, and consequently will return to daily life with fresh perception and understanding. Thus begins the reintegration process, which after some intense experiences, e.g., a pilgrimage or a marriage, may be quite demanding on one's time and commitment. But the integration is not focused on fresh understandings or new perceptions. The level of meaning itself — the spiritual unfolding — has shifted (at least in minute ways). My sense of the divine has changed, perhaps initially in a disturbing way, but eventually in a manner that enhances the process of integration that has been evoked. Quantum theology seeks to highlight both the grandeur and precariousness of the sacramental/ritual moment. Working on the assumption that (*a*) we humans are creatures of symbol and ritual, and (*b*) that we are forever inventing symbolic behavior to connect more meaningfully with each other and with life, the quantum theologian invites a more wholistic exploration of the sacramental experience. The current practice, whereby ritualistic or sacramental praxis is designed and structured in specific religious or ecclesiastical settings, creates a type of sacramental ghetto, reinforced by rules and regulations that denude many sacramental experiences of symbolic grandeur and personal transformation. We are in danger of undermining the rich potential of the sacramental tradition itself.

We cannot hope to revive and reinstate meaningful ritual and sacrament without a reeducation in the meaning and necessity of myth, symbol, and ritual. The spiritual imagination needs to be reawakened from its deadening and deadly entrenchment in mechanistic modeling, rational thought, and mental atrophy. The soul needs to rewaken to the God of surprises, to the light that shines even in darkness, to the light that ultimately cannot be extinguished. The final integration, which is focused on light — whether it be that of eternal life or the enlightenment of my inner being (which animates my life with fresh meaning) — is the goal of all sacramental experience. *Because we are primarily beneficiaries of light and not of darkness, and our final destiny — both here and in eternity — is that of enlightenment, we all need those sacred moments of ritualistic/sacramental space, serving as heightened encounters with the sustaining mystery that enfolds us.*

The scientific imagination has long sought to understand the nature of light. The human mind can scarcely grasp the speed at which light travels. The spiritual seeker engages unceasingly in the call to become enlightened. These are explorations that stretch the mind and the imagination, pointing us toward horizons of infinite possibility. Perhaps our ultimate destiny is as all-embracing as light itself — a topic we'll explore in the next chapter.

Chapter 13

Reaching toward Infinity

We are, as the aborigines say, just learning how to survive in infinity.
—MICHAEL TALBOT

Where the telescope ends, the microscope begins. Which of the two has the grander view?
—VICTOR HUGO

There are moments where time suddenly stands still and leaves space for eternity.
—FYODOR DOSTOYEVSKY

In Christian theology, "demythologization" became a central concept for much of the nineteenth and twentieth centuries. It was an attempt to strip away the mythic elements in the scholarly pursuit of pure, *factual* truth. Applied to the Bible and other sacred texts, it involved the recovery of historical facts over against the literary or cultural trappings that created an impressive story but not necessarily true-to-life history. Events in the Gospels, such as the birth of Jesus, the miracles, and the resurrection, came under intense scrutiny, and in the absence of hard historical data were often considered to be theological fabrications of no real factual significance and, therefore, not deserving of serious theological reflection.

This trend, more fashionable in Protestant than in Catholic theology, emulated the rational, scientific consciousness of the time. Pure truth was based on observation and measurement, carved out by the human mind, whose basic level of intelligence was assumed to be the ultimate barometer of verification and veracity. In this context, myth was considered to be the product of a fanciful imagination which added color, and perhaps excitement, to the facts, but deviated from the true nature of reality. Myth was deemed to be a primitive, infantile instinct which, in a mature, rational, developed culture should be outgrown and discarded.

Meanwhile, scholars of a different intellectual pursuit — especially anthropologists, psychologists, and social scientists — were proposing quite a different way of viewing reality. Facts were deemed to be superficial impressions; the real meaning resided much deeper, in the subtle and often undetectable realms of consciousness. Of particular interest to anthropologists were the great universal stories of beginnings and endings, which occur time and again across human cultures. There were universal and deeper truths which could be accessed only through a quality of story called "myth." Myth contained a depth and intensity of truth that no amount of scientific verification or rational thought could ever hope to explore.

All sacred texts — including the Christian Bible, the Muslim Koran, the Sikh Guru Granth, and the Indian Bhagavagita — are predominantly mythic in nature. This is what authenticates them as sacred texts. The historical facts are relatively unimportant; in themselves, they are incapable of eliciting or confirming genuine faith (belief). *It is the myth that awakens the sense of numinosity,* that evokes the spiritual energy, that empowers the person to respond to the divine urge (whether we consider that to come from within or from without).

Resurrection from the Dead

Among the better known mythic tales is that of resurrection from the dead. It occurs in many of the major religions in one form or another, and several examples occur in prehistoric belief systems. In the Christian Scripture, it provides the grand finale to the life and ministry of Jesus. "Finale" may be the wrong word, because, in fact, resurrection leaves everything open to fresh possibility, and the story of the Ascension in Luke's Gospel (Luke 24:50–53), which is intended to get Jesus back to heaven after the resurrection, is yet another mythic tale with the motif of *closure* or *completion* as its obvious goal.

The historical facts of the Christian resurrection narrative are a subject of intense debate among biblical scholars and theologians. Basically, we do not know when, where, or how Jesus was buried, nor have we any concrete, historical facts or artifacts to verify his miraculous rising from the dead. What we do have is the life-witness of a group of disenchanted followers, so transformed by the *experience* (whatever that was) that they give their very lives for their Christian convictions and, second, a Christian culture of two thousand years numbering today 1.5 billion people spread throughout the earth. It is hard to imagine that the totality of Christian culture, as we have known it to date, is based on a grand delusion.

The facts of the resurrection story are relatively unimportant. Even if some researcher of impeccable quality could prove that he or she had discovered the actual earthly remains of Jesus (thus negating the *fact* of resurrection), it would not undermine Christian faith in any serious way. What happens in the experience of the resurrection is that the close followers of Jesus begin to rediscover their Savior's presence with them, and they experience this presence with an intensity and reassurance that transcends the quality of his earthly/human presence among them. To make sense of this new experience, the frightened and excited disciples start telling a story: "It was as if...." The story helps to contain the vision, the dream, the myth. The mystery is made tangible and its challenge accessible. And the story spreads like wildfire, all the time gathering coherence and clarity. But the more the storytellers focus on the *meaning* of the story, the more the story loses its essential meaning. In time, logic threatens the myth, and historical fact distracts from the challenge of the mystery.

What is most gripping in the resurrection myth is its power to transform. At a personal level, it depicts the frayed, bruised, humiliated Jesus exonerated in his essential, human dignity. At a structural, systemic level, it signifies that the political, cultural forces of injustice and oppression do not win out in the end. And at the global (wholistic) level, it projects a world of unrealized possibilities, opening up into an eternal future. Resurrection elevates human yearning into infinite proportions and invites us to understand creation (the entire cosmos) as endowed with an eternal destiny. The myth of resurrection opens up global horizons for person and universe alike.

The great Eastern religions speak of reincarnation rather than resurrection. The Eastern spiritual vision comprises a cycle of eternal birth and rebirth. The underlying myth is not fundamentally different from that of Christian resurrection. The cultural expression is different, but not the fundamental mystery which the human heart seeks to comprehend. Whether we embrace resurrection (in the Christian sense) or reincarnation (in the Eastern sense), the important thing is that we do *not* dogmatize either. Once a myth becomes a dogma, it loses much of its capacity to inspire and to enlighten. If the dogma prevails it will eventually become an idolatrous ideology in which truth and meaning become largely, if not totally, subverted. At the end of the day, both resurrection and reincarnation are *human* namings, attempts to make human and earthly sense out of divine, eternal realities. A humble acknowledgment of this fact provides a far stronger guarantee of truth and doctrinal integrity than the many religious dogmas that have surfaced over the centuries.

The Universal Will to Life

Contemporary science has its own version of resurrection and re-incarnation, known as "autopoiesis" (see Jantsch, 1980, especially 10ff., 90ff., 187–91). The concept was introduced by the Chilean biologist Humberto Maturana in the early 1970s. Autopoiesis refers to the ability of living systems to renew themselves continuously and to regulate this process in such a way that the integrity of their structure is maintained and continuously enhanced.

Already in 1926, the South African statesman Jan Smuts was exploring the wholistic nature of evolution. It took a good fifty years for mainstream science to acknowledge his contribution; it will take at least another twenty before these creative insights are integrated in a coherent way. Meanwhile an all embracing concept such as autopoiesis projects the scientific pursuit toward new horizons whereby it becomes a key concept in one of the most promising and provocative interdisciplinary explorations of all time.

Autopoiesis incorporates a range of ideas which taken together gives the quantum vision substance and conviction:

a. It considers everything to be a living system. Dead, inert matter is a perception of the mechanistic worldview of classical science. From a quantum (wholistic) viewpoint, a stone is a crystallization (compaction) of energy, not a lifeless object. The universe itself is not a machine-like entity, but an organism endowed with a highly developed, self-organizing life system, outlined in the Gaia hypothesis (Lovelock, 1979, 1988). Living systems are essentially dynamic (as distinct from static). They grow, change, and adapt. They possess a will-to-live, an amazing and intriguing capacity to regenerate, usually through the cycle of birth-death-rebirth.

b. It holds that every living system has an inherent capacity for self-organization. Contrary to the long-established second law of thermodynamics, which postulates the gradual decline and ultimate extinction of all life forms, scientists are now beginning to acknowledge the capacity for self-regeneration as a more fundamental aspect of nature. In 1947, Conrad Waddington introduced the notion of the "epigenetic process," the selective and synchronized use of structurally coded genetic information (as in DNA and RNA) by the processes of life in interdependence with their relations to the environment. In the 1970s, Ilya Prigogine (1980, 1984), with his collaborators in Brussels and in Austin, Texas, introduced the notion of "autocatalysis": order through (chaotic) fluctuation, the inherent tendency of living systems to move beyond equilibrium, through instability, to adopt a totally new, life-enhancing structure. And at a cosmic level, Swimme and Berry (1992) postulate a similar self-regeneration process, which they call the "cosmogenetic principle," according to which the evolution of the universe is characterized by *differentiation, autopoiesis,* and *communion,* throughout time and space and at every level of reality.

   c. Living systems are rarely static, and if they are, they are likely to atrophy and die from stagnation. Living organisms do not thrive in a state of balanced equilibrium, but usually in a fluctuating restlessness often described as being "far from equilibrium." Living systems, therefore, are essentially *dissipative structures,* a concept introduced by Prigogine in the 1960s for which he won the Nobel prize in 1977.

   These are structures with an innate capacity to dissipate anything that comes in to disturb the system. The term "dissipate" is somewhat unfortunate, because what really occurs is *integration* and not *dissipation.* The system is shaken up — usually by an outside influence; a chaotic dysfunctional phase may ensue. The urge toward self-organization or regeneration is invoked (at a subtle, subconscious level, which nobody really understands) and the system evolves into a new and more creative way of being. At the human level, we see this process happen in the case of recovery from illness, trauma, or addiction. We also recognize that recovery may never happen, and death may ensue. But in quantum terms, death is not a meaningless termination; it is a transformation into a more wholistic way of being.

   d. Autopoiesis is essentially a learning process. According to Jantsch (1980, 8), evolution is open not only with respect to its products, but also with regard to the process within which it unfolds. Once the human body has developed an immunity to one or other illness, it retains that resource for a whole lifetime and uses it to recognize and ward off the intruding antigen. Proponents of the Gaia hypothesis claim that the same happens at the planetary and cosmic levels on a grand evolutionary scale. Chance and necessity are complementary principles (and not just a biological urge to survive) in what increasingly resembles a mystical, spiritual will-to-life.

   e. In quantum terms, the autopoietic process makes the notion of

an alive universe (Gaia) a great deal more meaningful and attractive than the more mechanistic concept of an external agent (God or
otherwise) empowering the unfolding process from without. This in
itself is not, nor is it intended to be, an argument against an external agent. Rather it is an invitation to take the focus off the *without*,
where so much energy and creativity is projected and dissipated, and
refocus on the *within* (of all things) where such a reservoir of life
and meaning awaits discovery. Once we begin to understand and internalize the sacredness of life from within — ourselves, our planet,
and our universe — then the classical academic search for an external agent may become quite irrelevant. Once we genuinely make the
connection, the deep realization of the interdependence of all things,
we readily endorse the quantum conviction that the *within* and the
without are, in fact, one and the same reality.

f. Finally, there are the quantum dimensions of autopoiesis itself,
a tendency that knows no boundaries, no before or after, a will-
to-life that stretches into infinity. The innate driving force of the
autopoietic process is something that science, by itself, can never
hope to comprehend fully, no more than theologians can ever fathom
fully what we understand by resurrection or reincarnation. These
concepts, at the different, but complementary, levels of science and
theology, are attempts to contextualize within our daily, earthly lives,
the pull (urge, desire) toward infinite horizons. St. Augustine seems
to have had a profound insight into our infinite yearnings when he
wrote: "You have made us for yourself, O Lord, and our hearts are
restless until they rest in you."

Whither Afterlife?

St. Augustine's cosmology had a simplicity to it that proved attractive
over subsequent centuries. It was a dualistic view of *this* world and
the *next* world. This domain of existence was considered transitory,
fragmentary, illusory, sinful, a place of pilgrimage to be endured until, in death, we escaped to the real life beyond. The *next* world was
deemed to be eternal, real, and complete in every sense. It, too, had
its dualistic poles of heaven (absolute happiness) and hell, (eternal
pain and suffering). In Catholic theology we added purgatory, as an
interim "place" of purification in preparation for heaven.

In Augustine's worldview, heaven, hell, and purgatory were real
physical places. Heaven was considered to be above the sky, hell be-
neath the earth, and purgatory in some unknown location. Although

only the soul left the body at the time of death, the joys or sufferings of the afterlife were considered to be physically real. Many of these ideas prevailed until the 1960s.

Our theology of afterlife developed under the influence of our changing cosmology. With the growing realization that our world is *one* in all its dimensions, the notion of a next world fell into disfavor. We have come to understand heaven, hell, and purgatory as states of being (not places) within the one world. According to the old theology, in death, we humans became *a-cosmic* (cut off from the cosmos). In our new understanding, we become *pan-cosmic;* we enter into a new relationship with the *whole* cosmos. In our earthly life, we were confined to one part of (and to a particular way of experiencing) the cosmos. In death, we are released into a potential relationship with the whole of universal life.

The quality of that cosmic relationship may be largely determined by how we live out our earthly life. If we alienate or estrange ourselves from the challenge of life while on earth, then we might be in an estranged relationship right through our eternal future, and this we call "hell": being permanently out of tune with our deepest meaning. "Heaven," on the other hand, refers to that harmonious state of being whereby we enjoy a permanent sense of attunement with the progressive, eternal nature of evolution itself.

The belief that heaven is a state of absolute happiness may be something of a misnomer, as indeed may be the view that God is incapable of experiencing pain and suffering. A sense of being eternally attuned to life does not mean escaping all pain and suffering, but rather being empowered to participate more wholistically in the mixture of agony and ecstasy which has characterized evolution from time immemorial.

Reincarnation offers more than one chance to work out our eternal destiny, until we eventually make the breakthrough that brings us to the ultimate happiness of Nirvana. This concept is not as alien to Christianity as is often suggested. In traditional Christian belief, a notion of a double resurrection prevailed, the first, at the time of one's own death, and the second at the "end of the world," when all the living and dead would be gathered for a final judgment, with some indication that there may be a reprieve, or a second chance, to obtain eternal happiness rather than eternal damnation. Some liberal theologians suggest that in the last judgment, the overwhelming power of God's love and forgiveness will conquer even hell itself.

Many of these ideas are highly speculative, but do embody spiritual aspirations of a profoundly primordial nature. One does not need to invoke theological or religious argument to defend the case for life after biological death. In the world of particle physics, all annihilation means transformation, not into nihilism, but into something radically new and vibrant. The cycles of life manifested in the seasons of nature, and in so many species within it, indicate that the spectrum of birth-death-rebirth evolves unceasingly. Change and decay are all around us in the visible spectrum, yet, at the unmanifest, quantum level, nothing is ever lost. Continuity, in a transformed state, seems to be the rule rather than the exception.

Scientifically, we can offer a number of explanations for the pervasiveness and endurance of life, our own included. We have touched already on the concept of the morphogenetic field, a reservoir of "information" which informs the life and behavior of a species over several generations. We have drawn attention to the notion of the quantum memory, whereby our whole universe is knitted together by a type of memory network, which builds matter around itself in various forms, ranging from molecules to plants, and to our own species as well. This closely resembles the conviction that consciousness is more fundamental than matter; in Bohm's terms, the unmanifest is what endures and continually unfolds in manifest forms. For many people, these controversial ideas, which mainstream science largely ignores, are now taking on a distinctive spiritual and religious import (see Tippler, 1994).

But more compelling than any logical or scientifically based argument, is the spiritual sense known to humans of all ages and cultures, that life — despite all its contradictions and paradoxes — is ultimately benign and benevolent. People who work closely with nature, especially in environmental and ecological settings, often attain a high level of this spiritual awareness. Their rootedness in creation awakens in them a sensitivity to the sacred, which then becomes a catalyst for spiritual or religious exploration. This spiritual journey is often characterized by an intense passion for justice and liberation, especially in the face of exploitation and deprivation. The desire for justice is motivated not merely by the plight of appalling suffering, but by a deeper sense that love and well-being must prevail in the end.

In traditional spirituality we call this the "providence of God." Today it is unfamiliar language. It smacks of escapism, irresponsibility, expecting the God of providence to work miracles that we humans should be working for ourselves, e.g., feeding the hungry peoples of our world. In fact, this is a theological concept of great age and profound depth of meaning. Our ancient ancestors, going back over some forty thousand years, based their entire spiritual meaning on the sense of a higher being who would see them through in the end, a conviction that life was endowed with an ultimate sense of purpose that would outgrow all its flaws and contradictions.

It is this deep, primordial conviction that underpins our notions of resurrection, reincarnation, and autopoiesis. These are attempts to contextualize our affinity to mystery, to make real and tangible the awe and apprehension that is deep within our being. Resurrection, reincarnation, and autopoiesis are mythic tales that embody our yearning for infinity, stretching back over billions of years and serving to connect us with the infinite aeons that still lie ahead. Yes, it's all about learning to live in infinity, as the scientist Michael Talbot suggests in our opening quote.

World without End?

So what about the end of the world? It is a dominant theme in the world's major religions, based, in most cases, on a highly problematic worldview. In an attempt to capture the moral high ground, all the religions have outstepped their limits and invoked dread and fear of divine punishment as strategies to compel allegiance. It has rarely worked to the long-term benefit of the religions themselves and usually has been counterproductive for the wider human and planetary culture.

Where the religions have failed most dismally is in their perception and understanding of the world, which they all tend to dismiss as an inferior, ungodly, and transitory reality. This cosmology goes right back to the Agricultural Revolution, which projected the original mechanistic image that the world was an object to be conquered and controlled. Adopting this worldview, the religions concocted a self-inflationary, eschatological myth, whereby the world would come to nothing and the religions themselves would triumph. What was intended to be an instrument of God became a God in its own right; religion became an outrageous form of idolatry.

Today the end of the world myth has fallen into disrepute. Only believers of a fundamentalist persuasion adopt it seriously. More enlightened people understand that the idea originated and prevailed within a faulty cosmology, rather than from within a spurious theology. In an autopoietic universe, life may go on unfolding forever. Infinity may well be our natural destiny.

Our human minds can scarcely grasp the idea of something being infinite, that is, lasting forever, or, perhaps more accurately, unfolding continuously into an open-ended future. In Western thought, infinity is considered to be a characteristic of God, in the sense that God is not limited in any way. In Eastern philosophy, it is often associated with the Void, where all dualisms cease and the eternal unity of life prevails into an indefinite and unceasing future.

Physicists seem to abhor infinities and have invented a questionable, scientific procedure called "renormalization" to eliminate them from calculations. What in effect happens is that the experiment is so construed that all the infinities cancel each other out. Although used to make some important predictions by such eminent scientists as Freeman Dyson, Richard Feynman, Julian Schwinger, and Mitchell Feigenbaum, some renowned theorists including Paul Dirac and Stephen Hawking do not find the notion attractive or useful. Infinity must somehow be included in scientific research, not conveniently circumvented. At this stage in our human evolution, the human mind can scarcely grasp the notion of the infinite, whether in its application to the unlimited power of the Godhead or the unlimited potential of our future evolution. However, we cannot evade nor avoid a concept that engages our imagination from within so many contemporary scientific and spiritual explorations. As horizons expand on so many fronts — theological and scientific alike — we must seek to imbibe a breadth and depth of wisdom which will stretch our intelligence and imagination to limits hitherto unknown. We must learn to feel at home with mystery unlimited.

The considerations of this chapter can be collated in what many will consider to be the most controversial principle of quantum theology: *The concepts of beginning and end, along with the theological notions of resurrection and reincarnation, are invoked as dominant myths to help us humans make sense of our infinite destiny in an infinite universe.*

These concepts can be employed usefully in our mythic narratives; they flesh out the human-planetary-cosmic story. To turn them into theological or scientific dogmas, however, is likely to convolute rather than illuminate their real truth or meaning. In learning to live in infinity we must also imbibe those attitudes and dispositions to live with the relativity of human ideas, including our theological and scientific dogmas. The future, which evokes and awaits our participation, will be characterized above all else by open-endedness and interconnectedness. The freedom to flow and connect, creatively and imaginatively, is a survival skill for the twenty-first century.

Part Seven

The Future

Perhaps the ultimate enterprise of the twenty-first century, will be the establishment of a tranquility base, not on the moon, but within humankind.

— KENNETH R. PELLETIER

Chapter 14

The Promise and the Peril

Our bodies are breaking down under the strain of the intoxication of our shared body, the Earth.

— ALBERT LA CHANCE

The New Cosmic Story emerging into human awareness overwhelms all previous conceptions of the universe for the simple reason that it draws them all into its comprehensive fulness.... Who can learn what this means and remain calm?

— BRIAN SWIMME

If we are lucky, mankind as it is, has about fifty years left. Most of the graphs on human development, population, ecology, nuclear proliferation and the spread of disease are on an explosive curve. The lines shoot off the graph somewhere in the middle of the next century.

— LORD REES-MOGG (1992)

We don't know how the dance will end. In fact, we suspect, it will never end. Endings and beginnings are constructs of the human mind; they provide boundaries that help us to make some degree of sense out of our dancing, vibrating world. At some stage in our future evolution — possibly within the next hundred years — we will shed many of these boundaries. Equipped with more sophisticated spiritual, intuitive, and psychic faculties, we may choose to participate more spontaneously in the great universal dance of being and becoming; if we choose not to, we may well spell perdition for Homo sapiens!

The evolutionary horizons which beckon us on are awesome, perilous, and promising. In this Calvary-moment of Western civilization, when we seem to have made an irredeemable mess of our earthly-cosmic project, our hopes dwindle and apathy prevails. Where do we even begin, if we wish to set things right? What's the point in beginning if — as many think — it is already too late?

From a quantum perspective, the impact of impending global disaster needs to be treated with profound theological seriousness. Central to the Christian faith is the Calvary experience, which we tend to explain in terms of personal (or interpersonal) redemption and salvation. But the Calvary experience — and its equivalents in other religious systems — has a symbolic meaning of planetary and global proportion, a dimension largely ignored by orthodox religion and theology.

Liberal theologians of the nineteenth century tended to distinguish between the particular (historical) Jesus and the Christ of faith. In other words, the actual, historical person of Jesus preached and embodied a vision for a new world that had an immediate application to the people of his time (and to those who, subsequently, aligned themselves with Christianity). That same Jesus, besides his specific, personal identity, has a cosmic significance for all people and for the whole of creation. Christian theologians tend to argue that the Cosmic Christ makes no sense apart from the particular, historical Jesus. Without the concrete person, we cannot imagine nor create the universal ideal.

This is where quantum theology differs radically. It considers the Cosmic Christ, the God of universal life and love, whose revelation unfolds over fifteen billion years of (known) evolution, to be the originating mystery from which we devise all our divine personages and images. All the god-figures of the different religions, including Christianity, emanate from this cosmic originating source.

Consequently, all the events narrated in the Christian Gospels, particularly those that impact upon universal human and planetary yearnings — beginnings (e.g., the Infancy Narratives) and endings (e.g., Calvary, resurrection), miracles, parables — are particularizations of a more universal narrative of faith and meaning. They point to something greater than their immediate terms of reference. They offer a universal symbolic significance as well as having an immediate, practical application.

Our Calvary Moment

Taken in its universal sense, the Calvary experience is a symbolic encapsulation of the breakdown and disintegration which is endemic to evolutionary unfolding and a prerequisite for a new evolutionary threshold from which higher forms of life emerge. In the great Eastern religions, this process is described as the cycle of birth-death-rebirth.

Our world today is in the throes of a Calvary disintegration. Death, destruction, and despair dominate our world scene. Exploitation, violence, and desecration are all around us. Our Western world has adopted a stance of outright denial: we don't want to know the real truth, and we'll do all in our power to subvert it by accommodating a range of addictive behaviors. Thus we trip headlong into chaos, destruction, and eventual annihilation.

It sounds too pessimistic to be taken seriously; so we resort to denial and rationalization. We choose to forget the thousands of species — animal, bird, and plant — that human interference has condemned to extinction. We fail to internalize the horror and disgust of tropical forests being eroded at the rate of one hundred hectares per week. We numb our intelligence to the realization that we have created enough bombs and nuclear arsenals to destroy the world, not once, but several times over. We are immersed in a cultural death-wish of the gravest proportion, one from which we can only hope to escape by some divine miracle.

From a quantum perspective, the miracle has already happened! The Christ-event, with its climax of death and resurrection, with a specific faith content for Christians, has a global symbolic significance of divine rescue. This can be understood as a once-and-for-all event (or experience) in the traditional Christian sense, or as an enduring quality of universal life, manifested in many spiritual trends and scientific discoveries of the recent past. The onus is not on some divine, external agent who can reverse, with sleight of hand, the cumulative destruction we humans have caused. The burden is ours to own and to bear. We are the stewards of creation and the time is at hand to render an account of our stewardship.

It is unlikely that we humans will survive the impending global crisis. Whether it be a nuclear holocaust (possible but unlikely), chronic oxygen-depletion due to pollution of air and water (quite possible), or mass extinctions due to global warming (likely), our species faces virtual extinction, possibly within the next *fifty* to *one hundred* years.

Rather than contemplate the enormity of the disaster, we continue to evoke human good will and some unexpected reprieve — from nature or from God. We need to recall that there have been, not one, but several mass extinctions in the history of our world, and climatic factors usually play a key role. We record destructive impacts like the extinction of the dinosaurs at the end of the Cretaceous Era (some sixty-six million years ago), but we fail to appreciate the larger more wholistic, interpretation that this is one of nature's strange and ingenious ways of withholding her creative energy for a new outburst of evolutionary life (Swimme and Berry, 1992, 50–60, 94–95, 118ff. are profoundly informative on this topic). Species emerge and become extinct, land masses surface and become submerged, cultures unfold and decline again, but the evolutionary story of creation moves unceasingly on its infinite trajectory.

We are a dimension of the evolutionary story, *co-creators* but not *masters*. As highlighted so often in this book, our lives make no sense apart from the planet and cosmos we inhabit. We take meaning from the larger reality to which we desperately try to give meaning. In our battle with the so-called "alien forces" of nature, we have now reached a nadir point where we could destroy the whole enterprise, ourselves included (as in a nuclear holocaust). In this grim scenario, we need to remember that the real loser would be our own species. Temporarily, but not permanently, we would have destroyed the processes of nature. However, we would not have destroyed the will-to-life which rapidly would reinvoke its self-organizing, autopoietic potential and begin the co-creative process all over again.

Within a short period of time, possibly within *one hundred* years (a mere millisecond on the evolutionary time scale), the cycle of life would recommence, regenerating human life, possibly within *one millennium*. What previously took billions of years would now happen in a few minutes of evolutionary time. And from the Calvary of Homo sapiens would emerge (in all probability) a new quality of human being, equipped emotionally, intellectually, psychically, and spiritually to become more attuned to the new evolutionary age. Not for the first time in the universe's story would death have given way to resurrection!

The quantum theologian needs to take extinction seriously. Without it the dance of life is fundamentally incomplete. The precise details are unimportant; scientific evidence, compulsively bent on controlling nature, is incapable of engaging with this dimension of our evolutionary story. Our patriarchal consciousness cannot confront the shadow, that dark pain and chaos that serves as a prerequisite for fresh possibilities. The insatiable desire to manipulate and control is the deadly addiction of our age, destined to reap havoc on planetary life. The crisis seems unavoidable; we may not be able to prevent it, but we can anticipate it, enter its painful and paradoxical life-giving energy, and in this way possibly survive it.

We cannot address the future in a serious or comprehensive way without embracing the dark and perilous threat that hangs over us as a human and planetary species. And in quantum terms, we are compelled to assert what seems initially to be an outrageous claim: a radically new future demands the destruction and death of the old reality. It is from the dying seeds that new life sprouts forth. Destruction becomes a precondition for reconstruction; disintegration undergirds reintegration; Calvary is a prerequisite for resurrection.

Quantum Yearnings: Within and Without

Our future, therefore, is about peril and promise, annihilation and fresh possibility. All fields of human learning offer dreams for a new future, and science has engendered some fascinating possibilities. These can be explored in terms of an *inward* and *outward* path, offering complementary rather than opposing strands of development. We have reviewed the imminent prospect of a universal Calvary, with the demise and likelihood of extinction for Homo sapiens. I suggest it will take nothing short of a universal resurrection if we humans are to retain some sense of sanity and hope in the future. Signs of this possible resurrection are already abundant for those who can see with the eyes of quantum vision.

In terms of the inward journey, scientific exploration has moved into the invisible realm of the subatomic world, a hybrid of intense and awesome activity which we can intuit in the heart long before we can, in any sense, apprehend with our human senses. We have shifted the quest for the origin of the universe from what happened in the first minute of time, to the first second, milli-second, and now we talk of the first billionth of a second, a concept which the human mind (at this stage of its evolution) cannot even remotely grasp. Biologically, we have probed the genetic code to a depth that is verging on mystery itself. The word "micro" is one of the most frequently used in modern technology.

Spiritually, the path of the inner journey is frequently traveled today. Religious adherents tend to judge prematurely and harshly the perceived secularism of our contemporary Western culture; this perception often betrays a myopic view that negates the spiritual search of our time in the nonreligious realm. As increasing numbers lose faith in the institutions of state and church alike, people often find themselves adrift in a spiritual wasteland. This is the mythic desert space, which, contrary to popular opinion, does not alienate people from God and from meaning, but awakens a renewed sense of the sacred, often setting the seeker on a lifelong journey of spiritual exploration. I believe that this sense of *interiority* is much more prevalent among today's people than is readily recognized. It is another dimension of the journey inward to the heart of reality, instigated I suggest by the "God who finds us" rather than the God *we* find at the end of some self-determined, anthropocentric search. This is the mysticism of our time, the pastoral landscape in which the vision of quantum theology makes a great deal of sense.

Alongside the *inward* journey with its various contemporary manifestations, there exists a range of challenges to think big and grapple with global, universal questions which were inconceivable just a few decades ago. With the landing on the moon in 1969, something changed in the collective consciousness of humanity. We began to perceive the earth differently, as a type of living creature rather than as dead, inert matter. We began to sense a unity within the whole cosmos. It is not by accident that the 1960s and 1970s were characterized by intense outer-space exploration on the one hand, and by the intense search of inner space (via the renewed interest in meditation, mysticism, new-age consciousness, etc.) on the other. Are these not likely to be two faces of the same reality?

As we moved into the 1990s, the last decade of the second millennium, the grand vision of outer space took on new impetus as we glimpsed novel mysterious horizons popularly known today as "dark matter." The detection by the Rosat X-ray satellite of a cloud of hot gas suffusing a seemingly empty region between two galaxies has led researchers to postulate the existence of an immense mass, stretching across the sky for some five hundred million light years, the so-called Great Wall. At a meeting of the American Astronomical Society in January 1993, a team of scientists confirmed the existence of dark matter, the equivalent of twenty trillion suns. Gravity working alone would have taken something like a hundred billion years to create the supercluster two and a half billion light years across (identified by the American and German observers). According to Boslough (1992, 220), this is a time scale at least five times longer than that permitted by even the most generous of the Big Bang models. Our single-cycle, Big-Bang universe cannot accommodate this recent discovery.

It is now estimated that at least 90 percent of the universe is made up of dark matter. Although the concept was first postulated in the 1930s by the astrophysicist Fritz Zwicky, it is only in the 1990s that we have succeeded in verifying its existence (see Krauss, 1989; Riordan and Schramm, 1991). Tentatively, scientists believe that the as yet undiscovered Weakly Interacting Massive Particles (WIMPS) may hold the secret to the nature of dark matter; others opt for the illusive particle the *neutrino,* which, if discovered to possess even tiny mass, will not merely help to unravel the mystery of dark matter, but may fundamentally change many cherished views of science and theology alike. In the light of these discoveries, the notion of a single-cycle universe has to be reconsidered. According to current mainstream cosmology, matter emerges from the quantum vacuum during the explosive burst of the Big Bang, and it vanishes back into the vacuum through black holes or a final implosion, in what is understood to be a *once-and-for-all* process. It now appears that the "once-and-for-all process" is only *one* of a number of evolutionary cycles, in a universe that may be trillions rather than billions of years old.

But why set time limits? Is this not another anthropomorphic quirk to abet our desire to keep a measure of control over the evolutionary process? Perhaps there are no time limits! Maybe we live in an infinite universe. Because of the creative potential of the quantum vacuum, cycles may be re-created infinitely (a notion that resonates with many Eastern philosophical and religious convictions). The cosmos itself would have neither beginning nor end. It would fold and unfold in the eternal, interweaving dance of cosmic creativity.

These ideas are still tentative and speculative but command a degree of interest and curiosity within the scientific community. Gunzig, Geheniau, and Prigogine (1987, 1988) have attempted a mathematical demonstration to illustrate the possibility of an infinite series of universal cycles. They suggest that not one but an infinite series of universes have existed. Each universe was generated in the context of its predecessor, from the enduring but periodically destabilizing quantum vacuum, and as each produced an instability in that vacuum, each gave rise to its successor. The ensuing cosmic vision is that of a cyclic, self-renewing, self-organizing whole, characterized by many features of David Bohm's implicate and explicate order, referred to in chapter 5.

God and Creation in Process

The possibility that we live in a universe without beginning or end is not totally new as a theological concept. It is the foundation-stone of process theology, founded by the philosopher and mathematician Alfred North Whitehead (1979) and developed by scholars such as

Charles Hartshorne, John Cobb, and David Griffin. Central to process theology is the conviction that God is responsible for ordering the world, not through direct action, but by providing the various potentialities which the physical universe is then free to actualize. Thus, God becomes a participator in the creative process rather than an omnipotent creator and ruler from without. In the very *becoming* of the universe God also becomes. God's creativity is manifested or revealed primarily in the process of creation itself.

Process theologians offer us the model of a *dipolar* God. The two poles are described by Whitehead as *primordial* and *consequent,* the former relating to the abstract essence of God: free, complete, eternal, immutable, and unconscious; and the latter, referring to God's concrete actuality: determined, dependent, incomplete, vulnerable, and conscious. Both aspects are necessary to comprehend God's activity at any moment in time.

Jantzen (1984) adopts a somewhat similar approach in proposing that we consider the world to be God's body, wherein God risks the embodiment of divine creativity, eliciting a perception of the divine as visible and present to all creation in a palpable way. McFague (1987, 1993) develops this idea at great length, describing such embodiment as a type of sacramentality, celebrating simultaneously something of the world's vulnerability and precariousness but also its uniqueness, beauty, and prodigious creativity.

The dipolar description, and its underlying sense of divine embodiment, is reminiscent of the Christian struggle to reconcile the divine and human aspects of Jesus. Our dualistic tendency is to oppose these two characteristics into conflicting positions which often become irreconcilable. The heart, mystery, and challenge of the Christian faith is that they are totally reconcilable, a conviction often articulated in mystical statements such as: "The glory of God is people fully alive" (St. Irenaeus) or, "God is what happens to people on the way to becoming human" (Gregory Baum).

Nonetheless, the concept of a dipolar God does disturb our desire for intellectual neatness and perceptual simplicity, but as Davies (1992, 183–84) remarks, this is an eminently appropriate model for our quantum age. In the domain of particle physics, we can no longer describe or perceive the electron as a simple object. It will manifest itself as a particle if we are observing its position and as a wavicle if we are observing its movement. At all times, it is a wave-particle duality, manifested only in one or other expression. Perhaps we have here a illustration of what *all* life is about, including God. We humans can grasp and comprehend only in a partial and fleeting way.

The "whole" is greater, more open-ended, and more creative than we can ever hope to observe or decipher. And it is precisely this greater whole that enlivens and energizes us toward a different and more creative future.

In this chapter, we have set out to achieve something verging on the impossible: to build a bridge between two possible futures for our planet and cosmos — *extinction* (at least of the human species) and *transformation* (by the co-creative forces of evolution itself). Paradoxically, with all the arguments in the melting pot, the challenge to perceive and understand our universe on the grand scale may yet prove to be the most rewarding pathway to the light of truth and to a real sense of hope for the future. At this juncture, there is increasing evidence to suggest that, for scientist and theologian alike, the breakthroughs of the future are more likely to be in the realms of global contemplation rather than in laboratory experimentation. In fact, the evidence is overwhelming, veering in the direction of that truth which asserts that the whole is greater than the sum of the parts.

What must be unmistakably clear at this juncture is that we humans have scarcely begun groping into the dark and mysterious power of universal life: that the arrogant intrusiveness with which we play God has made our very existence precarious and verging on meaninglessness; that we humans in the next few decades are in for a rude (and possibly highly destructive) awakening; that our only real hope for "salvation" and new life is to humbly acknowledge how little we are in it all, let go of our masculine will-to-power, and allow ourselves to become the co-creative beneficiaries of an evolutionary process that far outstretches anything we ever dreamed of. In that sublime and poignant moment of letting go, and letting "God," we'll rediscover who we really are.

The considerations of this chapter leave us with what may well be the most paradoxical of the twelve principles that underpin quantum theology: *Extinction and transformation, the evolutionary equivalents of Calvary and resurrection, are central coordinates of cosmic and planetary evolution. Their interplay at this historical moment — our "kairos" — provides the primary locus for the praxis of the quantum theologian.*

Chapter 15

No Greater Love...

The day will come when after we have mastered the winds, the waves, the tides and gravity, we shall harness for God the energies of love. Then for the second time in the history of the world, man[kind] will have discovered fire.
— PIERRE TEILHARD DE CHARDIN

In a time such as ours when the intrinsic value of our world must be stressed, eros as the love of the valuable is a necessary aspect of both divine and human love.
— SALLIE MCFAGUE

Human society, including its relationship to Planet Earth, will begin to transform only in relationship to the evolution of a new sexuality.
— ROBERT LAWLOR

People first began to use fire about six hundred thousand years ago. For our ancient ancestors, it became one of the greatest stories ever told. Not only did it provide new ways of cooking food and warding off the harsh winds of wintertime, but it became a life force that animated and united. The hearth became a new focal point for camaraderie, bonding, communicating, celebrating, and "praying." Around the bonfire, our ancestors came to know something of the meaning inherent in all things. And for possibly the first time in their existence, they consciously acknowledged the power of love. The warmth of fire awoke the inner flame that draws hearts closer together and unites people in true mutuality.

   Love is a central concept in all the great religions. But it always tends to be personalized, attributed to God(s) and people, but rarely to other species, and scarcely ever to the forces of universal life itself. Consequently, we have inherited in Christianity a focus on the inner forces of love and the outer forces of cold and darkness, another classic dualism that subverts deeper meaning.

With the discovery of the quarks (from the mid-1960s to the mid-1990s), we detect within nature itself tendencies toward mutuality. Because quarks are discernible only in relationships of diads or triads, we are confronted with what seems to be a fundamental truth about all life: connectedness and interrelatedness are interwoven throughout the entire fabric of creation. This imprint is not a cold inanimate force, but a vital, life-giving energy, perpetually destined toward co-creation. There are no limits to the energy of love which begets higher and more complex life forms, and in that very begetting we realize an essential benign quality with which all reality is endowed, in the face of which the "perpetuation of the species" and the "survival of the fittest" become motivating forces of secondary significance.

Power of Love or Love of Power?

At some moment in every human life, we each grasp something of love's own depth and beauty. Unfortunately, we are rarely sensitive enough to imbibe the experience for the future benefit of ourselves and others. Life forces us back to basics: the struggle to survive (for most in the Southern hemisphere) or the struggle to compete (for many in the West), or one or other of the destructive variants that lie in between. Our current travesty, as a human species, is that we have largely lost the capacity to love and to be lovely. We have succumbed to the crude and cruel functionalism of our mechanized culture. We are largely a people whose hearts are numb. We are children of an unloved and unlovable "God," which, in the West, we label "civilization."

In our civilized, mechanized culture, competition rather than co-operation is the dominant mode of action. From the internal bosom of the family to the geopolitical arena of nationalistic rivalry, there is an incessant drive of people seeking to outwit one another. Our culture is absorbed by a compulsive addiction where one has to be a winner or a loser. We are crazy for power, and to the same degree starved of love. And the more we seek to satisfy the power-drive, the more alienated we become in codependent systems that increasingly alienate us from other people, from nature, from the divine life force, and ultimately from our own selves.

In the power game, everything and everybody is an *object* to be manipulated and controlled, not a subject to be connected with or related to. Western imperialism — politically, scientifically, and religiously — always seeks to undermine subjectivity. Although many religions acknowledge and advocate "a personal relationship with God," they distrust human feeling and emotion. Love for most of the religions is a rather cerebral concept, often disembodied from real people in a real world. "God" is the object to be worshiped and obeyed, as prescribed in religious dogma, law, and ritual, rather than a life force (personal or otherwise) whose very essence is invitation into relationship (hence the notion of God as Trinity, the Old Testament idea of Covenant, or the Christian conviction that love is the first and greatest commandment).

Love is the life energy that animates everything that exists. Physiologically and psychologically, we can explain the urge to love in terms of various biochemical processes, such as phenylethylamine (PEA) and Oxytocin. These, I suggest, are *manifestations* rather than *causes* of loving, altruistic behavior. The love-energy is too complex, amorphous, and profound to be embodied in any one set of scientific explanations. It is probably more accurate — as Teilhard de Chardin observed — to compare it to fire, with the paradoxical combination of warmth, tenderness, care, and closeness, on the one hand, and an enormous power for destructibility, on the other.

Love sets the world on fire through the intimacy of sex and the compassion of justice. Only in recent times are we rediscovering that sexuality is the creative core of spirituality and theology (Eisler, 1995; Evola, 1983; Keen, 1985; Lawlor, 1989; Singer, 1990; Mollenkott, 1992). In prepatriarchal times, especially in the culture of the great Ice Age, 40,000–10,000 B.C.E., sexual union was frequently used as a symbolic expression of the divine-human relationship. Hinduism retains many features of this ancient wholism, where the beauty and sacredness of the body (human and earthly) are concomitant with the elegance and ecstasy of the divine energy. In the passion of human loving, the passionate God manifests the divine eros — in stark contrast to the *detached* God of later theistic religion.

The Embodiment of Love

McFague (1987, 1993) offers a contemporary theology of love that incorporates many of these insights. She suggests we adopt new metaphors to explore the meaning of God in the context of the emerging wholism which characterizes our age. She proposes that we image the world as God's body (see also Fox, 1991, 61ff.). The being and action of God are not limited to God's embodiment in the visible creation. Rather God "gives birth" to the world (universe) through divine self-expression and in doing so shapes an embodiment and generates the presence of, and relation to, all other embodiments which constitute God's body. Consequently, we are invited to see our own bodies as a dimension of a larger earthly and cosmic body which itself is divinely endowed and cherished as God's special mode of embodiment.

The model suggests — quite unambiguously — that God loves bodies, that bodies are worth loving, sexually and otherwise, that passionate love as well as attention to the needs of bodily existence are a part of divine fulfillment. It is to say further that the basic necessities of bodily existence, such as adequate food and shelter, are central aspects of God's love for all bodily creatures, and therefore should be central concerns of us, God's co-creators.

Beginning with the notion of the world as God's body, McFague suggests that we reimage the Trinity in terms of an embodiment that is characterized by love and nurturance. Instead of the traditional namings (metaphors) of Father, Son, and Spirit, she suggests Mother (parent), Lover, and Friend. The Mother-Creator image is offered as being more inclusive and wholistic than the patriarchal father metaphor, which has often been associated with subservience, royalty, power, and exclusion. God as Mother implies a cosmic generosity that gives life to all being with no thought of return and continues to *participate* in the unfolding dream of open possibility (hence the notion of the prodigious womb).

However, this is not a mother metaphor constructed on the traditional feminine stereotypes of softness, sentimentality, and pity. Instead, we are presented with a fiercely protective female, for whom passion and justice are paramount, a woman who rages with anger when her offspring (her very own body) are deprived of the basic essentials of love, care, and justice. Those who produce life have a stake in it and will judge, often with anger, what prevents its fulfillment.

In applying to Jesus the metaphor of *Lover,* McFague is touching base with one of the most profound and controversial movements of our time: the decadence of the *hero* and the upsurge of the *lover* as a dominant cultural metaphor (more on this topic in Keen, 1985). For McFague the love-energy of the lover is characterized particularly by *eros,* that quality of love that expresses personal affirmation of the worth and value of the beloved, the love that draws the beloved to

itself, seeking to bring about the beloved's wholeness and completion. This is the love of healing, the love that reconciles the alienated
and separated. It is the love of forgiveness that reaches to the depths
of the finite experience of fragility, worthlessness, willful rebellion,
or oppressed, silent passivity. God as lover has a particular desire for
union with these creatures who uniquely have the gifts of reflective
consciousness and finite freedom and the capacity to respond with
love in personal ways.

New Horizons of Human Sexuality

The lover is one of the most volatile metaphors of our time, loaded
with possibility and with peril. Eros as a love-energy is explosively
amorphous in today's world. There is an inordinate desire to connect
more deeply, not merely among humans, but also among so-called
inanimate entities — the quarks (hence, the provocative quip of the
1970s: "Nature seems to abhor naked quarks"). Consequently, we
find that human sexuality has outgrown its functional and exclusive
focus on the procreation of new life, adopting a more inclusive ambience of mutual enrichment of the spouses, as well as the possibility
of procreation within the context of monogamous marriage.

Throughout the 1980s, we experienced another quantum leap,
which as yet has not been acknowledged publicly: intimate relationships, whether between male and female, male and male, or female
and female tend to become quite erotic and veer toward genital
expression. Genitality is no longer reserved for heterosexual monogamous relationships, never mind for marital union. It has become
a dimension of human intimacy in the many different situations in
which people seek to express tenderness, affection, and mutuality.

There seems to be an enormous reluctance to acknowledge this
new development. Labels such as "premarital sex," "extramarital
relations," and "sexual acting-out" inhibit rather than encourage a
deeper analysis of this new sexual agenda. Culturally, politically, and
theologically, it has far more serious implications than the so-called
sexual revolution of the 1960s.

While churches and governments continue to bemoan the loss of
innocence, the promiscuity of the liberally minded, the immorality of
premarital sex and extramarital relationships, the new sexual agenda
continues to unfold, creating havoc and horror across our world.
The real havoc, I suggest, is not in the behavior itself (whether in its
range of delightful or deleterious consequences) but in the massive

denial whereby these new developments are perceived and treated as adversarial forces to be opposed, subdued, and conquered. We try to confront feminine *eros* with masculine *logos,* and in this post-patriarchal age, the *logos* is weary, deflated, and largely incapable of engaging meaningfully with the wildly creative and destructive power of eros.

June Singer is one of several modern writers who challenges us to engage more creatively with this new phenomenon:

> I sense a great void in the study of human psychosexual development. This void I see as the absence of an encompassing worldview that could provide a setting within which to discuss recent trends in sexual interaction. If a new worldview is in the making, as I believe it is, sexuality has not yet been incorporated into that vision. Current sexual practice can no longer be explained by the old theories and we do not yet understand it in the light of the new ones. Racing ahead of history we now find ourselves in new territory. We may as well begin drawing new maps. This is the first step in the process of revisioning sexuality, a step which I believe is necessary to our personal growth and collective evolution. (Singer, 1990, 10)

Questions of a highly complex nature ensue for cultural institutions such as monogamous marriage and the family. The breakdown in both spheres in recent times is not because of promiscuity, the emancipation of women, inadequate parenting, etc. No, it is a much deeper "revolution," a quantum transformation, whereby we are invited to reclaim the fundamentally amorphous creativity of our eros (comprehensively outlined by Evola, 1983), the fire of energizing love, and thus outgrow the mechanization of sex which patriarchy imposed on our world and which has dominated both our attitudes and behaviors since the rise of the Industrial Revolution in the sixteenth century.

It is against this background that contemporary writers (e.g., Eisler, 1995) strive to reclaim a spirituality of sexuality. Instead of eroticism being an obstacle (temptation) to spiritual growth, it may well be the creative wellspring of spiritual unfolding. Only an integrated spirituality can sustain us meaningfully today in the face of this massive upsurge of psychosexual creativity. The repressed psychic and sexual energies of centuries, especially the past few hundred years, explodes upon our world, releasing instinctual forces of unrestrained intimacy, passionate justice, unstinting compassion, but also of fiery eroticism, phallic projection, consuming passion, and self-destructive narcissism. Paradox abounds as an infertile desert sprouts forth an incomprehensible array of possibilities.

Never before have intimate relationships called on us to face ourselves with so much honesty and awareness. Maintaining an alive connection with an intimate partner today challenges us to free ourselves from old habits and blind spots and to develop the full range of our powers, sensitivities, and depths as human beings. Welwood (1991, 1) notes that if people of former times wanted to explore the deeper mysteries of life, they would often enter the seclusion of a monastery or a hermitage. For many of us today, however, intimate relationships have become the new wilderness that brings us face to face with all our gods and with all our demons.

Depicting the second person of the Trinity as Lover recaptures much of our lost Christian and spiritual heritage. It helps to reclaim the divine *embodiment* of godliness and goodness in the world, a salient theme of all the great religions — and of the prereligious worship of the goddess (see Eisler, 1987, 1995) — one that tends to be suppressed, or at least subdued, in the formal promulgation of Christian doctrine.

Perhaps the time is ripe for Christianity to reclaim its passionate commitment to embodiment, as mediated in persons, planets, and the divine unfolding (revelation) at the heart of creation. In evolutionary terms, this calls forth a fresh awareness of *relationship* as the dynamic context that begets all life, including divinity itself. The intensity of reciprocity and meaning within such relatedness is what we call "eros," the passionate will-to-life that underpins all reality, from the infinite grandeur of the divine, to the minute coexistence of subatomic particles, such as quarks and leptons.

The Spirit as Friend

There is a unifying principle that links the macro and the micro, across the aeons, and throughout the infinity of our universal potential, what Christians traditionally have called the "Holy Spirit," whom the theologian John Macquarrie (1966) describes as "unitive being," and to whom McFague attributes the metaphor of "Friend." The type of friendship attributed to the Spirit is characterized primarily by freedom and participation. God the lover of the world gave us the vision that God finds the world valuable and desires its wounds healed and its creatures free; God as friend asks us, as adults, to become associates in that work. McFague suggests that the right name for those involved in this ongoing, sustaining, trustworthy, committed work for the world is neither parents nor lovers, but friends.

There is something distinctively altruistic about the friendship of the Spirit. It operates outside the bounds of duty, function, or office. Of all our relationships, it is the most free, invoking neither the interdependence of the parent/mother (Creator) nor the mutuality of the lover (Eros), but offering a quality of presence and sustenance that allows and empowers the divine, evolutionary becoming. It evokes sentiments of the friend who remains a friend for life, although actual face-to-face encounters may happen only rarely. It is a powerfully feminine image of an intense, unrelenting presence, yet never interfering in the manipulative or intrusive manner which smacks of masculine, patriarchal religiosity.

The table below, based on McFague's trinitarian reconstruction and expanded by Fowler (1991, 67), provides a useful résumé of the material explored in this chapter. Something of the breadth, depth, profundity, and complexity of love are presented in this outline. I hope, too, the connections and paradoxes become clearer as the reader explores the various strands presented.

METAPHORICAL RECONSTRUCTION OF TRINITARIAN LOVE

Metaphor	Type of Love	Action (Power)	Form of Ethic	Root-Metaphor
Mother (Parent)	Agape	Creating Justice/ Judging	Organism	
Lover	Eros	Saving	Healing	Interpersonal relations
Friend	Philia	Sustaining	Companionship	Covenant faithfulness

A helpful example of what I mean by "paradox" is that of "saving" as the action (power) attributed to the divine eros. All the great religions refer to salvation as a gift freely offered by a higher power, with an abundance of love and generosity, yet all the religions convey an ambiguous sense of our having to "earn" our salvation. But there is an even deeper paradox, namely, that the divine, freely bestowed salvation is always mediated through pain and suffering. The bright light of salvation (fulfillment, nirvana, bliss, etc.) is attained only by traversing the dark alleyways of confusion, chaos, pain, and suffering (often to the point of martyrdom). It takes all the resources of our creative eros to negotiate this journey with integrity and hope. Indeed, it is only with the power of our divine-human eros that we eventually surrender to the true love which alone is our life and salvation.

The other dimension of the table which may need an explanatory note for nonreligious readers is the root metaphor of "covenantal faithfulness," attributed to the befriending Spirit. "Covenant" is a Judaeo-Christian concept, denoting a love of God for the people that remains faithful forever, inviting a similar response from those to whom this covenantal love is offered. I'd like to draw attention to the global ambience of this love and fidelity, which is apparent in the diagram in the series of metaphors offered. *Organism* can be understood as being on its own, complete within itself. The metaphorical range then widens beyond the "individual" to *interpersonal relations,* and again is expanded to assume global dimensions in the *covenantal faithfulness.* What in mainstream religion can seem an exclusive and limiting category, becomes in the quantum vision a threshold for openness to new possibilities and expanded horizons.

Love knows neither barriers nor boundaries. Mystics and novelists, artists and comedians all have had a go at exploring its mysterious power. From the basic particles that hold matter together (the bosons), to the divine energies that sustain our meaningfulness, we encounter a life force that lures and attracts, that underpins the polarities of attraction and repulsion, on which all human relationships are based. Our search for meaning compels us to probe this mysterious force. Yet all our probing leaves us only partially satisfied, if indeed satisfied at all. Perhaps the great Eastern mystics are the ones with the ultimate wisdom, which claims that it is only in the silence of the mystery that we can see the light, and from the darkness of the shadow we begin to glimpse its infinite meaning.

Inspired by these reflections, the quantum theologian invokes what seems to be a very old, yet radically new principle: *Love is an interdependent life force, a spectrum of possibility, from its divine grandeur to its particularity in subatomic interaction. It is the origin and goal of our search for meaning.*

The Love That Liberates

For the quantum theologian, the real question seeking understanding is not about our love for God, but God's love for us. From the totality of otherness, from which we often feel distanced and alienated, comes our ultimate meaning. It's not our individuality that matters (less so our independence and autonomy), but our personhood, which is meaningless apart from the relationships that beget and sustain each one of us. Even the child born from a pregnancy caused by rape is the product of a relationship yearning for love, in this case, the deep pain of love, a love thwarted and distorted, often because of an intense deprivation of love. Our human longings, dreams, hopes, aspirations, are focused on love as a goal; our anger, hatred, fear, disillusionment are inverted desires for a love that has been refused, or that we were unable to receive. Whatever our conditions or circumstances, love is the focal energy that holds the key to meaning.

In the fragmented world of our time, we are deeply aware of the lack of love and the abundance of hatred that prevails. But hatred is not the opposite of love; *indifference* is, just as spiritual indifference rather than atheism is the enemy of authentic religion. In our indifference we abdicate our divine will-to-life; we opt to disengage from the dialogue of life. We become love-less, and in a sense hate-less; we lose heart and begin to atrophy. It is this lack of passion, often provoked by patriarchal institutions and values, that denudes us of our dignity, value, and worth as human beings and poses the greatest threat to the future of humanity and to the future of our planet. This apathy often assumes masked and distorted power in the compulsions and addictions which are so prevalent in modern society. Our abdication of personal power disempowers us (and others) to the point where we become engulfed by "powers" which alienate us from our true selves.

Practically every approach to the treatment of addictions invokes, in one form or another, the twelve steps of Alcoholics Anonymous (A.A.). Central to this vision is an acknowledgment that we, individually, are no longer in control, and that we are not ultimately responsible for what we are or do. We learn, often slowly and painfully, to accept a "power" higher than ourselves, within whose love and energy we are not absorbed or consumed, but rediscover anew our true selves, as people born with the capacity to love and to be loved. It is in this rediscovery of love that we recapture something of our true nature. We come home to ourselves.

At this moment of homecoming, of reconnecting with the inner core of meaning, we don't become hermits cut off from the world, nor incestuous navel-gazers preoccupied with our own survival. No, it's precisely then, and only then, that we can embrace our world from that center of strength wherein we know we are loving and lovable. From that center point all things are possible. It is the greatest quantum leap we can ever hope to take.

Principles of Quantum Theology

Principle 1

Life is sustained by a creative energy, fundamentally benign in nature, with a tendency to manifest and express itself in movement, rhythm, and pattern. Creation is sustained by a superhuman, pulsating restlessness, a type of resonance vibrating throughout time and eternity.

NEW ELEMENTS:

a. God and the divine are described as a creative energy, which is perceived to include, but also supersede, everything traditional theology attributes to God.

b. The divine energy is not stable or unchanging, but works through movement, rhythm, pattern, and restlessness — within the evolving nature of life itself.

c. The divine co-creativity operates within the evolutionary process rather than as an external agent based on a cause and effect relationship.

d. Notions such as "God" and "divinity" are used sparingly, because these are human constructs (descriptions) that may limit rather than enhance our understanding of life's ultimate source and meaning.

Principle 2

Wholeness, which is largely unmanifest and dynamic (not static), is the wellspring of all possibility. In seeking to understand life, we begin with the whole which is always greater than the sum of the parts; paradoxically, the whole is contained in each part, yet no whole is complete in itself.

NEW ELEMENTS:

   a. No one source of knowledge, theological or otherwise, can provide a complete description of reality; the mystery of life is
   fundamentally open-ended.

   b. Theology is about opening up new horizons of possibility and
   ultimate meaning, and not about consigning truth to specific
   dogmas, creeds, or religions.

   c. Since the whole is understood to be contained in, but not by,
   each part, the dilemma of pantheism is resolved.

Principle 3

*Evolution is underpinned by a deep unfolding structure, character-
ized by design and purpose, necessitating an unceasing interplay of
order and disorder, randomness and creativity.*

NEW ELEMENTS:

   a. Evolution is considered to be the primary context of divine-
   human creativity in the world.

   b. Life, in its basic meaning, is blessed and not flawed (as in the
   original sin approach).

   c. In the divine-human unfolding, light and shadow always intermingle; quantum theology, while acknowledging the paradox of
   polarity, seeks to outgrow all dualisms, especially that of good
   vs. evil.

Principle 4

*The expanding horizon of divine belonging is the context in which
revelation takes place; all creatures are invited to respond, to engage
in the co-creative task of being and becoming. All life forms have
unique roles in this process, the primary focus of which is creation
itself rather than formal religion.*

NEW ELEMENTS:

   a. The primary context of divine revelation is the unfolding process of creation and not formal religion. Each religion is a
   particular crystallization of divine revelation. No one religion,
   not even all the religions together, could contain or explain the
   fulness of revelation.

b. All life forms, and not just humans, have a co-creative role in the divine plan for the world and in the responses it elicits and evokes.

c. Revelation is ongoing; it cannot be subsumed in any religion, creed, or cultural system.

Principle 5 _____

Because the capacity to relate is itself the primary divine energy, impregnating creation, we humans need authentic ecclesial and sacramental experiences to explore and articulate our innate vocation to be people in relationship.

NEW ELEMENTS:

a. The doctrine of the Trinity is a human attempt to describe God's fundamental relational nature.

b. The divine interaction within creation is that of subject to subject rather than subject to object.

c. The innate human desire and capacity for relationships is the experience in which we connect most authentically with the divine ambience of our existence.

d. Church and sacraments are key moments for exploring and articulating our relatedness, as a divine invitation to life and meaning, and not organizations and rituals commanding legal observance.

Principle 6 _____

Ultimate meaning is embedded in story, not in facts. All particular religious stories belong to a larger story, which includes but also transcends the specific religious traditions of any one historical or cultural epoch. All sacred texts are attempts at articulating ultimate truth and archetypal values, approximations that require fresh interpretation in each new cultural epoch.

NEW ELEMENTS:

a. Sacred story is our primary channel for accessing the divine source and ultimate meaning of life.

b. Sacred texts (e.g., the Bible) which seek to safeguard the story need to be interpreted afresh in each new age if they are to preserve the ever new challenge and inspiration of the sacred story.

c. Creation itself, and not we humans, is the primary narrator of the sacred story; we humans should be the supreme listeners.

d. Both the contemplation and narration of the sacred story require symbol and ritual if we are to engage meaningfully with its deep mythic and archetypal significance.

Principle 7

Redemption is planetary (and cosmic) as well as personal. Redemption is about reclaiming the darkness, the nothingness (void), and chaos of our world and celebrating the negative potential for new life and wholeness.

NEW ELEMENTS:

a. Redemption is a divine-human process of befriending those elements of our experience which threaten our security and integrity, rather than an act of rescue by an external, divine agent.

b. Redemption is a process of re-membering, highlighting the ultimate paradox of life that pain and extinction are prerequisites for fresh life and creativity.

c. Redemption is not just about personal salvation; it also concerns the healing and reinvigoration of planetary and universal life; there can be no personal salvation apart from the latter.

Principle 8

Structural and systemic sin abound in our world, often provoking people to behave immorally. To integrate the global shadow, we need fresh moral and ethical guidelines to address the structural and systemic sinfulness of our time. The formulation of these guidelines is as much a political as a religious duty.

NEW ELEMENTS:

a. Sin is a form of destructive collusion between people and systems. Consequently, systems, rather than individual people, become the instigators of immoral and irresponsible behavior.

b. The major sin of our time is *specieism,* the human-structural assumption that humans are the ultimate life form under God and are entitled to lord it over the rest of creation.

c. Morality is a universal, cultural requirement in the light of which the dualism between church and state becomes an anachronism.

Principle 9

Because we are primarily beneficiaries of light (and not of darkness), and our final destiny — both here and eternally — is that of enlightenment, we all need those sacred moments of ritualistic/sacramental space, serving as heightened encounters with the sustaining mystery that enfolds us.

NEW ELEMENTS:

a. Life is inherently destined toward the ultimate triumph of goodness, and not the ultimate catastrophe predicted by the second law of thermodynamics.

b. Humans are innately spiritual — so are all life forms — and if appropriate human and spiritual maturation takes place, humans feel a need to celebrate, in ritual and sacrament, their relationship with the ultimate mystery.

Principle 10

The concepts of beginning and end, along with the theological notions of resurrection and reincarnation, are invoked as dominant myths to help us humans make sense of our infinite destiny in an infinite universe.

NEW ELEMENTS:

a. We live in a world without beginning or end.

b. The "end of the world" is a human/theological myth whereby we humans tried to set boundaries on our infinite universe.

c. There is one world enfolded in eternity; heaven, hell, and purgatory are states of being within the one world. Our dead ones are all around us, living within a different plane of existence.

    d. Resurrection and reincarnation are not facts, but mental/ spiritual constructs that articulate both our paradoxical fear of, and yearning for, infinity.

Principle 11

Extinction and transformation, the evolutionary equivalents of Calvary and resurrection, are central coordinates of cosmic and planetary evolution. Their interplay at this historical moment — our "kairos" — provides the primary locus for the praxis of the quantum theologian.

NEW ELEMENTS:

    a. Theology no longer belongs to Christianity, not even to formal religion; it has become an agent for global transformation.

    b. We are invited to do theology at the heart of the world and not within the confines of church or formal religion.

    c. The theological encounter becomes most creative (and most perilous), when we engage with the pressing global issues of our time.

    d. In its global praxis, theology seeks to demolish all dualisms, outgrow all human constructs, and pursue ultimacy with the skills and discernments of a multidisciplinary imagination.

    e. Contemplation becomes the landmark of theology; the pursuit of justices becomes its dominant praxis. All the rest is window-dressing, useful, but not essential.

Principle 12

Love is an interdependent life force, a spectrum of possibility, ranging from its ultimate divine grandeur to its particularity in subatomic interaction. It is the origin and goal of our search for meaning.

NEW ELEMENTS:

    a. God is not a passive, detached, external ruler, but a passionate, relational presence, embodied in the creative, evolutionary process itself.

    b. God's passionate embodiment demands a whole new way of relating to bodies, through sexual tenderness, compassionate justice, and altruistic befriending.

   c. Sexuality, and its erotic creativity, for long perceived to be a major source of temptation, is emerging as a key dimension of authentic spirituality.

   d. Our world will become a new place when we choose to take love seriously.

Doing Theology in a Space-Time Continuum

The notion of "expanded horizons" occurs on practically every page of this book. The reader has been invited to expand horizons of mind, intellect, and especially imagination, and to stretch perceptions, feelings, and images to what at times must have seemed like the breaking point. Yes, the quantum world is immensely vast and profoundly complex at both the micro and macro levels.

The quantum vision shatters many of our accepted and cherished norms and opens us up to another worldview. This view of reality is not entirely new, nor indeed is it alien to what we humans strive to become in the depth of our being. On the contrary, it invites us to ways of perceiving and interrelating which ground us in reality rather than alienate us from it.

The scientific discoveries of the twentieth century have altered, quite radically, our understanding of the world we inhabit and our role within it as co-creators. Above all else we must change our mindset, our perceptions of how we comprehend and understand the world of our time. The following are some of the major challenges facing us:

a. There is a fundamental *unity* to our universe, transcending all the divisions and distinctions developed by the human mind. The oneness of life is far more fundamental than the many divisions and categories we humans have invented.

b. On the micro scale, e.g., at the level of subatomic particles, there is an unceasing buzz of energy, operative at time scales and space dimensions that our minds (at this stage of our evolution) cannot even remotely grasp. Actions, with life and death implications, happen at time scales as small as a billionth of a second and in spaces that totally defy any attempt at human measurement. And all those minute actions profoundly affect you, me, and everything in the world that we inhabit.

    c. On a macroscale, we have been challenged to stretch every dimension of spirit and mind in order to comprehend:

    i. A world which is at least fifteen billion years old, and that refers only to the presently known cycle of evolution. Even a million years is a bewildering concept for many people to entertain.

    ii. An evolutionary story that unfolded for 95 percent of that time without any assistance from us humans.

    iii. A human-evolutionary time scale that is itself somewhere in the region of three to four million years, with Homo sapiens emerging about a hundred thousand years ago.

    iv. A spiritual time scale of at least seventy thousand years, predating the presently known formal religions (which we often assume to be eternal) by at least sixty-five thousand years.

    v. A space dimension of 90 percent void (emptiness) and only about 10 percent matter; we now believe that up to 90 percent of the matter in the universe is dark and, as yet, we know virtually nothing about it.

    vi. A species diversity of incomprehensible variety and elegance, with an intriguing and often paradoxical interdependence. Of all the species that have ever inhabited our universe, at least 50 percent are now extinct. New species emerge on a daily basis; we ourselves also change and mutate, but over centuries rather than over days or years.

    vii. And on top of all that, we inhabit a world of 90 percent empty space, with most of the "matter" possibly yet to be discovered, a discovery that may well take place in the transformative process of matter becoming conscious, rather than continuing to be the "object" we humans seek to analyze and manipulate.

The Challenge of Theology

No serious theologian can ignore these new horizons. These are the revelatory thresholds of our time, calling us to encounter ultimacy and meaning in a novel and challenging context. God comes alive in our world, and the divine permeates on a scale our limited imaginations can only vaguely comprehend. Our world is narrating the sacred story with new symbols, new language, and above all with a new cosmology.

It is this *cosmology* more than anything else that dictates the future. For much of the past five thousand years, theology (and formal religion) was deemed to be the queen of the sciences. For a brief period of about three hundred years, classical science tried to usurp that privilege, but with only limited success. Today *cosmology* and not *theology* is the queen of the sciences. The cosmos — understood in the open-ended and wholistic context explored in the present work — is the ultimate point of reference against which we explore meaning and truth. Even our most mystical and highly developed notions of God are mediated for us cosmologically. All the major moral, political, social, interpersonal, and personal decisions confronting us today demand a cosmological referent. Despite all our attempts to objectify the cosmos (and creation), the *cosmos as subject* is winning out and will rescue us (from ourselves) in the end.

If theology wishes to retain a degree of relevance and meaning it must now adopt the great paradoxical pathway it has so often advocated for its adherents: it must die to its own supremacy. It must become the servant of a higher and more embracing wisdom. It must learn to mediate new truth for the new age that is dawning upon our world. It must allow itself — in conjunction with all the other sciences — to be born anew!

And for the theologian — which is each one of us at one level or another — it is another of those painful and challenging conversion moments. Keen (1985, 146) offers the poignant insight that the Greek word *metanoia* (conversion), a word with several parallels in the great religions, is the etymological opposite of *paranoia* (fear). Often it is our fears that cripple us — fear of the new, of letting go of the old, of being challenged, of taking risks, of broadening our visions and horizons. The call to conversion is an invitation to outgrow our fears and trust ourselves to the unfolding process of life and meaning. Once we realize that the unfolding process itself is fundamentally benign and benevolent, then we begin to realize the profound meaning of the words: "Perfect love casts out fear" (1 John 4:18).

When we let go of our patriarchal props, categories, labels, powers, and "certainties," we don't abandon ourselves to the "forces of evil." Perhaps for the first time, we encounter the relational God at the heart of a relational universe, albeit one that today is emaciated with the pain of so much wrecked relatedness. We too are relational creatures. We belong to a greater whole, held forever in the gracious embrace of divine abandonment. In letting go of our patriarchal securities, we come home to where we really belong, to the universe itself. Here, *love*, and not *fear*, is the enduring reality!

Notes

1. It is fashionable in current anthropological studies to attribute positive rather than negative qualities to our ancient ancestors. Many scholars are loath to use words like "primitive" and "prelogical." Direct comparisons between ancient and modern cultures are meaningless, but proportionately and contextually, it is simplistic to demean and denounce ancient and prehistoric culture compared with the so-called sophisticated and developed standards of our time. Ancient cultures also manifest traits and attitudes which we humans today could beneficially reclaim, e.g., ecological and spiritual sensitivities (see especially Eisler, 1987).

2. Many problems of the present time, global and personal, are often blamed on the one-sided emphasis of classical science and the technology that prevailed from the seventeenth century until about 1960. Of much greater significance, it seems to me, is the Agricultural Revolution and its major impact upon global culture since about 8000 B.C.E. down to the sixteenth century (and later in some parts of the world). This is when patriarchy emerged as a dominant cultural orientation, seeking to conquer and control everything, including the divine power itself. On this subject also see Bronowski (1973), Eisler (1987), Hemming (1986), and Leakey (1992).

3. See O'Murchu, 1986; 1988. For the purposes of the present work, I adopt Katherine Zappone's description of spirituality as "the relational component of lived experience" (1991, 12). For a survey of recent developments in spirituality, see Jon Alexander, "What Do Recent Writers Mean by Spirituality?" in *Spirituality Today* 32, no. 3 (September 1980): 247–56.

4. The notion of dualism occurs many times in this book. It refers to the human tendency to construe reality as if everything was divided into pairs of adversarial opposites, e.g., good vs. evil; God vs. human(kind); heaven vs. earth. Life consists of polarities rather than dualities. What are often construed as *opposites* are, in fact, complementary, polar values. The way to understanding is not via either-or dualities but through both-and polarities.

5. To most people, the word "evolution" signifies the gradual development of many living species, one from another, probably along the lines that Charles Darwin proposed in his treatise *On the Origin of Species* (1859). Darwin's key notion — the survival of the fittest — was an economic, mechanistic concept which he borrowed from the work of Thomas Malthus, *An Essay on the Principle of Population*. Fifty years previously, in 1809, Jean Lamarck (1744–1829) published his *Philosophie zoologique* outlining his evolutionary theory, based on the teleological urge to unfold and develop. This developmental approach rapidly lost favor in the mechanistic culture of the nineteenth century while

the Darwinian theory continued to flourish — well into the twentieth century. Lamarck has made something of a comeback in recent years.

Many contemporary theorists have moved beyond both Darwin and Lamarck, espousing a new concept called "co-evolution," originally developed in 1965 by the American biologists Paul Ehrlich and Peter Raven. In co-evolutionary terms, no one species or system evolves in isolation. Evolution, at every level, from the cosmic to the subatomic, is a cooperative, interdependent, unceasing process. Evolution does not take place *in* the universe; all life co-evolves *with* the universe (see Jantsch, 1980; Sahtouris, 1989; Fagan, 1990; Laszlo, 1993).

6. Many contemporary compendia of theology either ignore or underestimate the important contribution of African and Asian theologians (see Abraham, 1990). (*a*) *Black* theology sprang up initially in the U.S., with James H. Cone as its most versatile proponent, but today black theology tends to be synonymous with African theology, claiming John S. Pobee and Allan Boesak among its most ardent advocates (see the comprehensive overview by Patrick Kalilombe in Ford, 1989, 193–216). (*b*) *Asian* theology seeks to enculturate the Christian message in a genuinely Asian context. Leading names include Stanley J. Samartha of India, Choan-Seng Song of Taiwan, Hyun Younghak of Korea, and Kosuke Koyama of Japan.

7. Aristotle believed that nowhere on a line drawn from the smallest atom of hydrogen to the most complex human creature is it possible to say where nonlife ends and life begins. Contemporary scientists have not advanced much further; they perceive living systems to be highly complex and do not tend to employ descriptions, definitions, or even the use of the word "life." Throughout the present work, I use the word in a generic sense to denote the "power of spirit" which seems to underpin the creative vacuum (see pp. 70, 102–3), potentiating field influence (described in chapter 6), which in turn empowers the propensity for self-reproduction and self-renewal. I suggest that human life is a dimension of the greater whole, not an exalted form superior to all others, and I suggest that the divine is to be perceived more as a co-creative, synchronistic life force, rather than a mechanistic, clockwork God operating from without (see Margulis and Sagan, 1995, for further elucidation of these ideas).

8. In scientific terms, a quantum leap (or jump) refers to an abrupt, unpredictable transition from an atom's initial state to another one: "Suppose you measure the state of a single atom repeatedly, always getting the same result. Then, suddenly between two successive measurements, there is a spontaneous internal rearrangement, and the next measurement records a change. That, in modern parlance, is a quantum jump" (Von Baeyer, 1992, 100).

In the present work, however, I use the phrase in its popularly acquired *metaphorical* meaning to denote a radical shift of emphasis with often unforeseen and unpredictable consequences, not just on the microscopic sphere of quantum physics, but also on the macroscopic scale of cosmic and planetary evolution.

9. In 1927, Werner Heisenberg formulated the uncertainty principle, noting that in our descriptions of atomic phenomena there are pairs of concepts, or aspects which are interrelated, and precision in the measurement of one quantity is

possible only with a measure of uncertainty in the other. It was one of the more important landmarks in relegating classical determinism to a secondary role.

10. Adherents of the Baha'i faith, which originated in the Middle East in the 1860s, would consider theirs to be the last of the great religions. It numbers around three million followers.

11. Consequently, in order to make the message of this book accessible to a wide and inclusive readership, I have attempted to keep concepts and language as simple as possible. This, I expect, will prove irritating to both scientists and theologians, and possibly to all readers of a more scholarly ilk.

12. The metaphor of the "machine" belongs to the era of Newtonian science and Cartesian philosophy (seventeenth and eighteenth centuries). One of its more influential articulations was that of Julian de la Mettrie's *Man a Machine,* initially published in French in 1748. Although immediately rebutted by a plethora of publications with titles such as *Denial of Man a Machine* (Frantzen), *On Man's Machine and Soul* (Tralles), *Refutation of Man a Machine* (Hollmann), de la Mettrie's influence prevailed into the twentieth century and today is reechoed in works such as those of the biologist Richard Dawkins (*The Selfish Gene* [New York: Oxford University Press, 1976]; *The Blind Watchmaker* [London: Longman, 1986]).

13. *Gravity* is a universal force field. Nothing in the cosmos escapes its influence. It acts as a force of attraction, drawing things together in a relational capacity within the space-time curvature (see Swimme and Berry, 1992, 24–27, 260). At the level of particle interaction, it is a very feeble force, difficult to measure or even observe. At the macroscopic level, it also tends to escape our attention. When you walk down a street, the large buildings exert minute gravitational tugs, but they are too small to be felt.

After gravity, the *electromagnetic force* is the one that exerts the greatest influence, which we experience in X-rays, heat, light, radio waves, etc. It is also the glue that holds everyday objects in their solid state.

In contrast to the long-range nature of gravity and electromagnetism, the *weak force* is inoperative beyond about 10^{-16} cm of its source. It seems to manifest itself in particle decay (as with beta radioactive atoms) and in this way contributes to certain transmutations in the identity of particles, often propelling the products to high speed.

The *strong force* is the most virulent of all forces. It is the glue that holds together the nucleus of the atom. It is the energy released through sunlight. The cores of the sun and other stars are nuclear fusion reactors under the control of the strong force field. It is also the force that activates the nuclear bomb.

How these forces interact and affect life universally is one of the keenest pursuits of contemporary science. Einstein himself, toward the end of his life, hoped that one day we could understand all the forces within a grand unified theory. Quite a lot has been achieved on how electromagnetism combines with the weak and strong forces, but so far gravity has defied all attempts at a total unification of the forces.

14. The problem with a disease like AIDS (and with various forms of cancer) is that they succeed in conquering the memory itself and change the information template. As yet, we don't understand why or how this happens. What is

clear is that it happens much more rapidly in a weak immune system than in a healthy one.

15. Among mainstream Christian theologians, the one who seems to come closest to this understanding of the Trinity is Jürgen Moltmann in his *The Trinity and the Kingdom of God* (London: SCM Press, 1981).

16. It is assumed that a black hole comprises at least three times the mass of the sun; one of the most persuasive cases for the existence of black holes, namely, the constellation V404 Cygni, which erupted in 1989, is estimated to be 6.3 times the mass of the sun. Contemporary scholars are also keenly pursuing the nature and purpose of *quasars* — believed to be luminous cores of young galaxies at the edge of the universe — many of which are brighter than a hundred billion stars, and may be powered by black holes. See Rees (1990).

17. I draw the reader's attention to an important distinction between *complexity* and *complicatedness* (see Davies, 1987, 94). The human body (and indeed the universe itself) is highly complex, because it is so richly and diversely endowed. Nonetheless, it exhibits a sense of pattern and purpose which transcends complicatedness in the negative connotation we often attribute to that word. Classical rational thought, in both science and theology, strove to keep everything very simple, perceiving the absence of simplicity to be an aberration. Contemporary science can no longer exclude a consideration of complexity; neither can theology or spirituality. In our attempts to include complexity, we tend to confuse it with things being complicated, and this often militates against the quality of attention and exploration that the study of complexity deserves. On the modern understanding of complexity, see Lewin, 1993. On the work of the Santa Fe Institute in New Mexico, which specializes in the study of complexity, see Waldrop, 1992.

18. The list enumerated in this section largely reflects the Eight Deadly Sins of the Fathers enumerated by Mary Daly (1978, 30–31): Processions, Professions, Possession, Aggression, Obsession, Assimilation, Elimination, Fragmentation.

19. For information on the various practices and methods of meditation, Christian and otherwise, there is a great deal of written material. For beginners, I recommend Anthony de Mello, *Sadhana: A Way to God* (London and New York: Doubleday, 1984); Lawrence Le Shan, *How to Meditate* (London: Turnstone, 1983; Boston: Little Brown & Co.); Laurence Freeman, *Light Within: The Inner Path of Meditation* (London: Darton, Longman & Todd, 1986).

Bibliography

Abraham, K. C. 1990. *Third World Theologies: Commonalities and Divergences.* Maryknoll, N.Y.: Orbis Books.

Alston, William P. 1989. *Divine Nature and Human Language: Essays in Philosophical Theology.* Ithaca, N.Y.: Cornell University Press.

Arbuckle, Gerald. 1988. *Out of Chaos.* London: Chapman.

Barbour, Ian. 1990. *Religion in an Age of Science.* San Francisco: HarperSanFrancisco.

Barrow, John D. 1990. *Theories of Everything.* New York: Vintage Books.

Barrow, John D., and Frank F. Tippler. 1986. *The Anthropic Cosmological Principle.* New York: Oxford University Press.

Bausch, William. 1984. *Storytelling: Imagination and Faith.* Mystic, Conn.: Twenty-Third Publications.

Bevans, Stephen B. 1992. *Models of Contextual Theology.* Maryknoll, N.Y.: Orbis Books.

Birch, C., W. Eakin, and J. B. McDaniel. 1990. *Liberating Life: Contemporary Approaches to Ecological Theology.* Maryknoll, N.Y.: Orbis Books.

Boff, Leonardo. 1987. *The Maternal Face of God.* New York: Harper & Row.

———. 1995. *Ecology and Liberation: A New Paradigm.* Maryknoll, N.Y.: Orbis Books.

Bohm, David. 1980. *Wholeness and the Implicate Order.* New York: Routledge & Kegan Paul.

Bohm, David, and F. David Peat. 1988. *Science, Order and Creativity.* New York: Bantam Books.

Boslough, John. 1992. *Masters of Time.* London: J. M. Dent.

Brock, Rita N. 1992. *Journeys by Heart.* New York: Crossroad.

Bronowski, Jacob. 1973. *The Ascent of Man.* Boston: Little Brown.

Burnham, John. 1986. *Family Therapy.* London and New York: Tavistock.

Campbell, Joseph. 1976. *The Masks of God: Primitive Mythology.* London: Penguin Books.

Capra, Fritjof. 1976. *The Tao of Physics.* London: Fontana/Flamingo.

———. 1982. *The Turning Point.* London: Fontana/Flamingo.

Chopra, Deepak. 1989. *Quantum Healing.* New York: Bantam Books.

Chorafas, Dimitris. 1994. *Chaos Theory on the Financial Market.* London: Probus Books.

Cobb, John, and John Boswell. 1982. *Process Theology as Political Theology.* Manchester: Manchester University Press.

Collins, Michael. 1974. *An Astronaut's Journey.* New York: Farrar, Straus & Giroux.

Collins, Paul. 1995. *God's Earth.* Melbourne.: Dove/HarperCollins.

213

Conlon, James. 1990. *Geo-Justice*. San Jose, Calif.: Resource Publications.

Coveney, Peter. 1990. "Chaos, Entropy and the Arrow of Time." *New Scientist* 29, no. 9: 49–52.

Coveney, Peter, and Roger Highfield. 1991. *The Arrow of Time*. London: HarperCollins.

Cupitt, Don. 1988. *The New Christian Ethics*. London: SCM Press.

Daly, Gabriel. 1988. *Creation and Redemption*. Dublin: Gill & Macmillan.

Daly, Mary. 1973. *Beyond God the Father*. Boston: Beacon Press.

———. 1978. *Gyn/Ecology: The Metaethics of Radical Feminism*. Boston: Beacon Press.

Davidson, John. 1989. *The Secret of the Creative Vacuum*. London: C. W. Daniel.

Davies, Paul. 1983. *God and the New Physics*. New York: Simon & Schuster.

———. 1984. *Superforce*. London: Unwin Books.

———. 1987. *The Cosmic Blueprint*. London: Heinemann.

———. 1992. *The Mind of God*. New York: Simon & Schuster.

Donovan, Vincent. 1989. *The Church in the Midst of Creation*. London: SCM Press; Maryknoll, N.Y.: Orbis Books.

Eisler, Riane. 1987. *The Chalice and the Blade*. San Francisco and London: HarperCollins.

———. 1995. *Sacred Pleasure: Sex, Myth and the Politics of the Body*. New York: HarperCollins.

Eliade, Mircea. 1965. *The Two and the One*. New York: Harper & Row.

Evola, Julius. 1983. *The Metaphysics of Sex*. London: East-West Publications.

Fagan, Brian M. 1990. *The Journey from Eden*. London: Thames & Hudson.

Feigenbaum, Mitchell. 1978. "Quantitative Universality for a Class of Nonlinear Transformations." *Journal of Statistical Physics* 19: 25–52.

———. 1979. "The Universal Metric Properties of Nonlinear Transformations." *Journal of Statistical Physics* 21: 669–706.

Fell, Nolan, and Peter Liss. 1993. "Can Algae Cool the Planet?" *New Scientist* 21, no. 8: 34–38.

Ferguson, Kitty. 1994. *The Fire in the Equations*. New York: Bantam Books.

Ferm, Dean William. 1986. *Third World Liberation Theologies: An Introductory Survey*. London: SCM Press; Maryknoll, N.Y.: Orbis Books.

Ford, David F. 1988–89. *The Modern Theologians*. 2 vols. Oxford: Blackwell.

Fowler, James W. 1991. *Weaving the New Creation*. San Francisco: Harper.

Fox, Matthew. 1984. *Original Blessing: A Primer in Creation Spirituality*. Santa Fe: Bear & Co.

———. 1991. *The Coming of the Cosmic Christ*. San Francisco: Harper & Row.

Frohlich, Herbert. 1968. "Long-Range Coherence and Energy Storage in Biological Systems." *International Journal of Quantum Chemistry* 2:641–49.

Frohlich, H., and F. Kremer. 1983. *Coherent Excitations in Biological Systems*. New York: Springer-Verlag.

Fuellenbach, John. 1995. *The Kingdom of God*. Maryknoll, N.Y.: Orbis Books.

Gleick, James. 1987. *Chaos*. New York: Simon & Schuster.

Goldbrunner, Josef. 1955. *Individuation: A Study of the Depth Psychology of Jung*. London: Hollis & Carter.

Greenstein, George. 1988. *The Symbiotic Universe*. New York: William Morrow & Co.

Grey, Mary. 1989. *Redeeming the Dream*. London: SPCK.

———. 1993. *The Wisdom of Fools? Seeking Revelation for Today*. London: SPCK.

Gribbin, John. 1988. *In Search of Schrodinger's Cat*. London: Pan/Macmillan.

Griffiths, Bede. 1989. *A New Vision of Reality*. London: Collins.

Gunzig, E., J. Geheniau, and I. Prigogine. 1987. "Entropy and Cosmology." *Nature* 330: 621–24.

———. 1988. "Thermodynamics of Cosmological Matter Creation." *Proceedings of the National Academy of Sciences 85*.

Gutzwiller, Martin C. 1992. "Quantum Chaos." *Scientific American* 266 (January): 26–32.

Guthrie, S. E. 1993. *Faces in the Clouds: A New Theory of Religion*. New York: Oxford University Press.

Halkes, Catharina. 1991. *New Creation: Christian Feminism and the Renewal of the Earth*. London: SPCK; Louisville: Westminster/John Knox Press.

Hardy, Alistair. 1979. *The Spiritual Nature of Man: A Study of Contemporary Religious Experience*. New York: Oxford University Press.

Harris, Errol. 1991. *Cosmos and Anthropos*. London: Humanities Press International.

Hawking, Stephen. 1988. *A Brief History of Time*. New York: Bantam Books.

———. 1993. *Worm Holes and Baby Universes*. New York: Bantam Books.

Hayes, Michael. 1994. *Musical Structures in Science and Theology*. London: Weidenfeld & Nicolson.

Hayles, N. Katherine. 1991. *Chaos and Order: Complex Dynamics in Literature and Science*. Chicago: University of Chicago Press.

Helsel, S. K., and J. P. Roth. 1991. *Virtual Reality: Theory, Practice and Promise*. Westport, Conn., and London: Meckler Publications.

Hemming, James. 1986. *Instead of God*. London: Marion Boyars.

Henderson, Hazel. 1981. *The Politics of the Solar Age*. New York: Anchor Books.

Herbert, Nick. 1985. *Quantum Reality: Beyond the New Physics*. London: Rider Publications.

Heyward, Carter. 1982. *The Redemption of God: A Theology of Mutual Relation*. Washington: University Press of America.

Hick, John, and Paul Knitter. 1988. *The Myth of Christian Uniqueness*. London: SCM Press.

Hoffman, Virginia. 1988. *Birthing a Living Church*. New York: Crossroad.

Ho, Mae-Wan, and Fritz-Albert Popp. "On the Coherent Lightness of Being." *Caduceus* (Leamington Spa) 13: 28–31.

Hopper, Jeffrey. 1987. *Understanding Modern Theology*, vol. 1. Philadelphia: Fortress Press.

Horgan, John. 1992. "Quantum Philosophy." *Scientific American* 267 (July): 72–80.

Huizinga, Johan. 1950. *Homo Ludens: A Study of the Play Element in Culture*. Boston: Beacon Press.

Jantsch, Erich. 1980. *The Self-Organizing Universe*. New York: Pergamon Press.

Jantzen, Grace M. 1984. *God's World, God's Body*. London: Darton, Longman & Todd.

Jung, C. G. 1968. *Man and His Symbols*. New York: Dell.

Jürgens, Harmut, et al. 1990. "The Language of Fractals." *Scientific American* 363 (August): 40–47.

Keen, Sam. 1985. *The Passionate Life*. London: Gateway Books.

Kelly, Kevin W. 1988. *The Home Planet: Images and Reflections of Earth from Space Explorers*. London: Macdonald.

Kimel, Alvin F., ed. 1992. *Speaking the Christian God: The Holy Trinity and the Challenge of Feminism*. Grand Rapids, Mich.: Eerdmans; Leominster, U.K.: Gracewing.

King, Ursula. 1989. *Women and Spirituality: Voices of Protest and Promise*. London: Macmillan.

Koestler, Arthur. 1978. *Janus*. London: Hutchinson.

Krauss, Lawrence M. 1989. *The Fifth Essence: The Search for Dark Matter in the Universe*. New York: Basic Books.

Krieger, David J. 1991. *The New Universalism: Foundations for a Global Theology*. Maryknoll, N.Y.: Orbis Books.

Kroh, Werner. 1991. "Foundations and Perspectives for an Ecological Ethics." *Concilium* 4: 79–93.

Küng, Hans, and David Tracy. 1989. *Paradigm Change in Theology*. Edinburgh: T. & T. Clark.

Kuhn, Thomas. 1970. *The Structure of Scientific Revolutions*. Chicago: University of Chicago Press.

La Chance, Albert. 1991. *Green Spirit: Twelve Steps in Ecological Spirituality*. Shaftsbury, Dorset: Element Books.

La Cugna, Catherine Mowry. 1991. *God for Us: The Trinity and Christian Life*. San Francisco: HarperSanFrancisco.

Lash, Nicholas. 1986. *Theology on the Way to Emmaus*. London: SCM Press.

Laszlo, Erwin. 1993. *The Creative Cosmos*. Edinburgh: Floris Books.

Lawlor, Robert. 1989. *Earth Honoring: The New Male Sexuality*. Rochester, Vt.: Park St. Press.

Leakey, Richard. 1992. *Origins Reconsidered: In Search of What Makes Us Human*. London: Abacus Books.

Lewin, Roger. 1993. *Complexity: Life at the Edge of Chaos*. London: J. M. Dent.

Liechty, Daniel. 1990. *Theology in Postliberal Perspective*. London: SCM Press; Philadelphia: Trinity Press International.

Lockwood, Michael. 1989. *Mind, Brain and the Quantum*. Oxford: Blackwell.

Lovelock, James. 1979. *Gaia: A New Look at Life on Earth*. New York: Oxford University Press.

———. 1988. *The Ages of Gaia*. New York: Oxford University Press.

Macquarrie, John. 1966. *Principles of Christian Theology*. London: SCM Press.

Mandelbrot, Benoit. 1977. *The Fractal Geometry of Nature*. San Francisco: W. H. Freeman & Co.

————. 1990, "Fractals — A Geometry of Nature." *New Scientist* 15, no. 9: 38–43.

Margulis, Lynn, and Dorian Sagan. 1995. *What Is Life?* London: Weidenfeld & Nicolson.

McDonagh, Sean. 1986. *To Care for the Earth*. London: Chapman.

McFague, Sallie. 1987. *Models of God*. Philadelphia: Fortress Press.

————. 1993. *The Body of God: An Ecological Theology*. London: SCM Press.

McGovern, Arthur F. 1989. *Liberation Theology and Its Critics*. Maryknoll, N.Y.: Orbis Books.

Metzner, Ralph. 1987. "Resonance as Metaphor and Metaphor as Resonance." *ReVision* 10: 37–44.

Mollenkott, Virginia R. 1992. *Sensuous Spirituality*. New York: Crossroad.

Moltmann, Jürgen. 1985. *God in Creation*. London: SCM Press.

Miller, James. 1978. *Living Systems*. New York: McGraw-Hill.

Murchie, Guy. 1979. *The Seven Mysteries of Life*. London: Rider/Hutchinson.

Nye, Andrea. 1990. *Words of Power*. New York: Routledge.

O'Murchu, Diarmuid. 1986. *The God Who Becomes Redundant*. Cork, Ireland: Mercier Press; Leominster: Fowler Wright.

————. 1988. *Coping with Change in the Modern World*. Cork: Mercier Press; Leominster: Fowler Wright.

————. 1992. *Our World in Transition*. London: The Book Guild.

Orenstein, Gloria F. 1990. *The Reflowering of the Goddess*. New York: Pergamon Books.

Pagels, H. 1985. *Perfect Symmetry*. New York: Penguin Books.

Peacock, Arthur. 1979. *God and the New Biology*. London: J. P. Dent.

Penrose, Roger. 1990. *The Emperor's New Mind*. New York: Oxford University Press.

Peters, Edgar E. 1991. *Chaos and Order in the Capital Markets*. New York: John Wiley & Sons.

Peters, Tom. 1988. *Thriving on Chaos*. London: Pan Books.

Pines, Malcolm. 1992. *Bion and Group Psychotherapy*. London: Tavistock/Routledge.

Polkinghorne, J. C. 1984. *The Quantum World*. New York and London: Penguin Books.

Powell, Corey S. 1993. "Inconstant Cosmos." *Scientific American* 268 (May): 69–76.

Pribram, Karl. 1971. *The Language of the Brain*. Englewood Cliffs, N.J.: Prentice-Hall.

Prigogine, Ilya. 1980. *From Being to Becoming*. San Francisco: W. H. Freeman.

Prigogine, Ilya, and Isabelle Stengers. 1984. *Order out of Chaos*. New York: Bantam Books.

Rahner, Karl. 1969. *Hearers of the Word*. New York: Herder & Herder.

Rein, Glen. 1992. *Quantum Biology: Healing with Subtle Energy*. Palo Alto, Calif.: Quantum Biology Research Labs.

Rees, Martin J. 1990. "Black Holes in Galactic Centers." *Scientific American* 263 (November): 69–76.

Riordan, M. 1987. *The Hunting of the Quark*. New York: Simon & Schuster.

Riordan, M., and D. Schramm. 1991. *The Shadows of Creation: Dark Matter and the Structure of the Universe*. New York: Oxford University Press.

Rolston, Holmes. 1987. *Science and Religion: A Critical Survey*. New York: Random House.

Ross, Susan A., and Mary Catherine Hilkert. 1995. "Feminist Theology: A Review of Literature." *Theological Studies* 56: 327–52.

Ruether, Rosemary Radford. 1992. *Gaia and God: An Ecofeminist Theology of Earth Healing*. San Francisco: HarperSanFrancisco.

Russell, Peter. 1982. *The Awakening Earth*. New York: Routledge & Kegan Paul.

———. 1992. *The White Hole in Time*. London: Aquarian Press.

Russell, Robert John, Nancey Murphy, and C. J. Isham, eds. 1993. *Quantum Cosmology and the Laws of Nature*. Vatican City: Vatican Observatory Publications; Berkeley, Calif.: Center for Theology and the Natural Sciences.

Sahtouris, Elizabet. 1989. *Gaia: The Human Journey from Chaos to Cosmos*. New York and London: Pocket Books.

Satir, Virginia. 1964. *Conjoint Family Therapy*. Palo Alto, Calif.: Science and Behavior Books.

Shea, John. 1978. *Stories of God*. Chicago: Thomas More Press.

———. 1980. *Stories of Faith*. Chicago: Thomas More Press.

Sheehan, Thomas. 1986. *The First Coming: How the Kingdom of God Became Christianity*. New York: Random House.

Sheldrake, Rupert. 1988. *The Presence of the Past*. London: Collins.

———. 1991. *The Rebirth of Nature*. London: Collins.

Shlain, Leonard. 1991. *Art and Physics*. New York: William Morrow.

Singer, June. 1990. *Love's Energies*. Boston: Sigo Press.

Stewart, Ian. 1989. *Does God Play Dice? The Maths of Chaos*. Oxford: Blackwell.

Stewart, Ian, and Martin Golubitsky. 1992. *Fearful Symmetry*. Oxford: Blackwell.

Swimme, Brian, and Thomas Berry. 1992. *The Universe Story*. San Francisco: HarperSanFrancisco.

Talbot, Michael. 1991. *The Holographic Universe*. London: Grafton Books.

Taylor, Roger. 1991. "Scalar Fields, Subtle Energy and the Multidimensional Universe." *Caduceus* (Leamington Spa, Autumn Ed.): 28–30.

Teilhard de Chardin, Pierre. 1968. *Science and Christ*. New York: Harper & Row.

———. 1971. *Christianity and Evolution*. New York: Harcourt Brace Jovanovich; London: Collins.

Thompson, Ross. 1990. *The Spirituality of Matter*. London: SPCK.

Thompson, William. 1977. *Christ and Consciousness*. New York: Paulist Press.

Tippler, Frank J. 1994. *The Physics of Immortality*. New York: Doubleday.

Toffler, Alvin. 1990. *Power Shift: Knowledge, Wealth and Violence at the Edge of the 21st Century*. New York: Bantam Books.

Tracy, David. 1990. *Dialogue with the Other*. Grand Rapids, Mich.: Eerdmans.

Trussell, Denys. 1989–90. "The Arts and Planetary Survival." *The Ecologist* 19: 170–76 and 20: 4–8.

Turner, Victor and Edith. 1969. *The Ritual Process.* Chicago: Aldine.

Van Beeck, F. J. 1979. *Christ Proclaimed: Christology as Rhetoric.* New York: Paulist Press.

Verschuur, Gerritl. 1978. *Cosmic Catastrophes.* London: Addison-Wesley.

Von Baeyer, Hans Christian. 1992. *Taming the Atom.* New York: Viking.

Von Bertalanffy, L. 1968. *General Systems Theory.* New York: Braziller.

Wach, Joachim. 1958. *The Comparative Study of Religions.* New York: Columbia University Press.

Waldrop, M. Mitchell. 1992. *Complexity: The Emerging Science at the Edge of Chaos.* New York and London: Viking.

Weber, Renee. 1986. *Dialogues with Scientists and Sages.* New York: Routledge and Kegan Paul.

Welwood, John. 1991. *Journey of the Heart.* London: Grafton Books; San Francisco: Harper & Co.

Wheatley, Margaret J. 1992. *Leadership and the New Science.* San Francisco: Berrett-Koehler.

Whitehead, Alfred. 1979. *Process and Reality.* New York: Free Press.

Wiener, Norbert. 1965. *Cybernetics.* New York: Wiley.

Wilber, Ken. 1982. *The Holographic Paradigm and Other Paradoxes.* London and Boulder, Colo.: New Science Library.

Wilson, Kenneth. 1983. "The Renormalization Group and Critical Phenomena." *Reviews of Modern Physics* 55: 583–600.

Wilson-Schaef, Anne. 1987. *When Society Becomes an Addict.* San Francisco: Harper & Row.

Wolf, Fred Alan. 1985. *Mind and the New Physics.* London: Heinemann.

Woods, Richard. 1980. *Understanding Mysticism.* New York: Image Books.

Wosien, Maria-Gabriele. 1974. *Sacred Dance: Encounter with the Gods.* London: Thames & Hudson.

Wright, T. R. 1988. *Theology and Literature.* Oxford: Blackwell.

Yalom, Irwin D. 1985. *The Theory and Practice of Group Psychotherapy.* 3d ed. New York: Basic Books.

Zappone, Katherine. 1991. *The Hope for Wholeness.* Mystic, Conn.: Twenty-Third Publications.

Zohar, Danah. 1990. *The Quantum Self.* London: Bloomsbury.

———. 1993. *The Quantum Society.* London: Harper Collins.

Zukav, Gary. 1979. *The Dancing Wu Li Masters.* London: Penguin/Flamingo.

Index

Of Related Interest